TRADE AND PAYMENTS ADJUSTMENT UNDER FLEXIBLE EXCHANGE RATES

Also published for the Trade Policy Research Centre by Macmillan

TOWARDS AN OPEN WORLD ECONOMY
by Frank McFadzean *et al.*

WORLD AGRICULTURE IN DISARRAY
by D. Gale Johnson

THE ESSENTIALS OF ECONOMIC INTEGRATION
by Victoria Curzon

NEGOTIATING ON NON-TARIFF DISTORTIONS OF TRADE
by Robert Middleton

TRADE EFFECTS OF PUBLIC SUBSIDIES TO PRIVATE ENTERPRISE
by Geoffrey Denton, Seamus O'Cleireacain and Sally Ash

INVISIBLE BARRIERS TO INVISIBLE TRADE
by Brian Griffiths

TECHNOLOGY AND ECONOMIC INTERDEPENDENCE
by Harry G. Johnson

THE ECONOMICS OF THE OIL CRISIS
edited by T. M. Rybczynski

PUBLIC ASSISTANCE TO INDUSTRY
edited by W. M. Corden and Gerhard Fels

MEETING THE THIRD WORLD CHALLENGE
by Alasdair MacBean and V. N. Balasubramanyam

AGRICULTURE AND THE STATE
edited by Brian Davey, T. E. Josling and Alister McFarquhar

PRICE ELASTICITIES IN INTERNATIONAL TRADE
by Robert M. Stern, Jonathan Francis and Bruce Schumacher

TARIFF PREFERENCES IN MEDITERRANEAN DIPLOMACY
by Alfred Tovias

NUCLEAR POWER AND THE ENERGY CRISIS
by Duncan Burn

NORTH SEA OIL IN THE FUTURE
by Colin Robinson and Jon Morgan

Trade and Payments Adjustment under Flexible Exchange Rates

Papers of the Second Annual Conference of the International Economics Study Group

Edited by
JOHN P. MARTIN AND ALASDAIR SMITH

for the
Trade Policy Research Centre
London

First published 1979 by
THE MACMILLAN PRESS LTD
London and Basingstoke
Associated companies in Delhi
Dublin Hong Kong Johannesburg Lagos
Melbourne New York Singapore Tokyo

Printed in Great Britain by
Redwood Burn Ltd
Trowbridge and Esher

British Library Cataloguing in Publication Data

International Economics Study Group
Annual Conference, 2nd, Isle of Thorns, 1977
Trade and payments adjustment under flexible exchange rates
1. Foreign exchange – Congresses
I. Title II. Martin, John P. III. Smith, Alasdair
IV. Trade Policy Research Centre
332.4′5 HG3821

ISBN 0–333–21705–5

TO THE MEMORY OF HARRY G. JOHNSON (1923–1977)

International Economics Study Group

The International Economics Study Group (IESG), administered by the Trade Policy Research Centre, London, from 1975 to 1978 is one of several study groups in economics supported in the United Kingdom by grants from the Social Science Research Council. The IESG was founded on the initiative of Max Corden and David Wall in 1972, the founding committee also including John Dunning, Brian Hindley, Tim Josling and the late Harry G. Johnson. Through the programme of eight or nine regular seminars in the academic year, held at the London School of Economics, and an annual conference each September, held at the Isle of Thorns, University of Sussex, the IESG provides a forum in which professional international economists in British universities, polytechnics, government departments and business can meet and discuss research papers presented by members and visiting faculty from abroad. The Committee for 1977–78 included John Black, Chairman; David Wall, Secretary; Brian Hindley, Alasdair Smith and Alec Chrystal.

Contents

List of Tables

List of Figures

Biographical Notes

RICHARD BLACKHURST: Senior Economist, Secretariat of the General Agreement on Tariffs and Trade, Geneva.

WILLIAM H. BRANSON: Professor of Economics, Princeton University.

WILLEM BUITER: Assistant Professor of Economics and Public Affairs, Princeton University; previously Lecturer in Economics, London School of Economics and Political Science.

STEPHEN CARSE: Lecturer in Economics at Leicester Polytechnic; formerly Research Associate, University of Warwick, Coventry.

K. ALEC CHRYSTAL: Lecturer in Economics, University of Essex, Colchester.

ALAN V. DEARDORFF: Associate Professor of Economics, University of Michigan.

MARK N. GREENE: Research Fellow, Department of Economics, University of Michigan.

HANNU HALTTUNEN: Economist, Bank of Finland, Helsinki.

BRIAN HINDLEY: Lecturer in Economics, London School of Economics and Political Science, and Counsellor for Studies, Trade Policy Research Centre, London.

MALCOLM D. KNIGHT: Economist, the International Monetary Fund, Washington.

STEPHEN P. MAGEE: Professor of Finance, University of Texas at Austin; formerly Associate Professor of Economics, University of Chicago.

JOHN P. MARTIN: Economist, Secretariat of the Organisation for Economic Cooperation and Development, Paris; previously Research Fellow, Nuffield College, Oxford.

DONALD J. MATHIESON: Economist, the International Monetary Fund, Washington.

ALASDAIR SMITH: Lecturer in Economics, London School of Economics and Political Science.

ROBERT M. STERN: Professor of Economics, University of Michigan.

GEOFFREY E. WOOD: Lecturer in Economics, the Centre for Banking and International Finance, City University, London.

List of Abbreviations

BTN	Brussels Tariff Nomenclature
CES	constant elasticity of substitution
c.i.f.	prices including cost, insurance and freight
EREO	exchange-rate elasticities of output
FE	foreign exchange
f.o.b.	free-on-board prices
GATT	General Agreement on Tariffs and Trade
GNP	gross national product
IMF	International Monetary Fund
ISIC	International Standard Industrial Classification
MLR	minimum lending rate
OECD	Organisation for Economic Cooperation and Development
OLS	ordinary least squares
PPP	purchasing power parity
QR	quantitative restrictions
RHS	right-hand side
ROW	rest of the world
SDR	special drawing right
SITC	Standard International Trade Classification

Introduction

The nine papers which make up this book were presented at the second annual conference of the International Economics Study Group at the Isle of Thorns, Sussex, 16–18 September 1977.

In seeking to organise a conference around a specific theme, one immediately has the problem of selecting a coherent and topical theme. In this case we were faced with no such difficulty, given the current interest both of academic economists and policy-makers in the workings of a system of flexible exchange rates. All the papers in this volume are concerned with various aspects of the economics of flexible exchange rates but they address a rich variety of topics under that general subject and choose different methods of approach.

The first two papers concern themselves with purely theoretical issues of exchange-rate management. Buiter's model tackles the question of the optimal exchange-rate policy for a small open economy that is subject to stochastic disturbances arising from both foreign and domestic sources. The analysis suggests that some degree of intervention in foreign exchange markets is superior to no intervention – for example, managed floating is superior to free floating. Hindley's paper addresses itself to the topical problem of real-wage rigidity. He adopts a particular definition of the real wage and considers the implications of the real-wage rigidity hypothesis for macro-policy under the two polar exchange-rate regimes.

The papers by Branson and Halttunen, Knight and Mathieson, and Deardorff *et al.*, although very different from each other in most detailed respects, can all be described as empirical models of the interaction between goods markets and financial markets. Branson and Halttunen build on the so-called 'asset market' approach to derive a simple model for explaining monthly movements in bilateral exchange rates. For such a simple model the preliminary econometric results are not unpromising. They then go on to demonstrate how the results can be blended with simple reaction functions to highlight the policy problems facing the authorities under flexible rates. Knight and Mathieson's aim is more ambitious: to construct and estimate a macro-economic model that (i) takes account of the major elements of international interdependence via commodity and financial markets; and (ii) is sufficiently general that it can be applied to different countries. The exchange rate plays a key role in the model; the exchange-rate determination process reflects the insights of the asset–market approach, although allowance is made for excess demands in commodity markets to have a separate influence. Careful attention is given to modelling the intervention strategies of the central authorities in foreign exchange markets. The approach adopted has the merit of stressing the fact, often overlooked, that the move to greater flexibility of exchange rates since 1972–73 was not a dichotomous jump but a shift along the spectrum of exchange-rate regimes. Deardorff *et al.*, specifically consider the interaction between commodity markets and exchange rates in a general equilibrium model of world output and trade. A unique feature of this model is the combination of a multilateral structure with a high level of industry disaggregation between tradeables and non-tradeables. The model is used to simulate the responsiveness of output and employment across countries to changes in exchange rates.

The next two papers focus on aspects of the pricing policies adopted by traders and firms under flexible rates. Magee is concerned with the operation of the 'law of one price' at a micro-economic level. Using United States–Japanese price data he attempts to test whether international commodity arbitrage is more effective under fixed or flexible exchange rates. Carse and Wood, on the other hand, analyse currency invoicing practices using United Kingdom data. They then consider the implications of their findings for exchange-market stability. Evidence is also provided on the degree to which British firms had recourse to forward markets.

The concluding papers are concerned with institutional arrangements in a world of flexible rates. Chrystal's paper builds on the vehicle currency hypothesis to argue that the world economy needs an international medium of exchange even under floating rates and that natural economic forces would lead to the currency of the dominant economic power (presently the United States dollar) being used for the purpose. He casts a cold eye on the special drawing rights (SDR) and argues that such a centrally-created reserve asset cannot hope to challenge the pre-eminence of the dollar as the international money. Indeed, he goes so far as to suggest that the SDR, as presently constituted, may actually lower world welfare. Blackhurst focuses on the principle of reciprocity, which played a major role in tariff negotiations under the Bretton Woods system. He argues that a policy of reciprocity has significant advantages over unilateral tariff reductions under fixed exchange rates but that these advantages disappear under flexible exchange rates.

In sum, we believe these papers provide an interesting cross-section of current work in international economics, representing the type of work which the International Economics Study Group exists to promote. We make no apology for the fact that a high proportion of the authors come from outside Britain: visitors from abroad have an important role in our programme throughout the year, and the annual conference provides a further welcome opportunity for international cross-fertilisation of ideas.

Nor do we apologise for the fact that several of the papers (Branson and Halttunen, Knight and Mathieson, Deardorff *et al.*, and Carse and Wood are reports of work in progress: again it is one of the important aspects of a conference that this should be so. No one who reads this book will be surprised to learn that several papers provoked sharp discussion from the floor: Chrystal's attack on the SDR was criticised not only by the defenders of the SDR but also by those who felt that there were stronger grounds for attack; Deardorff *et al.*'s unusual blending of theory, empirical estimation and simulation was the subject of some controversy; and so on.

We did not keep, and therefore cannot publish, a formal record of the discussion. Instead, the authors were asked in preparing their papers for publication to take account of points made at the conference. We are grateful to all who participated in the conference, but especially to those who acted as principal discussants of papers: John Black, Tony Bottrill, Koichi Hamada, Jocelyn Horne, Vijay Joshi, Seamus O'Cleireacain, John Spraos, and Alan Winters.

We also wish to express our gratitude to those who made the conference possible from a financial point of view: notably the Shell International Petroleum Company, who provided the funds for inviting one American visitor, and the Social Science Research Council, who finance the regular programme of the Study Group as well as the annual conference.

The Study Group would probably not exist, certainly not in its present healthy form, without the organisational support of the Trade

Policy Research Centre. We are grateful for their efforts at every stage of the long process that began with the initial planning for the conference and ended with the production of this volume.

JOHN P. MARTIN
ALASDAIR SMITH

London
March 1978

1

Optimal Foreign Exchange Market Intervention with Rational Expectations

WILLEM BUITER

This paper deals with a number of related issues. The main substantive problem analysed is the derivation, using simple stochastic control theory, of the optimal foreign exchange market intervention policy from the point of view of a small open economy.[1]

PRICES VERSUS QUANTITIES

The extensive literature on the comparative merits of fixed and floating exchange-rate regimes[2] and the proliferation of proposals for gliding, sliding and crawling pegs, intervention bands, snakes and other animals, all deal with special cases of this general problem. We can distinguish between 'price-setting policies' or *exchange-rate management policies*, and 'quantity-setting policies' or *reserve management policies*.[3] With exchange-rate management policies a value for the exchange rate is chosen each period (at each point in time in the continuous case) by the policy authority, which then buys or sells reserves in the amount required to realise that exchange rate, given the behaviour of the domestic private sector and the external sector.[4] The fixed exchange-rate regime is the special case where the exchange rate is set at the same level each period (at each point in time). With reserve management policies the authority decides each period how much it wishes to add to or subtract from its stock of foreign exchange reserves. The exchange rate is then left free to find the level required to achieve that objective. Freely-floating exchange rates are the special case where the amount of reserves bought or sold each period is zero.

Clearly the issue of price management versus quantity management is a trivial one in a world without risk or uncertainty. Only differences in the costs associated with using the two instruments can lead one to favour the one over the other. The question as to what constitutes the best exchange-market intervention policy can therefore only be analysed properly in an explicitly stochastic model. This paper considers a number of very simple stochastic open-economy models. The uncertainty is due to a variety of domestic and foreign disturbances.

RULES VERSUS DISCRETION

In addition to analysing the 'prices versus quantities' issue in the context of foreign exchange market intervention, the paper also addresses the 'rules versus discretion' issue. This is rather a misnomer. 'Open-loop' or 'no-feedback' policies versus 'non-trivial closed-loop' or 'feedback' policies would be a more appropriate description of this debate. With open-loop policies the values of the time paths of the policy variables are specified at the beginning of a planning period. These paths are to be followed by the policy-maker without regard to future events. Closed-loop policies specify the policy variables as functions of observations yet to be made, that is the values of the policy variables in the future will depend on future observations, which will reflect the results of current policy.[5] The best-known example of an open-loop policy prescription is Milton Friedman's advocacy of a fixed growth rate for some monetary aggregate.[6] Formally, consider a first-order system of linear difference equations

$$Y_t = AY_{t-1} + CX_t + b + U_t.$$

Y_t is a vector of endogenous variables, X_t a vector of controls and U_t a serially uncorrelated vector with mean 0 and covariance matrix V.

A policy rule

$$X_t = G_t Y_{t-1} + g_t$$

is a non-trivial closed-loop policy if $G_t \neq 0$ and an open-loop policy if $G_t = 0$.

In this paper, a result favourable to the 'fixed rule' school of thought would be that the optimal exchange-rate management policy is the fixed exchange rate and that the optimal reserve management policy is the freely-floating exchange rate.

Two comparatively new approaches in the economic policy literature appear to give different answers to the open-loop versus feedback control question. The optimal control literature seems to suggest that, even for imperfect econometric models, optimal policy rules can be derived that will significantly improve performance in terms of some explicit objective functional over any fixed rule. These optimal rules can, in the case of stochastic models, only be expressed in terms of feedback control rules, which make explicit the dependence of the optimal values assumed by the policy instruments on the past states of the economy.[7] This paper uses the linear-quadratic framework of optimal control: a linear model with additive noise and a (finite) multi-period quadratic objective functional.

In contrast, the rational expectations literature seems to suggest that if economic agents form expectations in a way that is rational (that is, using all 'available' information optimally),[8] the scope for policy-makers to exert a beneficial impact upon economic welfare through stabilisation policy is pretty well eliminated.[9] Rational expectations are the stochastic analogue of perfect foresight. Rational expectations are optimal predictions conditional on all the information 'available' to the economic agent in question. In practice, unbiased (least squares) estimators are always used. Rational expectations do not have to be good forecasts although they are the best forecasts. In the simple models considered in this paper, rational expectations will indeed be very good forecasts; the information assumed to be available to private economic agents is considerable: they know the structure of the economy, including the stochastic processes and the government's objective function. They can solve simultaneously for their expectations of the behaviour of the economy and for the behaviour of the economy that is affected by these expectations. The main implication of the rational expectations hypothesis for macro-modelling is this necessity to solve simultaneously for the currently anticipated value of a variable and its future value calculated from the model.

There are a host of practical and conceptual problems associated with rational expectations theory. The assumption of perfect knowledge of probability distributions of outcomes is substituted for the assumption of perfect knowledge of the outcomes themselves. Obvious questions are whether these probability distributions are stable (stationary) and can be estimated. Problems of model selection do not arise in most rational expectations papers because the 'correct' model used for forecasting is the author's model in the paper. In practical applications this will be a major problem. The issue of learning behaviour when the 'environment' of an economic agent (the model) changes is another critical issue.[10] Economic agents do not just have to know the objective model; they must believe in rational expectations theory itself for it to work!

The problem of *non-existence* of a rational expectations equilibrium arises when the same information is not available to all economic agents and strategic behaviour is permitted: economic agents may allow for the fact that their actions will affect the expectations and actions of other economic agents, and deliberately act so as to influence expectations. Situations of *inconsistent expectations*—a bargaining stand-off in which each party confidently expects the other(s) to cave in—cannot, by definition, be modelled with rational expectations. *Non-uniqueness* of the rational expectations equilibrium trajectory raises serious conceptual problems. It is especially likely to arise when economic agents forecast many periods into the future.[11]

A practical problem is that, while rational expectations allow one to get away from the usual *ad hoc* distributed lag expectation functions, ad-hockery re-enters with a vengeance through the specification of the information set assumed to be available to economic agents. In other words, the hypothesis that economic agents use all available information optimally cannot be tested independently of a hypothesis about the economic agents' information set.

In addition to rational expectations, the models that have generated results that suggest the irrelevance of optimal feedback controls incorporate a number of further assumptions, each one of which is necessary for those results.[12] They are:

(*a*) Absence of static or dynamic money illusion.

(*b*) Instantaneous market clearing. More precisely, all markets are efficient auction markets: prices adjust to clear markets with a frequency no less than the frequency with which new information accrues to private and public economic agents. The 'market period' for each good or service equals the 'information period'. In reality, many implicit or explicit contracts extending over time intervals much longer than the 'information period' exist and these contracts are not complete contingent contracts in the sense of contingent on any new information that might accrue.

(*c*) No differential access to (and capacity to utilise) different kinds of information as between private and public economic agents. This does not only rule out the possibility that uniformly better information is available to the government, it also excludes the possibility of private and public economic agents having comparative advantages in gathering, processing and analysing different kinds of information.

(*d*) The frequency with which prices adjust to clear markets (or more generally the frequency with which private economic agents can react to new events) is no less than the frequency with which the public authority can adjust at least one of its controls and influence some economic variable that affects private-sector behaviour.[13]

In this paper, all four of these further assumptions are made. The result is that, while the choice between price-setting (exchange-rate management) policies and quantity-setting (reserve management) policies does affect the stochastic process governing the behaviour of real output, the actual values assigned to the exchange rate (if exchange-rate management is chosen) or to reserve sales or purchases (if a reserve management policy is chosen) will have no further effect on the probability distribution of real output. Appendix I (page 31) shows that if output is also a function of the stock of real reproducible capital, its probability distribution is affected by the values assigned to the foreign exchange market instruments when there is no perfect capital mobility. The external disequilibrium and the variability of the price level, however, will be always affected by the time path of the exchange rate or of reserve sales and purchases, as will real absorption. That this is possible under rational expectations is a consequence of the inability of the private sector to 'undo' every government action through market actions. While there are many plausible ways of ensuring that there is no 'Modigliani-Miller Theorem' for the private sector *vis-à-vis* the public sector,[14] in our models the not unreasonable assumption that the policy authority controls the nominal stock of money and the quite common assumption that foreign exchange is held only by the policy authority provide two reasons—each sufficient by itself—for the non-neutrality of foreign exchange market intervention. In two recent papers, Fischer (1977b) and Phelps and Taylor (1977) have demonstrated how multi-period wage contracts, or price-setting in advance of the period to which the price will apply, may cause the information set available at the time of the current money supply decision to be larger than the information set available when the current wage or price was decided on. Monetary feedback rules can then affect the probability distributions of real output and employment even with rational expectations.

The paper considers different domestic and foreign sources of disturbances. Three models are analysed. In order of increasing complexity they are:

1. A model without international financial flows and without an explicitly specified domestic financial sector.

2. A model without international financial flows but with an explicit domestic financial sector.

3. A model with an explicit domestic financial sector and international financial flows.

RESULTS

The main results of the paper are the following.

In the absence of international financial flows, freely-floating exchange rates and, more generally, reserve management policies, insulate the domestic economy from foreign disturbances. In the one-commodity models of the paper, foreign disturbances take the form of random variations in the world price level. The result, however, can be extended to a world with import and export demand functions and random shifts in the export demand function, as long as relative prices are not affected. This insulation of the domestic economy from foreign disturbances is a mixed blessing. 'Locking out' foreign disturbances means 'locking in' or 'bottling up' domestic disturbances, whose full effect will be felt in the home economy without any spillover abroad through external leakages. If domestic and foreign disturbances are appropriately correlated, the total variability of the target variables may be less if the foreign disturbances are allowed to enter freely.

When there is international integration of financial markets,[15] reserve management policies (including a freely-floating exchange rate) no longer insulate the domestic economy from foreign disturbances. Variations in 'the' world interest rate will have obvious direct effects, but world price disturbances too will lead to changes in the real rate of interest. The exchange rate still adjusts to the level required to generate the policy-determined change in reserves, but this exchange-rate adjustment cannot fully negate the effect of world price changes on the rate of return.

Open-loop controls are in general inferior to closed-loop feedback rules that can take into account new information as it becomes available. Once the price versus quantity-management choice has been made, the probability distribution of real output is unaffected by the values assigned to the exchange rate or the reserve sales or purchases, except in the case considered in Appendix I, but the price level, the external position and real absorption can be stabilised by 'active' optimal feedback controls.

The assumption of rational expectations (and the exact specification of the information available to the private and public economic agents) is crucial. Substituting *ad hoc* expectations functions for rational expectations will give the policy authority scope to affect the probability distribution of real output as well.

Minor changes in the specification of the objective functional will significantly affect the relative desirability of fixed and floating exchange rates. For example, having the level of the stock of foreign exchange reserves rather than the change in the level as an argument in the objective functional tilts the balance against the fixed exchange-rate regime.[16]

While the optimal reserve management policy will in general be superior to the freely-floating exchange-rate policy and the optimal exchange-rate management policy superior to the fixed exchange rate, we cannot rank the optimal reserve management policy and the optimal exchange-rate management policy without additional information about the exact numerical values of the coefficients of both the deterministic and the stochastic parts of the model. The ranking of fixed and freely-floating exchange-rate regimes depends in a more transparent manner on the structural coefficients of the model.

NOTATION

Y = real output
A = real absorption
X = net exports
R = reserves
p = log of the price level
e = log of the exchange rate
i = interest rate
m = log of the nominal stock of money balances
B = stock of real-valued bonds
$\hat{p}(t-1, t)$ = expected value, as of $t-1$, of p at t
$\hat{e}(t-1, t)$ = expected value, as of $t-1$, of e at t
$\varepsilon_s(t)$ = domestic supply disturbance
$\varepsilon_d(t)$ = domestic demand disturbance
$\varepsilon_m(t)$ = domestic monetary disturbance
$\eta_p(t)$ = foreign price disturbance
$\eta_f(t)$ = foreign interest-rate disturbance
σ_i^2 : variance of i, $i = \varepsilon_s, \varepsilon_d, \varepsilon_m, \eta_p, \eta_f$
ρ_{ij} : correlation coefficient between i and j, $i,j = \varepsilon_s, \varepsilon_d, \varepsilon_m, \eta_p, \eta_f$
E: the mathematical expectation operator

I THE SIMPLEST MODEL

In this section we consider the simplest small-country open-economy model. There is one traded commodity whose world price in terms of foreign currency is given. There are no international financial flows. The domestic financial sector is not represented explicitly (the *LM* curve is solved for the interest rate which is substituted into the *IS* curve). There is only one domestic disturbance, an aggregate demand shock, ε_d and one foreign disturbance, a world price shock, η_p. Throughout this paper it is assumed that there is complete sterilisation of reserve flows, for instance, by open-market operations. In addition, the government always balances its budget. The nominal quantity of money balances is therefore constant throughout.[17] All foreign exchange is held by the government.[18] As it is assumed that the government holds all its monetary and fiscal policy instruments constant, any 'optimal' foreign-exchange market intervention rule that may be derived will be optimal only in a very limited sense. The pursuit of a multi-dimensional vector of objectives through the manipulation of a multi-dimensional vector of controls, while not conceptually more complicated than the single instrument—multiple objective case analysed in the paper is too unwieldy for analytical treatment.[19]

The model can be summarised as follows:

(1) $Y(t) = a(p(t) - \hat{p}(t-1, t))$ $\qquad a > 0$

(2) $A(t) = b_1(m - p(t)) + \varepsilon_d(t)$ $\qquad b_1 > 0$

(3) $p(t) = e(t) + \eta_p(t)$

(4) $X(t) = Y(t) - A(t)$

(5) $\Delta R(t) \equiv R(t+1) - R(t) = X(t)$

(6) $\hat{p}(t-1, t) = E_{t-1}(p(t) | I(t-1))$

(7a) $E\varepsilon_d(t) = E\eta_p(t) = 0$

(7b) $E(\varepsilon_d(t), \eta_p(t))' (\varepsilon_d(s), \eta_p(s))$

$$= \begin{cases} \begin{bmatrix} \sigma^2_{\varepsilon_d} & \rho_{\varepsilon_d \eta_p} \sigma_{\varepsilon_d} \sigma_{\eta_p} \\ \rho_{\varepsilon_d \eta_p} \sigma_{\varepsilon_d} \sigma_{\eta_p} & \sigma^2_{\eta_p} \end{bmatrix} & \text{if } t = s \\ \mathbf{0} \qquad \begin{bmatrix} 0 & 0 \\ 0 & 0 \end{bmatrix} & \text{if } t \neq s. \end{cases}$$

The government's objective is to minimise[20]

$$(8)\ L = E_0 \sum_{t=1}^{T} \{w_1 Y(t)^2 + w_2(\Delta R(t))^2 + w_3(\Delta p(t))^2\}.$$

Equation (1) is a Phelps-Friedman[21] aggregate supply function. Current output, $Y(t)$, expressed in terms of the deviation from its normal or natural level, is an increasing function of the excess of this period's price over the price that last period was expected to prevail during the current period. $p(t)$ is the natural log of the price level, $\hat{p}(t-1, t)$ is the expectation, as of $t-1$, of the natural log of the price level at t. The natural level of output is independent of the capital stock. The role of the Phelps-Friedman production function in generating the result that the probability distribution of real output is not affected by foreign-exchange market intervention is crucial. With a Phelps-Friedman production function, deviations of actual output from its natural level occur, *if and only if*, the actual price differs from the expected price. Given expectations, demand equals supply in the output market (and in the suppressed labour market). Notional and effective demand and supply schedules coincide. Perfectly competitive markets clear instantaneously and all of the time. Thus neither 'target' output nor variations about that target level can be affected by government policy.

Equation (2) specifies aggregate demand or real domestic absorption (expressed in terms of deviations from the normal or natural level of output) as an increasing function of the real money stock. m is the natural log of the constant nominal supply of money balances. Aggregate demand is affected by a random error term ε_d. Expenditure could be made to depend on actual income, with a marginal propensity to spend between zero and one without changing any of the results in the paper. Our choice of units to measure Y and A permits us to economise on the number of constants to be carried around. It leads to a few *prima facie* unfamiliar results which will be pointed out below.

Equation (3) is the 'law of one price'; perfect commodity arbitrage equates the domestic currency price of output, $P(t)$, to the foreign currency price $P^*(t)$ multiplied by the foreign exchange rate, $\Pi(t)$. Taking logs on both sides, we get $p(t) = e(t) + p^*(t)$. The log of the world price level is assumed to be a random variable $\eta_p(t)$.

Equation (4) states that net exports are the excess of domestic production over domestic absorption.

Equation (5) states that in the absence of international capital flows the real value of the net increase in reserves is equal to the trade balance surplus.

Equation (6) is the rational expectations hypothesis. The price level expected in period $t-1$ to prevail in period t is the mathematical expectation of the price level at period t, conditional on the information available to the economic agents at $t-1: I(t-1)$.

Equations (7a) and (7b) give the known mean vector and variance-covariance matrix of the disturbances. Both have zero means and are mutually serially independent.[22]

The specification of the objective function (8) requires some justification. It is a special case of the T period sum of quadratic functions:

$$E_0 \sum_{t=1}^{T} (Y(t)-a(t))'K(t)(Y(t)-a(t)).$$

The objections to a quadratic single-period loss function are well known. It exhibits 'satiation', that is, it achieves a minimum or maximum at $a(t)$, and it is 'symmetric', that is, it assigns the same cost to a positive deviation from the ideal path, $a(t)$, as to a negative deviation of equal magnitude. The satiation problem can be avoided by setting the optimum, $a(t)$, at so unrealistic a level that the actual solution will always stay on the 'right' side of the ideal path. The symmetry problem has been tackled by B. Friedman. He generalised the linear constraint-quadratic objective optimal control framework to piecewise linear constraints and piecewise quadratic objectives without losing the major advantage of the linear-quadratic framework – the simplicity of the optimal linear feedback rules it generates.[23]

It is not true, as is sometimes argued, that a quadratic specification means that the policy authority attaches utility only to reducing the variance of its objectives. While utility is attached to *stabilisation*, the ideal path around which target variables are to be stabilised (which could, for example, in the case of absorption be chosen to be the golden rule path) and the weights attached to deviations from the ideal path at different dates, given by the weighting matrices $K(t)$, are equally important in determining the optimal trajectory. It is appropriate to view the quadratic function as a (second-order) approximation to a more general non-linear objective function.

If we accept the quadratic specification, the choice of variables to be included in the objective function, of ideal paths for these variables and of weights to be attached to deviations of the objectives from their ideal or target values still remains to be made. While our objectives may have comparatively weak 'welfare foundations', in the rather limited sense of being different from the most common arguments found in the normative macro-economic literature (essentially current and future—*per capita*—consumption paths), they are descriptively realistic in the sense that they correspond to the well-publicised proximate aims of demand management policy in advanced capitalist economies.

The government has three objectives: two 'internal balance' objectives – stabilisation of output (employment) at normal capacity (at the 'natural' rate of unemployment) and price level stability – and one external balance objective. We specify this in terms of minimisation of the balance-of-payments deficit or surplus. If the *level* of the stock of reserves relative to some target level, $R - R^*$, rather than the *change* in the reserves, ΔR, is the external balance objective, fixed exchange rates become a less attractive proposition, as will be demonstrated below. The government minimises the expectation, as of time O, of the T period sum of squared deviations of the objectives, Y, ΔR and Δp from their target values (zero for all three). Without in any way weakening the main conclusions of the paper, we can substitute deviations of domestic absorption (A) from its target (zero) for deviations of Y from its target. Indeed, our conclusions as regards the existence of non-trivial optimal feedback controls would be strengthened, as the stochastic process for $A(t)$, unlike that for $Y(t)$, is not independent of the values assumed by the controls, $\Delta R(t)$ or $e(t)$.

The information available to economic agents when forming their expectations about $p(t)$ during period $t-1$ is very rich. They know the structure of the model, and the joint density of the disturbances (only the first two moments of which matter for our analysis). In addition, they know the government's objective function. They also know all past values of the endogenous variables and the policy instruments, up to and including those in period $t-1$. This allows them to derive the values of the disturbances in period $t-1$ and in all earlier periods.

When the government chooses, at the beginning of period t, the value for its control during period t, it does not know the current (period t) values of the disturbances but it does know all past states of the model.

THE FIXED EXCHANGE-RATE REGIME

Consider the case where $e(t)$ is set at the same level $\bar{e}$ each period. $\bar{e}$ has been chosen optimally so as to minimise (8). The private sector knows that the government follows a fixed exchange-rate policy, believes it to be viable because $\bar{e}$ has been chosen optimally and reserves are large enough to withstand a run of bad luck, and knows that the price level is generated according to (3). Thus

$$\hat{p}(t-1, t) = E_{t-1}p(t) = E_{t-1}(e(t) + \eta_p(t)) = \bar{e}.$$

With a fixed exchange rate, the behaviour of the target variables is given by

(9) $Y(t) = a\eta_p(t)$

(10) $\Delta R(t) = -b_1(m-\bar{e}) + \Psi\eta_p(t) - \varepsilon_d(t)$

(11) $\Delta p(t) = \eta_p(t) - \eta_p(t-1)$,

where $\Psi = a + b_1$. Neither the behaviour of output nor that of the price level can be affected by the choice of the fixed value $\bar{e}$. Real output and rate of inflation are given by stochastic processes determined only by the foreign price disturbances.[24]

From equation (10) and the objective function, it is clear that $\bar{e} = m$ is the optimal fixed exchange rate; when $\bar{e} = m$ the expected external deficit $(E\Delta R(t))$ equals zero. This justifies the assumption that the private sector has confidence that the fixed exchange-rate regime will not break down. The coefficient of unity on m is a result of our choice of units for Y and A.

The minimum expected loss equals

(12) $L^*_{\text{Fixed}} = T\{(w_1a^2 + w_2\Psi^2 + 2w_3)\sigma^2_{\eta_p} + w_2\sigma^2_{\varepsilon_d} - 2w_2\Psi\rho_{\eta_p\varepsilon_d}\sigma_{\eta_p}\sigma_{\varepsilon_d}\}$.

THE FREELY-FLOATING EXCHANGE-RATE REGIME

When $\Delta R(t)$ is set equal to zero each period, domestic production equals domestic absorption and $Y(t) = A(t)$ can be solved for the domestic price level. The exchange rate required to clear the foreign exchange market is then determined via equation (3). By equating (1) and (2), we obtain:

$$p(t) = \frac{b_1}{\Psi}m + \frac{a}{\Psi}\hat{p}(t-1,t) + \frac{1}{\Psi}\varepsilon_d(t).$$

According to the rational expectations assumption, private economic agents know this equation. Using $\hat{p}(t-1,t) = E_{t-1}p(t)$, we find:

$$\hat{p}(t-1,t) = m.$$

Our choice of units for Y and A accounts for the coefficient of unity on m here as well. Substituting this into the previous equation, we get

$$p(t) = m + \frac{1}{\Psi}\varepsilon_d(t).$$

The floating-rate model can now be summarised as:

(13) $Y(t) = \frac{a}{\Psi}\varepsilon_d(t)$

(14) $\Delta R(t) = 0$

(15) $p(t) = \frac{1}{\Psi}(\varepsilon_d(t) - \varepsilon_d(t-1))$.

The economy is completely insulated from foreign disturbances. The freely-floating exchange-rate policy is simpler to execute than the fixed exchange-rate policy as the level of the fixed rate needs to be chosen optimally while all the government has to do under floating rates is announce its absence from the foreign exchange market.

The expected loss is

(16) $L^*_{\text{Float}} = T\left(\frac{w_1 a^2 + 2w_3}{\Psi^2}\right)\sigma^2_{\varepsilon_d}$.

Comparing (16) and (12), we note the following:

if there are no domestic disturbances ($\sigma^2_{\varepsilon_d} = 0$) the freely floating exchange rate regime dominates with an expected loss of zero.

if there are no foreign disturbances, sign $[L^*_{\text{Fixed}} - L^*_{\text{Float}}]$ = sign $\left[w_2 - \left(\frac{(w_1 a^2 + 2w_3)}{\Psi}\right)\right]$. Without foreign disturbances, only $\Delta R(t)$ is subject to shocks under a fixed rate while both Y and Δp are subject to shocks with the floating rate. The relative weights of the three targets will then clearly play a role in determining the ranking of the two regimes.

$\eta_p(t)$ and $\varepsilon_d(t)$ affect the external deficit in opposite directions. A positive correlation between the two will therefore reduce the minimum expected loss with a fixed rate.

the larger b_1, which measures the responsiveness of domestic absorption to changes in the real stock of money balances, the lower the minimum expected loss under a floating rate. When b_1 is small, a domestic demand shock requires a large change in the price level and a large change in domestic output to re-equilibrate the goods market (to keep output and absorption equal to each other). Such changes in p and Y are penalised in the loss function.

THE SPECIFICATION OF THE LOSS FUNCTION

Consider an alteration, at first sight minor, in the specification of the loss function, consisting of the substitution of the deviation of the stock of reserves from its target level, $R-R^*$ for the change in the level of reserves, ΔR.

$$L' = E_0 \sum_{t=1}^{T} \{w_1 Y(t)^2 + w_2 (R(t+1) - R^*)^2 + w_3 (\Delta p(t))^2\}.$$

With a fixed exchange rate, we can write the model as:

$$Y(t) = a\eta_p(t)$$

$$R(t) = R(t-1) - b_1 m + b_1 \bar{e} + \Psi\eta_p(t-1) - \varepsilon_d(t-1)$$

$$\Delta p(t) = \eta_p(t) - \eta_p(t-1).$$

The optimum value for $\bar{e}$ is easily found to be:

$$\bar{e} = m + \frac{2(R^* - R_0)}{b_1(T+1)}.$$

Assuming the policy authority not to be excessively silly, the exchange rate will not be fixed at $t=0$ unless $R^* = R(0)$. The optimum value of the fixed exchange rate is therefore again $\bar{e} = m$. The minimum expected loss under the fixed exchange-rate regime is then equal to:

$$L^*_{\text{Fixed}} = T\{w_1 a^2 \sigma^2_{\eta_p} + w_2 \frac{(T+1)}{2} \Psi^2 \sigma^2_{\eta_p} + \sigma^2_{\varepsilon_d} - 2\Psi \rho_{\eta_p \varepsilon_d} \sigma_{\eta_p} \sigma_{\varepsilon_d})$$
$$+ 2w_3 \sigma^2_{\eta_p}\}.$$

Comparing this with (12), we find that the minimum loss when $R-R^*$ rather than ΔR is in the objective function is greater because each one-period loss associated with a change in reserves due to random disturbances: $w_2(\Psi^2\sigma^2_{\eta_p} + \sigma^2_{\varepsilon_d} - 2\Psi\rho_{\eta_p\varepsilon_d}\sigma_{\eta_p}\sigma_{\varepsilon_d})$ is multiplied by the average number of periods that each disturbance stays in the system by being 'carried forward' in R, that is, $\frac{T+1}{2}$.

Assuming a free float is not initiated unless $R(o) = R^*$, the expected loss under freely-floating exchange rates is the same as when ΔR was in the objective functional. Having the level rather than the change in reserves in the objective function will make a floating exchange rate more attractive relative to a fixed exchange rate.

OPTIMAL CLOSED-LOOP EXCHANGE-RATE AND RESERVE-MANAGEMENT POLICIES

A fixed exchange rate is but the extreme case of the class of exchange-rate management policies which in principle allow a different value for the exchange rate to be set each period. A freely-floating rate is the extreme case of the class of reserve management policies.

The optimal exchange rate and reserve management policies for the simple model given by equations (1) to (8) are derived here. The derivation of our optimal policies requires the minimisation of a quadratic objective functional subject to constraints that are represented by a set of finite order linear difference equations. Such a control problem can always be written in the form of equations (17) and (18) below.[25]

$$(17) \qquad \min_{\{\mathbf{x}(t);t=1,2,\ldots T\}} \quad E_0 \sum_{t=1}^{T} (\mathbf{y}(t)-\mathbf{a}(t))'\mathbf{K}(t)(\mathbf{y}(t)-\mathbf{a}(t))$$

subject to

$$(18a) \quad \mathbf{y}(t) = \mathbf{A}(t)\mathbf{y}(t-1)+\mathbf{C}(t)\mathbf{x}(t)+\mathbf{b}(t)+\mathbf{u}(t)$$

$$(18b) \quad E\mathbf{u}(t) = \mathbf{0} \text{ for all } t$$

$$(18c) \quad E\mathbf{u}(t)\mathbf{u}(s)' = \begin{cases} \mathbf{V} & \text{if } t = s, \ V \text{ a known positive definite matrix.} \\ \mathbf{0} & \text{if } t \neq s. \end{cases}$$

$$(18d) \quad \mathbf{y}(O) = \mathbf{y}_0.$$

$\mathbf{y}(t)$, the state vector, can contain current and lagged target variables, current and lagged intervening or intermediate variables (those endogenous variables that are neither targets nor instruments), current and lagged values of the instruments and current and lagged disturbances. $\mathbf{x}(t)$ is the vector of current instruments, $\mathbf{b}(t)$ is a vector of exogenous variables and $\mathbf{u}(t)$ is a vector of mutually serially independent disturbances. $\mathbf{A}(t)$ and $\mathbf{C}(t)$ are known coefficient matrices.[26] The $\mathbf{K}(t)$ are known symmetric (usually diagonal) positive semi-definite matrices and the $\mathbf{a}(t)$ are known vectors of desired values for the target variables.

The optimal control rule that minimises (17) subject to (18) is:[27]

$$(19a) \quad \mathbf{x}(t) = \mathbf{G}(t)\mathbf{y}(t-1)+\mathbf{g}(t)$$

$$(19b) \quad \mathbf{G}(t) = -[\mathbf{C}'(t)\mathbf{H}(t)\mathbf{C}(t)]^{-1}\mathbf{C}'(t)\mathbf{H}(t)\mathbf{A}(t)$$

$$(19c) \quad \mathbf{H}(t-1) = \mathbf{K}(t-1)+\mathbf{A}'(t)\mathbf{H}(t)[\mathbf{A}(t)+\mathbf{C}(t)\mathbf{G}(t)]$$

$$(19d) \quad \mathbf{g}(t) = -[\mathbf{C}'(t)\mathbf{H}(t)\mathbf{C}(t)]^{-1}\mathbf{C}'(t)[\mathbf{H}(t)\mathbf{b}(t)-\mathbf{h}(t)]$$

(19e) $\mathbf{h}(t-1) = \mathbf{K}(t-1)\mathbf{a}(t-1) - \mathbf{A}'(t)\mathbf{H}(t)(\mathbf{b}(t) + \mathbf{C}(t)\mathbf{g}(t)) + \mathbf{A}(t)'\mathbf{h}(t)$

(19f) $\mathbf{H}(T) = \mathbf{K}(T)$

(19g) $\mathbf{h}(T) = \mathbf{K}(T)\mathbf{a}(T)$.

This solution is identical to the one obtained when the random disturbance vector is ignored (replaced by its expected value). When we minimise the expectation of a multi-period quadratic loss function subject to a known linear model with additive random disturbances, multi-period certainty equivalence exists if the solution is expressed in the form of feedback control equations. The importance of equations (19a) to (19g) for our problem is that the current period value of the optimal control, $\mathbf{x}(t)$, depends only on last period's state of the model, $\mathbf{y}(t-1)$, which we assume to be known when economic agents form their expectations, at time $t-1$, about the current period value of the control, and on the known coefficient matrices. In other words, $\mathbf{x}(t)$ is known with certainty to private economic agents at time $t-1$. Any effect that the active use of these controls may have can therefore certainly not be attributed to the government 'fooling' the people. In our models the foregoing implies $E_{t-1}e(t) = e(t)$ and $E_{t-1}\Delta R(t) = \Delta R(t)$.

THE OPTIMAL EXCHANGE-RATE MANAGEMENT POLICY

With rational expectations the general exchange-rate management model can be written as:

(20) $Y(t) = a\eta_p(t)$

(21) $\Delta R(t) = -b_1 m + b_1 e(t) + \Psi\eta_p(t) - \varepsilon_d(t)$

(22) $\Delta p(t) = e(t) - e(t-1) + \eta_p(t) - \eta_p(t-1)$.

The objective is to minimise, by choice of $e(t)$, $t = 1, 2, \ldots, T$,

$$E_0 \sum_{t=1}^{T} [w_1 Y(t)^2 + w_2(\Delta R(t))^2 + w_3(\Delta p(t))^2].$$

If we rewrite this in the format provided by equations (17) and (18), we obtain the following. Minimise

$$(23)\quad E_0 \sum_{t=1}^{T} \begin{bmatrix} Y(t) \\ \Delta R(t) \\ \Delta p(t) \\ e(t) \\ \eta_p(t) \end{bmatrix} \begin{bmatrix} w_1 & 0 & 0 & 0 & 0 \\ 0 & w_2 & 0 & 0 & 0 \\ 0 & 0 & w_3 & 0 & 0 \\ 0 & 0 & 0 & 0 & 0 \\ 0 & 0 & 0 & 0 & 0 \end{bmatrix} \begin{bmatrix} Y(t) \\ \Delta R(t) \\ \Delta p(t) \\ e(t) \\ \eta_p(t) \end{bmatrix}$$

Subject to:

$$(24)\quad \begin{bmatrix} Y(t) \\ \Delta R(t) \\ \Delta p(t) \\ e(t) \\ \eta_p(t) \end{bmatrix} = \begin{bmatrix} 0 & 0 & 0 & 0 & 0 \\ 0 & 0 & 0 & 0 & 0 \\ 0 & 0 & 0 & -1 & -1 \\ 0 & 0 & 0 & 0 & 0 \\ 0 & 0 & 0 & 0 & 0 \end{bmatrix} \begin{bmatrix} Y(t-1) \\ \Delta R(t-1) \\ \Delta p(t-1) \\ e(t-1) \\ \eta_p(t-1) \end{bmatrix} + \begin{bmatrix} 0 \\ b_1 \\ 1 \\ 1 \\ 0 \end{bmatrix} e(t) + \begin{bmatrix} 0 \\ -b_1 m \\ 0 \\ 0 \\ 0 \end{bmatrix} + \begin{bmatrix} a\eta_p(t) \\ \eta_p(t) - \varepsilon_d(t) \\ \eta_p(t) \\ 0 \\ \eta_p(t) \end{bmatrix}.$$

(23) and (24) represent a simple version of (17) and (18) with all the $\mathbf{A}(t)$, $\mathbf{C}(t)$, $\mathbf{b}(t)$ and $\mathbf{K}(t)$ matrices time-invariant and the $\mathbf{a}(t)$ vectors all equal to zero.

A hard look at (23) to (24) suggests immediately that the fixed exchange-rate policy, $e(t) = e(t-1) = m$, will not be optimal, because the authorities at time t know $\eta_p(t-1)$ and can therefore stabilise the price level by adjusting $e(t)$ upwards whenever $\eta_p(t-1)$ is positive and vice versa. (If $e(t)$ were kept constant when $\eta_p(t-1)$ is positive, the price level in period t would be expected to fall as $E_{t-1}\,\eta_p(t) = 0$.) It also suggests that if no weight were attached to price stability ($w_3 = 0$), the optimal exchange-rate management policy will in fact be the fixed exchange-rate policy. The formal analysis bears this out. The explicit solutions of $\mathbf{g}(t)$ and $\mathbf{G}(t)$ for the last two periods (T and $T-1$) are given below:

$$(25a)\quad \mathbf{G}(T) = \begin{bmatrix} 0 & 0 & 0 & \dfrac{w_3}{\Psi_0} & \dfrac{w_3}{\Psi_0} \end{bmatrix}$$

$$(25b)\quad \mathbf{g}(T) = \frac{b_1^2 w_2 m}{\Psi_0}$$

that is,

$$(26)\quad e(T) = \frac{w_3}{\Psi_0} e(T-1) + \frac{w_3}{\Psi_0}\eta_p(T-1) + \frac{b_1^2 w_2 m}{\Psi_0}$$

Since $\eta_p(T-1) = p(T-1) - e(T-1)$, (26) can be rewritten as:

$$(26')\quad e(T) = \frac{w_3}{\Psi_0} p(T-1) + \frac{b_1^2 w_2 m}{\Psi_0}$$

$\Psi_0 = b_1^2 w_2 + w_3.$

Note that e(T) increases with $\eta_p(T-1)$ and that if $w_3 = 0$, $e(T) = m$, as expected.

$$(27a)\ \mathbf{G}(T-1) = \left[\begin{array}{ccccc} 0 & 0 & 0 & \dfrac{w_3\Psi_0}{\Psi_1} & \dfrac{w_3\Psi_0}{\Psi_1}\end{array}\right]$$

$$(27b)\ \mathbf{g}(T-1) = \frac{b_1^2 m\Psi_2}{\Psi_1}$$

that is,

$$(28)\ e(T-1) = \left(\frac{w_3\Psi_0}{\Psi_1}\right)e(T-2) + \left(\frac{w_3\Psi_0}{\Psi_1}\right)\eta_p(t-2) + \frac{b_1^2 w_2\Psi_2}{\Psi_1}.$$

Using $\eta_p(T-2) = p(T-2) - e(T-2)$, (28) can be rewritten as:

$$(28')\ e(T-1) = \frac{w_3\Psi_0}{\Psi_1}p(T-2) + \frac{b_1^2 w_2\Psi_2 m}{\Psi_1}$$

$$\Psi_1 = b_1^4 w_2^2 + 3w_2w_3b_1^2 + w_3^2;\ \Psi_2 = b_1^2 w_2 + 2w_3.$$

Again we note that $e(T-1)$ moves with $\eta_p(T-2)$ and that when $w_3 = 0$, $e(T-1) = m$.

THE OPTIMAL RESERVE MANAGEMENT POLICY

With rational expectations we can solve the equation $Y(t) - A(t) = \Delta R(t)$ for the actual and expected price level. We find

$$\hat{p}(t-1, t) = m + \frac{\Delta R(t)}{b_1}$$

$$p(t) = m + \frac{\Delta R(t)}{b_1} + \frac{\varepsilon_d(t)}{\Psi}.$$

Under general reserve management policies, the model can then be written as:

$$(29)\ Y(t) = \frac{a}{\Psi}\varepsilon_d(t)$$

$$(30)\ \Delta R(t) = \Delta R(t)$$

$$(31)\ \Delta p(t) = \frac{1}{b_1}(\Delta R(t) - \Delta R(t-1)) + \frac{1}{\Psi}(\varepsilon_d(t) - \varepsilon_d(t-1)).$$

Note that the economy is still insulated from foreign disturbances.

The first-order representation of this system with serially independent disturbances is:

$$(32)\quad \begin{bmatrix} Y(t) \\ \Delta R(t) \\ \Delta p(t) \\ \frac{a}{\Psi}\varepsilon_d(t) \end{bmatrix} = \begin{bmatrix} 0 & 0 & 0 & 0 \\ 0 & 0 & 0 & 0 \\ 0 & -\frac{1}{b_1} & 0 & 0 \\ 0 & 0 & 0 & 0 \end{bmatrix} \begin{bmatrix} Y(t-1) \\ \Delta R(t-1) \\ \Delta p(t-1) \\ \frac{a}{\Psi}\varepsilon_d(t-1) \end{bmatrix} + \begin{bmatrix} 0 \\ 1 \\ \frac{1}{b_1} \\ 0 \end{bmatrix} \Delta R(t) + \begin{bmatrix} \frac{a}{\Psi}\varepsilon_d(t) \\ 0 \\ \frac{1}{\Psi}\varepsilon_d(t) \\ \frac{a}{\Psi}\varepsilon_d(t) \end{bmatrix}.$$

The objective functional is: minimise

$$(33)\quad E_o \sum_{t=1}^{T} \begin{bmatrix} Y(t) \\ \Delta R(t) \\ \Delta p(t) \\ \frac{a}{\Psi}\varepsilon_d(t) \end{bmatrix} \begin{bmatrix} w_1 & 0 & 0 & 0 \\ 0 & w_2 & 0 & 0 \\ 0 & 0 & w_3 & 0 \\ 0 & 0 & 0 & 0 \end{bmatrix} \begin{bmatrix} Y(t) \\ \Delta R(t) \\ \Delta p(t) \\ \frac{a}{\Psi}\varepsilon_d(t) \end{bmatrix}.$$

Casual inspection of equations (30) and (31) suggests that the optimal value of $\Delta R(t)$ will move positively with $\varepsilon_d(t-1)$, but that if no weight is attached to price instability ($w_3 = 0$), the optimal foreign exchange reserve management policy is the floating exchange rate. This is again confirmed by the formal solution for $\Delta R(t)$ for the last two periods. The intuitive reason is that a positive domestic demand shock in period $t-1$ will, given $\Delta R(t-1)$, cause a depreciation of the exchange rate (a rise in the price level). As $E_{t-1}\varepsilon_d(t) = 0$, we would expect an appreciation of the exchange rate (a fall in the price level) during period t. The policy authority should therefore purchase foreign exchange to prevent this appreciation of the exchange rate.

$$(34a)\quad \mathbf{G}(T) = \begin{bmatrix} 0 & \frac{w_3}{\Psi_0} & 0 & \frac{w_3 b_1}{a\Psi_0} \end{bmatrix}$$

$$(34b)\quad \mathbf{g}(T) = 0$$

that is,

$$(35)\ \Delta R(T) = \frac{w_3}{\Psi_0}\Delta R(T-1) + \frac{w_3 b_1}{\Psi\Psi_0}\varepsilon_d(T-1).$$

As $\dfrac{\varepsilon_d(T-1)}{\Psi} = p(T-1) - m - \dfrac{\Delta R(T-1)}{b_1}$

we can rewrite this as:

$$(35)\ \Delta R(t) = \frac{w_3 b_1}{\Psi_0}(p(T-1) - m),$$

Equation (35) shows that $\varepsilon_d(t)$ and $\Delta R(T)$ will move together and that $\Delta R(T) = 0$ if $w_3 = 0$.

$$(36a)\ \mathbf{G}(T-1) = \begin{bmatrix} 0 & \dfrac{w_3\Psi_0}{\Psi_3} & 0 & \dfrac{w_3 b_1 0}{a\Psi_3} \end{bmatrix}$$

(36b) $\mathbf{g}(T-1) = 0$,
that is,

$$(37)\ \Delta R(T-1) = \frac{w_3\Psi_0}{\Psi_3}\Delta R(T-2) + \frac{w_3 b_1 \Psi_0}{\Psi\Psi_3}\varepsilon_d(T-2).$$

As $\dfrac{\varepsilon_d(T-2)}{\Psi} = p(T-2) - m - \dfrac{\Delta R(T-2)}{b_1}$, we can rewrite this as:

$$(37')\ \Delta R(t-1) = \frac{w_3 b_1 \Psi_1}{\Psi_3}(p(T-2) - m)$$

$$\Psi_3 = b_1^4 w_2^2 + 2w_2 w_3 b_1^2 + w_2 w_3 b_1 + w_3^2.$$

Equation (37) shows, as expected, that $\varepsilon_d(T-2)$ and $\Delta R(T-1)$ move together and that $\Delta R(T-1) = 0$ if $w_3 = 0$.

NON-RATIONAL EXPECTATIONS

The rational expectations assumption is central and the consequences of abandoning it are far-reaching. In general, the trajectory (the probability distribution function) or real output will now be affected by the values assigned to the policy instrument. The optimal feedback control will depend on the lagged value of $Y(t)$ and on w_1, the weight attached to output instability in the objective function. A frequently used *ad hoc* expectations mechanism is the following:

$$\hat{p}(t-1, t) = p(t-1) + v(p(t-1) - \hat{p}(t-2, t-1)).$$

This includes as special cases, static expectations ($v = 0$), mildly regressive expectations ($-1 < v < 0$), strongly regressive expectations ($v < -1$), mildly extrapolative expectations ($0 < v < 1$) and strongly extrapolative expectations ($v > 1$).

The first order representation with serially independent disturbances of the exchange-rate management model is:

$$\begin{bmatrix} Y(t) \\ \hat{p}(t,t+1) \\ \Delta R(t) \\ \Delta p(t) \\ e(t) \\ \eta_p(t) \end{bmatrix} = \begin{bmatrix} 0 & -a & 0 & 0 & 0 & 0 \\ 0 & -v & 0 & 0 & 0 & 0 \\ 0 & -a & 0 & 0 & 0 & 0 \\ 0 & 0 & 0 & 0 & -1 & -1 \\ 0 & 0 & 0 & 0 & 0 & 0 \\ 0 & 0 & 0 & 0 & 0 & 0 \end{bmatrix} \begin{bmatrix} Y(t-1) \\ \hat{p}(t-1,t) \\ \Delta R(t-1) \\ \Delta p(t-1) \\ e(t-1) \\ \eta_p(t-1) \end{bmatrix}$$

$$+ \begin{bmatrix} a \\ 1+v \\ a+b_1 \\ 1 \\ 1 \\ 0 \end{bmatrix} e(t) + \begin{bmatrix} 0 \\ 0 \\ -b_1 m \\ 0 \\ 0 \\ 0 \end{bmatrix} + \begin{bmatrix} a\eta_p(t) \\ (1+a_1)\eta_p(t) \\ (a+b_1)\eta_p(t)-\varepsilon_d(t) \\ \eta_p(t) \\ 0 \\ \eta_p(t) \end{bmatrix}$$

With $Y(t)$ depending on current and lagged values of the instrument $e(t)$, the scope for stabilisation policy is greatly enhanced. With a fixed exchange rate, the only non-zero characteristic root of the system is $-v$. Static expectations or mildly regressive or extrapolative expectations are therefore necessary and sufficient for stability under a fixed exchange-rate regime.

The first order representation with serially independent disturbances of the reserve management model is:

$$\begin{bmatrix} Y(t) \\ \hat{p}(t,t+1) \\ \hat{p}(t-1,t) \\ \Delta p(t) \\ \Delta R(t) \\ \varepsilon_d(t) \end{bmatrix} \begin{bmatrix} 0 & \dfrac{-ab_1}{a+b_1} & 0 & 0 & 0 & 0 \\ 0 & \dfrac{a-vb_1}{a+b_1} & 0 & 0 & 0 & 0 \\ 0 & 1 & 0 & 0 & 0 & 0 \\ 0 & \dfrac{a}{a+b_1} & \dfrac{-a}{a+b_1} & 0 & \dfrac{-1}{a+b_1} & \dfrac{-1}{a+b_1} \\ 0 & 0 & 0 & 0 & 0 & 0 \\ 0 & 0 & 0 & 0 & 0 & 0 \end{bmatrix} \begin{bmatrix} Y(t-1) \\ \hat{p}(t-1,t) \\ \hat{p}(t-2,t-1) \\ \Delta p(t-1) \\ \Delta R(t-1) \\ \varepsilon_d(t-1) \end{bmatrix}$$

$$+\begin{bmatrix} \dfrac{a}{a+b_1} \\ \dfrac{1+v}{a+b_1} \\ 0 \\ \dfrac{1}{a+b_1} \\ 1 \\ 0 \end{bmatrix} \Delta R(t) + \begin{bmatrix} \dfrac{ab_1 m}{a+b_1} \\ \dfrac{b_1(1+v)m}{a+b_1} \\ 0 \\ 0 \\ 0 \\ 0 \end{bmatrix} + \begin{bmatrix} \dfrac{a}{a+b_1}\varepsilon_d(t) \\ \dfrac{(1+v)}{a+b_1}\varepsilon_d(t) \\ 0 \\ \dfrac{1}{a+b_1}\varepsilon_d(t) \\ 0 \\ \varepsilon_d(t) \end{bmatrix}$$

Again, the probability distribution of real output depends on current and lagged values of $\Delta R(t)$, enhancing the scope for active feedback stabilisation policy. It is also clear that the insulation of the domestic economy from foreign disturbances under reserve management policies in the absence of international financial flows does not depend on the rational expectations hypothesis. With a freely-floating exchange rate, the only non-zero characteristic root is $\dfrac{a-vb_1}{a+b_1}$. The necessary and sufficient condition for stability, $|v| < 1$, is the same as under a fixed rate. Even without going through the unrewarding hard slog of deriving the expected T-period loss under fixed and freely-floating exchange rates, it would seem to be clear that the introduction of *ad hoc* expectations mechanisms *per se* will not lead one to favour the one regime over the other.

While we shall not pursue the issue of non-rational expectations any further here, it is important to be aware of the tremendous power of the rational expectations assumption in 'auction market' models.[28]

ALTERNATIVE SPECIFICATIONS OF THE OBJECTIVE FUNCTION

The existence of non-trivial feedback control rules is not affected by substituting $R - R^*$ for ΔR in the objective function, although the form of the feedback control will of course be different.

If real absorption rather than real output is included as an argument in the objective function, the scope for active feedback stabilisation policy is enhanced. With exchange-rate management policies, $A(t)$ is given by:

$$A(t) = b_1 m - b_1 e(t) - b_1 \eta_p(t) + \varepsilon_d(t),$$

while with reserve management policies we get:

$$A(t) = -\Delta R(t) + \frac{a}{\Psi}\varepsilon_d(t).$$

In the absence of international capital mobility, domestic absorption will only depend on the current value of the controls. With international capital mobility, current absorption will depend on current and lagged values of controls, as will be shown below.

II A MODEL WITH AN EXPLICIT DOMESTIC FINANCIAL SECTOR

In this section of the paper, three domestic sources of disturbances are considered: ε_s, supply shocks, which can be interpreted as random events affecting the production function or the labour market, ε_d, demand shocks, the random shifts of the *IS* curve considered in the previous section and ε_m: financial market disturbances, or random shifts of the *LM* curve. These disturbances are assumed to have zero means and to be mutually serially independent. The assumptions of complete sterilisation of reserve flows and absence of international financial flows continue to be maintained. $i(t)$ denotes the real rate of interest.

(38) $Y(t) = a(p(t) - \hat{p}(t-1, t)) + \varepsilon_s(t) \qquad a > 0$

(39) $A(t) = b_1(m - p(t)) + b_2 i(t) + \varepsilon_d(t) \qquad b_1 > 0;\ b_2 < 0$

(40) $m - p(t) = c_1(i(t) + \hat{p}(t, t+1) - p(t)) + c_2 Y(t) + \varepsilon_m(t)$
$c_1 < 0;\ c_2 < 0$

(41) $p(t) = e(t) + \eta_p(t)$

(42) $X(t) = Y(t) - A(t)$

(43) $\Delta R(t) = X(t)$

Domestic absorption varies inversely with the rate of interest [equation (39), $b < 0$]. Equation (40) is the *LM* curve.

Under general exchange-rate management policies, the model can be summarised as follows; if the government adopts feedback policies for $e(t)$.

$$Y(t) = a\eta_p(t) + \varepsilon_s(t),$$

$$\Delta R(t) = -\Psi_4 m + b_2 e(t+1) + \Psi_5 e(t) + \Psi_6 \varepsilon_s(t) - \varepsilon_d(t) + \frac{b_2}{c_1}\varepsilon_m(t) + \Psi_7 \eta_p(t)$$

$$\Delta p(t) = e(t) - e(t-1) + \eta_p(t) - \eta_p(t-1).$$

The fixed exchange-rate model is the special case when $e(t+1) = e(t) = e(t+1) = \bar{e}$.[29]

Comparing this model with the general exchange-rate management model in the absence of an explicit domestic financial sector, equations (20) to (22), we see that here too the authorities' knowledge of $\eta_p(t-1)$ when they decide on $e(t)$ permits them to improve on the fixed exchange-rate policy.

To obtain the model for general reserve management policies, we solve the equation $\Delta R(t) = Y(t) - A(t)$ for $\hat{p}(t-1, t)$ and $p(t)$, obtaining (if we assume stability):

$$\hat{p}(t-1,t) = m + \frac{1}{\Psi_5}\Delta R(t) + \frac{1}{\Psi_5}\sum_{i=1}^{\infty}\left(\frac{-b_2}{\Psi_5}\right)^i \Delta\hat{R}(t-1,t+i)$$

$$p(t) = m + \frac{\Delta R(t)}{\Psi_5} - \frac{\Psi_6}{\Psi_8}\varepsilon_s(t) + \frac{1}{\Psi_8}\varepsilon_d(t) - \frac{b_2/c_1}{\Psi_8}\varepsilon_m(t) + \frac{a\Psi_6}{\Psi_8\Psi_5}\sum_{i=1}^{\infty}\left(\frac{-b_2}{\Psi_5}\right)^i$$

$$\Delta\hat{R}(t-1,t+i)\frac{-b_2}{\Psi_8\Psi_5}\sum_{i=0}^{\infty}\left(\frac{-b_2}{\Psi_5}\right)^i \Delta\hat{R}(t,t+1+i)$$

Thus $Y(t)$ is given by:

$$Y(t) = a\frac{1}{\Psi_8}\sum_{i=1}^{\infty}\left(\frac{-b_2}{\Psi_5}\right)^i [\Delta\hat{R}(t,t+i) - \Delta R(t-1,t+i)]$$

$$+\frac{\Psi_5}{\Psi_8}\varepsilon_s(t) + \frac{a}{\Psi_8}\varepsilon_d(t) - \frac{ab_2/c_1}{\Psi_8}\varepsilon_m(t)$$

$$\Psi_4 = b_1 + \frac{b_2}{c_1};\quad \Psi_5 = b_1 + \frac{b_2}{c_1} - b_2;\ \Psi_6 = \frac{b_2 c_2}{c_1} + 1$$

$$\Psi_7 = b_1 + \frac{b_2}{c_1} + \frac{b_2 c_2 a}{c_1} - b_2;\ \Psi_8 = a\left(1 + \frac{b_2 c_2}{c_1}\right) + b_1 + \frac{b_2}{c_1} - b_2$$

The freely-floating-exchange rate model is the special case when $\Delta R(t) = \Delta R(t-1) = 0$. With any reserve management policy, the economy is insulated from foreign disturbances, in the absence of international capital flows. Comparing this model with the reserve management model without an explicit domestic financial sector (equations 29 to 31), we can conclude that because $\varepsilon_S(t-1)$, $\varepsilon_d(t-1)$ and $\varepsilon_m(t-1)$ are known to the policy authority when it decides on $\Delta R(t)$, a closed-loop (feedback) control rule that permits such new information to be taken into account will dominate the freely-floating exchange-rate policy.[30]

In the final section of this paper, I shall deal with a model in which there are international financial flows. The special case considered is that of 'perfect capital mobility': there exists a foreign asset that is a perfect substitute in private portfolios for a domestic bond. For simplicity the real rate of interest rather than the nominal rate is included as an argument in the money demand function.

III A MODEL WITH INTERNATIONAL FINANCIAL FLOWS

Equations (44) to (51) represent the model under 'perfect capital mobility'.

(44) $Y(t) = a(p(t) - \hat{p}(t-1,t)) + \varepsilon_s(t)$ $\qquad a > 0$

(45) $A(t) = b_1(m - p(t)) + b_2 B(t) + b_3 i(t) + \varepsilon_d(t)$

$b_1 > 0;\ b_2 > 0;\ b_3 < 0$

(46) $m - p(t) = c_1 i(t) + c_2 Y(t) + c_3 B(t) + \varepsilon_m(t)$

$c_1 < 0;\ c_2 > 0;\ c_3 > 0$

(47) $X(t) = Y(t) - A(t).$

(48) $p(t) = e(t) + \eta_p(t)$

(49) $i(t) = \bar{i}^* + \eta_f(t) + \hat{e}(t,t+1) - e(t) - (\hat{p}(t,t+1) - p(t))$

(50) $\Delta R(t) = X(t) + rB(t-1) - \Delta B(t)$ $\qquad r > 0$[31]

(51a) $\hat{p}(t-1,t) = E_{t-1}(p(t)|I(t-1))$

(51b) $\hat{p}(t,t+1) = E_t(p(t+1)|I(t))$

(51c) $\hat{e}(t,t+1) = E_t(e(t+1)|I(t))$

Domestic bonds are real-valued short bonds. $B(t)$ denotes net domestic claims on the rest of the world by the private sector. $i(t)$ is the real rate of return on these bonds. $i^*(t)$ is the exogenously given world rate of return, in terms of foreign exchange, on a claim that is a perfect substitute in private portfolios for the real-valued bond. For simplicity we assume that the domestic private sector does not hold claims denominated in foreign exchange. The rest of the world holds the mixed portfolio that permits it to conduct the arbitrage operations reflected in the international interest arbitrage condition (49). $i^*(t) = \bar{i}^* + \eta_f(t)$. $\eta_f(t)$ is a foreign financial disturbance. All disturbances, the three domestic ones, $\varepsilon_s(t)$, $\varepsilon_d(t)$ and $\varepsilon_m(t)$ and the two foreign ones, $\eta_p(t)$ and $\eta_f(t)$ have zero means and are mutually serially independent.

Equation (50) states that the official financing balance is the sum of the current account $X(t)+rB(t)$ and the capital account $-\Delta B(t)$. $rB(t)$, net interest income from abroad, should more properly be $i(t)B(t)$. To preserve linearity, $i(t)$ is replaced by the constant r. r can be taken to be positive; $r = i^*$ might be an attractive compromise. The substitution of r for i is just a fudge for technical reasons, but could be 'justified' by postulating a sufficiently bizarre policy of official transfers and remittances.

Under rational expectations, $\hat{p}(t,t+1) = E_t(e(t+1)+\eta_p(t+1))$ $= E_t e(t+1)$. Equation (49) therefore reduces to:

$$(49)\quad i(t) = \bar{i}^* + \eta_f(t) + \eta_p(t).$$

The interest parity condition (49), which holds under both exchange-rate management and reserve management policies, makes it clear that, with international mobility of financial claims, reserve stock management policies (including a freely-floating exchange rate) no longer insulate the domestic economy from foreign disturbances. Not only foreign interest rate disturbances but foreign price disturbances as well are transmitted to the domestic economy. The reason is that a random increase in the world price level, $\eta_p(t) > 0$, will raise the current domestic price level relative to the current exchange rate, as $p(t) = e(t) + \eta_p(t)$. Since these foreign price disturbances are serially uncorrelated with mean zero, next period's exected price level will be lower, relative to next period's expected exchange rate, than the current price level is relative to the current exchange rate ($\hat{p}(t,t+1) = \hat{e}(t,t+1)$). To satisfy the interest parity condition, which can be rewritten as

$$i(t) + (\hat{p}(t,t+1) - \hat{e}(t,t+1)) - (p(t) - e(t)) = \bar{i}^* + \eta_f(t),$$

the domestic real rate of interest will have to increase. This will affect both real output and the rate of inflation under reserve management policies.

The trade account surplus under exchange-rate management policies is given by:

$$(52a)\quad X(t) = Y(t) - A(t) = \left(\frac{b_2 c_1}{c_3} - b_3\right)\bar{i}^* - \left(b_1 + \frac{b_2}{c_3}\right)m$$
$$+ \left(b_1 + \frac{b_2}{c_3}\right)e(t) + \left(1 + \frac{b_2 c_2}{c_3}\right)\varepsilon_s(t)$$
$$- \varepsilon_d(t) + \frac{b_2}{c_3}\varepsilon_m(t) + \left[a + b_1 - b_3 + \frac{b_2}{c_3}\Psi_9\right]\eta_p(t)$$

$$+\left(\frac{b_2c_1}{c_3}-b_3\right)\eta_f(t)$$

$$\Psi_9 = 1 + c_1 + ac_2.$$

The current account surplus is given by:

$$\text{(52b)}\quad X(t)+rB(t) = \left[(b_2-r)\frac{c_1}{c_3}-b_3\right]\bar{i}^* - \left(b_1+\frac{b_2-r}{c_3}\right)m$$

$$+\left(b_1+\frac{b_2}{c_3}\right)e(t)-\frac{r}{c_3}e\,(t-1)$$

$$+\left(1+\frac{b_2c_2}{c_3}\right)\varepsilon_s(t)-r\frac{c_2}{c_3}\varepsilon_s(t-1)$$

$$-\varepsilon_d(t)+\frac{b_2}{b_3}\varepsilon_m(t)-\frac{r}{c_3}\varepsilon_m(t-1)$$

$$+\left[a+b_1-b_3+\frac{b_2}{c_3}\Psi_9\right]\eta_p(t)$$

$$-\frac{r}{c_3}\Psi_9\eta_p(t-1)+\left(\frac{b_2c_1}{c_3}-b_3\right)\eta_f(t)$$

$$-r\frac{c_1}{c_3}\eta_f(t-1).$$

The capital account surplus is given by:

$$\text{(52c)}\quad -\quad \Delta B(t) = \frac{1}{c_3}e(t)-\frac{1}{c_3}e(t-1)+\frac{\Psi_9}{c_3}\eta_p(t)$$

$$-\frac{\Psi_9}{c_3}\eta_p(t-1)+\frac{c_1}{c_3}\eta_f(t)$$

$$-\frac{c_1}{c_3}\eta_f(t-1)+\frac{c_2}{c_3}\varepsilon_s(t)$$

$$-\frac{c_2}{c_3}\varepsilon_s(t-1)+\frac{\varepsilon_m(t)}{c_3}-\frac{\varepsilon_m(t-1)}{c_3}.$$

The overall balance-of-payments surplus is $\Delta R(t) = X(t) + rB(t) - \Delta B(t)$. Under general exchange-rate management policies, the model with perfect international capital mobility can be summarised as follows:

(53) $Y(t) = a\eta_p(t) + \varepsilon_s(t)$

(54)
$$\Delta R(t) = \left[(b_2 - r)\frac{c_1}{c_3} - b_3\right]i^* - \left(b_1 + \frac{b_2 - r}{c_3}\right)m$$
$$+\left(b_1 + \frac{1+b_2}{c_3}\right)e(t) - \frac{(1+r)}{c_3}e(t-1) + \left(1 + \frac{(1+b_2)}{c_3}c_2\right)\varepsilon_s(t)$$
$$-\frac{(c_2+r)}{c_3}\varepsilon_s(t) - \varepsilon_d(t) + \frac{(1+b_2)}{c_3}\varepsilon_m(t) - \frac{(1+r)}{c_3}\varepsilon_m(t-1)$$
$$+\left[a + b_1 - b_3 + \frac{(1+b_2)}{c_3}\Psi_9\right]\eta_p(t) - \frac{(1+r)\Psi_9}{c_3}\eta_p(t-1)$$
$$+\left[\frac{(1+b_2)}{c_3}c_1 - b_3\right]\eta_f(t) - (1+r)\frac{c_1}{c_3}\eta_f(t-1)$$

(55) $\Delta p(t) = e(t) - e(t-1) + \eta_p(t) - \eta_p(t-1)$.

If current-account equilibrium is considered a more appropriate long-run policy objective than equilibrium in the official financing account, (52b) could be substituted for (54).

The fixed exchange rate is the special case when $e(t) = \bar{e}$ for all t. The optimal fixed exchange rate is given by

$$\bar{e} = m - \left[\frac{(b_2 - r)c_1 - b_3 c_3}{b_1 c_3 + b_2 - r}\right]\bar{i}^*.$$

With international capital mobility, a change in the exchange rate affects the external equilibrium in the current period and, by changing net private sector claims on the rest of the world, also in the next period. Without international financial flows, an 'active' feedback stabilisation policy can only stabilise the price level and does so at the expense of some increase in the degree of external imbalance. With international financial flows, 'active' stabilisation policy will be optimal even if we assign zero weight to stabilisation of the price level.

Real output again cannot be stabilised. It is shown in Appendix I that when we introduce durable capital into the model and make output dependent on the stock of capital, the probability distribution of real output will be affected by the value assumed by the exchange rate in the absence of perfect international capital mobility. Through sterilisation policies and exchange-rate management, the government can determine the real quantity of money and thus the interest rate and the volume of investment. With perfect international capital mobility, the real interest rate is not under the control of the policy authority.

With general reserve management policies, we use the identity

$$\Delta R(t) = X(t) + rB(t-1) - \Delta B(t)$$

to solve for $p(t)$ and $\hat{p}(t-1,t)$. This gives us:

$$\hat{p}(t-1,t) = m + \frac{\Delta R(t)}{\Psi_{10}} + - \left(\frac{\Psi_{11}}{\Psi_{10}}\right)\bar{i}^* - \frac{(1+r)}{\Psi_{10}}B(t-1)$$

and

$$p(t) = m + \frac{\Delta R(t)}{\Psi_{10}} + - \left(\frac{\Psi_{11}}{\Psi_{10}}\right)\bar{i}^* - \frac{(1+r)}{\Psi_{10}}B(t-1)$$

$$- \left[\frac{\Psi_{12}}{\Psi_{13}}\right]\varepsilon_s(t) + \frac{1}{\Psi_{13}}\varepsilon_d(t) - \frac{(b_2+1)}{\Psi_{13}c_3}\varepsilon_m(t)$$

$$- \frac{\Psi_{11}}{\Psi_{13}}\eta_p(t) - \frac{\Psi_{11}}{\Psi_{13}}\eta_f(t)$$

where

$$\Psi_{10} = b_1 + \frac{b_2+1}{c_3}; \quad \Psi_{11} = (b_2+1)\frac{c_1}{c_3} - b_3;$$

$$\Psi_{12} = 1 + \frac{(b_2+1)}{c_3}c_2; \quad \Psi_{13} = a + b_1 + \frac{(b_2+1)}{c_3}(1+c_2a).$$

The behaviour of the model is summarised in equations (56) to (59).

(56) $$Y(t) = \left(1 - \frac{a\Psi_{12}}{\Psi_{13}}\right)\varepsilon_s(t) + \frac{a}{\Psi_{13}}\varepsilon_d(t) - \frac{a(b_2+1)}{\Psi_{13}c_3}\varepsilon_m(t)$$

$$- \frac{a\Psi_9}{\Psi_{11}}\eta_p(t) - \frac{\Psi_9}{\Psi_{11}}\eta_f(t)$$

(57) $\Delta R(t) = \Delta R(t)$

(58) $$\Delta p(t) = \frac{\Delta R(t)}{\Psi_{10}} - \frac{\Delta R(t-1)}{\Psi_{10}} - \frac{(1+r)}{\Psi_{10}}\Delta B(t-1)$$

$$-\frac{\Psi_{12}}{\Psi_{13}}\varepsilon_s(t)+\frac{1}{\Psi_{13}}\varepsilon_d(t)-\frac{(b_2+1)}{\Psi_{13}c_3}\varepsilon_m(t)$$
$$-\frac{\Psi_{11}}{\Psi_{13}}\eta_p(t)-\frac{\Psi_{11}}{\Psi_{13}}\eta_f(t)+\frac{\Psi_{12}}{\Psi_{13}}\varepsilon_s(t-1)$$
$$-\frac{1}{\Psi_{13}}\varepsilon_d(t-1)+\frac{(b_2+1)}{\Psi_{13}c_3}\varepsilon_m(t-1)$$
$$+\frac{\Psi_{11}}{\Psi_{13}}\eta_p(t-1)+\frac{\Psi_{11}}{\Psi_{13}}\eta_f(t-1)$$

$$(59)\quad \Delta B(t) = -\frac{1}{c_3}\Delta p(t)-\frac{c_2}{c_3}Y(t)+\frac{c_2}{c_3}Y(t-1)-\frac{c_1}{c_3}\eta_p(t)$$
$$-\frac{c_1}{c_3}\eta_f(t)-\frac{1}{c_3}\varepsilon_m(t)+\frac{c_1}{c_3}\eta_p(t-1)$$
$$+\frac{c_1}{c_3}\eta_f(t-1)+\frac{1}{c_3}\varepsilon_m(t-1).$$

We can substitute from equation (56) for $Y(t)$ and $Y(t-1)$ and from equation (58) for $\Delta p(t)$ to obtain $\Delta B(t)$ exclusively in terms of its own lagged value and current and lagged values of the disturbances and the instruments.

Both foreign disturbances, $\eta_p(t)$ and $\eta_f(t)$ will affect the domestic economy under reserve management policies (including the freely floating rate given by $\Delta R(t)=0$, for all t), when there is international capital mobility. The insulation provided by reserve management is gone, for better or worse.

IV CONCLUSION

The scope for active feedback stabilisation policies is enhanced when the extent to which past events affect present and future states of the economy is increased by the existence of international capital market integration. International financial integration permits foreign-exchange market intervention to have a favourable effect on external stability. In its absence, the only reason for not sticking to open-loop rules is price stabilisation. Real output continues to be unaffected by the values assigned to the controls but real absorption depends on both current and lagged values of the controls – see equations (45), (58) and (59). The assumption of complete sterilisation of reserve flows, maintained throughout the paper, is one of convenience only. In Appendix II, our qualitative results as regards open-loop versus closed-loop policies are confirmed for a model with no reserve flow sterilisation.

APPENDIX I

When there is durable capital in the model, the conclusion that the probability distribution function of output is independent of the values assigned to the policy instruments no longer holds. Consider the model given by equations (38) to (43), modified to include durable reproducible capital. $K(t)$ denotes the stock of capital at the beginning of period t, $Z(t)$ denotes net investment and $C(t)$ consumption.

$$Y(t) = a_1(p(t) - \hat{p}(t-1,t)) + a_2K(t) + \varepsilon_s(t); \qquad a_1 > 0 \; a_2 > 0$$

$$A(t) \equiv C(t) + Z(t) + \varepsilon_d(t)$$

$$C(t) = b_0 + b_1(m - p(t)) \qquad b_0 > 0 \; b_1 > 0$$

$$Z(t) = z_0 + z_1 i(t) \qquad z_0 > 0 \; z_1 < 0$$

$$m - p(t) = c_1 i(t) + c_2 Y(t) + \varepsilon_m(t) \qquad c_1 < 0 \; c_2 > 0$$

$$p(t) = e(t) + \eta_p(t)$$

$$X(t) = Y(t) - A(t)$$

$$\Delta R(t) = Y(t)$$

$$K(t) = K(t-1) + Z(t-1)$$

Under an exchange rate management regime

$$Y(t) = a_1\eta_p(t) + a_2K(t) + \varepsilon_s(t).$$

Since

$$K(t) = K(t-1) + z_0 + z_1 i(t-1)$$

and

$$i(t-1) = \frac{m}{c_1} - \frac{1}{c_1}e(t-1) - \frac{(1+c_2a_1)}{c_1}\eta_p(t-1) - \frac{1}{c_1}\varepsilon_m(t-1)$$

$$-\frac{c_2}{c_1}\varepsilon_s(t-1) - \frac{c_2}{c_1}a_2K(t-1),$$

it is clear that the probability distribution function of the stock of capital depends on the lagged values of the exchange rate. Changes in $e(t)$ and the associated changes in $p(t)$ will change the real quantity of money (given m), the rate of interest and the rate of investment. Current output is not affected by the current choice of $e(t)$, but next period's capital stock and level of real output will be affected. Similar conclusions can be drawn for reserve management policies. The reason for this result, which contrasts with those obtained for a closed economy by, for instance, Barro (1976), is that through sterilisation and exchange market operations the policy authority can control the real quantity of money. In an economy without perfect international mobility of capital, this permits the authorities to influence the real rate of interest. With perfect capital mobility, $i(t) = \bar{i}^* + \eta_f(t) + \eta_p(t)$ and the behaviour of the capital stock cannot be affected by the policy authority.

APPENDIX II

If reserve flows are not sterilised, we can represent the simplest model by the following equations: (It is convenient to represent the external balance target in terms of $\Delta m(t)$, as there is no domestic credit creation.)

$$Y(t) = a(p(t) - \hat{p}(t-1,t)) \qquad a > 0$$

$$\Delta m(t) = d_1(p(t) - \hat{p}(t-1,t)) + d_2(m(t) - p(t)) - \varepsilon_d(t) \qquad d_1 > 0;\ d_2 < 0$$

$$p(t) = e(t) + \eta_p(t)$$

$$m(t) = m(t-1) + \Delta m(t-1)$$

$$\min E_0 \sum_{t=1}^{T} [w_1(Y(t))^2 + w_2(\Delta m(t))^2 + w_3(\Delta p(t))^2]$$

With general exchange-rate management policies, this can be summarised as:

$$Y(t) = a\eta_p(t)$$

$$\Delta m(t) = (d_1 - d_2)\eta_p(t) - d_2 e(t) - \varepsilon_d(t) + d_2 \sum_{i=0}^{t-2} [(1+d_2)^i (d_1 - d_2)\eta_p(t-i-1) - d_2 e(t-i-1) - \varepsilon_d(t-i-1)] + d_2(1+d_2)^t m_0 + d_2(1+d_2)^{t-1}(d_0 - d_2)(\eta_p(o) - \varepsilon_d(o)).$$

$$\Delta p(t) = e(t) - e(t-1) + \eta_p(t) - \eta_p(t-1).$$

The current external deficit or surplus depends on current and lagged values of the disturbances and the exchange rate, and on the initial condition, m_0. 'Active' feedback controls will again be optimal.

With general reserve management policies, or more precisely, general money management policies the model becomes (using $\hat{p}(t-1;t) = -\frac{1}{d_2}m(t+1) + \left(1+\frac{1}{d_2}\right)m(t)$ and $p(t) = -\frac{1}{d_2}m(t+1) + \left(1+\frac{1}{d_2}\right)m(t) + \frac{\varepsilon_d(t)}{d_1-d_2}$:

$$Y(t) = \frac{a}{d_1-d_2}\varepsilon_d(t)$$

$$\Delta m(t) = \Delta m(t)$$

$$\Delta p(t) = -\frac{1}{d_2}\Delta m(t) + \left(1+\frac{1}{d_2}\right)\Delta m(t-1) + \frac{\varepsilon_d(t)}{d_1-d_2} - \frac{\varepsilon_d(t-1)}{d_1-d_2}.$$

As in the case of complete sterilisation of reserve flows, active feedback control can be used to stabilise the price level. With international capital mobility, both the price level and the external deficit can be stabilised.

NOTES

1. I would like to thank critical participants in seminars at University College, London, the London School of Economics and SEAE in Paris for useful and penetrating comments on earlier drafts of this paper. John P. Martin's comments have improved the substance and presentation of the paper considerably. Alasdair Smith has saved me from a few embarrassing errors and has offered detailed and wide-ranging suggestions for improvements. Financial support from the Social Science Research Council is gratefully acknowledged.
2. Some well-known references are: Fellner (1966), Friedman (1953), and Meade (1955). Some recent contributions are Kindleberger (1972), Argy and Porter (1972), Fischer (1977a) and Turnovsky (1976).
3. This 'prices versus quantities' approach was first developed formally by Weitzman (1974).
4. The official stock of foreign exchange reserves must be adequate to meet any likely demand on it.
5. Chow (1975) and Aoki (1976).
6. Friedman (1968).
7. Chow (1975), Cooper and Fischer (1972a), (1972b), (1972c), B. Friedman (1973), Turnovsky (1975), Pindyck (1973).
8. 'Available' is unsatisfactorily vague. It can only be defined with reference to the costs of and uncertain return to gathering additional information.
9. See Muth (1961), Lucas (1972a), (1972b), (1973), (1975), (1976), Sargent and

Wallace (1975, 1976), Sargent (1976), Gordon (1976), Barro (1976), Barro and Fischer (1976), and Poole (1976).
10. Taylor (1975).
11. See Black (1974), Taylor (1977).
12. Baily (1974), (1976), Azariadis (1975), D. F. Gordon (1974).
13. Both inside and outside policy lags must be taken into account. I am indebted to William Branson for this point.
14. See Modigliani and Miller (1958).
15. For a useful survey of the theory of international financial integration, see Kenen (1976). The paper considers the case in which there exists a foreign asset that is a perfect substitute in private portfolios for the domestic asset, that is, 'perfect' international capital mobility.
16. See Levin (1977).
17. Government interest-bearing debt is assumed not to be part of perceived private-sector net worth.
18. Public-sector holdings of foreign exchange reserves are assumed not to be part of perceived private-sector net worth.
19. The supposed advantage of floating over fixed exchange rates in restoring the power of the domestic monetary authority to influence the domestic level of economic activity is not analysed in this model, which treats all policy instruments other than the foreign exchange market intervention instrument, as constant.
20. $\Delta p(t) = p(t) - p(t-1)$.
21. See Phelps (1970) and Friedman (1968).
22. More complicated mixed moving average—autoregressive schemes for the disturbances could be incorporated at the cost of greater notational and arithmetic complexity without altering any of the main conclusions. Consider, for example, the simple first-order autoregressive scheme:

$$\eta_p(t) = \rho\eta_p(t-1) + v(t);\ Ev(t) = 0;$$

$$Ev(t)v(s) = \begin{cases} \sigma_v^2 & \text{if } t = s \\ 0 & \text{if } t \neq s \end{cases}.$$

In this case, $E_{t-1}\eta_p(t) = \rho_{\eta_p}(t-1)$ if $\eta_p(t-1)$ is known at $t-1$, or $\rho^2_{\eta_p}(t-2)$ if $\eta_p(t-1)$ is not known, but $\eta_p(t-2)$ is, *etcetera*. [$v(t)$ is assumed to be independent of all other disturbances].
23. B. Friedman (1972).
24. Output will of course also be affected by domestic supply disturbances, if there are any. See Section II.
25. See Chow (1975).
26. Chow (1975) also treats the case where $A(t)$ and $C(t)$ are stochastic.
27. For a discussion of the existence and uniqueness of this solution, see Garbade (1976).
28. The term is from Okun (1975).
29. A detailed discussion of the behaviour of the model under fixed and freely floating exchange rates is available from the author on request.
30. The explicit solution is omitted for reasons of space.
31. $\Delta B(t) \equiv B(t) - B(t-1)$. Note that $B(t)$ is an endogenous variable in period t. Under exchange rate management policies, it adjusts instantaneously to

clear the money market. If we substitute $rB(t)$ for $rB(t-1)$ in (54), nothing essential changes.

REFERENCES

M. AOKI, *Optimal Control and System Theory in Dynamic Economic Analysis* (Amsterdam: North-Holland, 1976).

V. ARGY and M. G. PORTER, 'The Forward Exchange Market and the Effects of Domestic and External Disturbances under Alternative Exchange Rate Systems', *International Monetary Fund Staff Papers*, Washington, Vol. 19, 1972, pp. 503–32.

C. AZARIADIS, 'Implicit Contracts and Underemployment Equilibria', *Journal of Political Economy*, Chicago, Illinois, Vol. 83, December 1975, pp. 1183–202.

M. N. BAILY, 'Wages and Employment under Uncertain Demand', *Review of Economic Studies*, Edinburgh, Vol. 41, January 1974, pp. 37–50.

——'Contract Theory and the Moderation of Inflation by Recession and by Controls', *Brookings Papers on Economic Activity*, Washington, No. 3, 1976, pp. 585–622.

R. J. BARRO, 'Rational Expectations and the Role of Monetary Policy', *Journal of Monetary Economics*, Amsterdam, Vol. 2, January 1976, pp. 1–32.

——and S. FISCHER, 'Recent Developments in Monetary Theory', *Journal of Monetary Economics*, Vol. 2, April 1976, pp. 133–67.

R. BLACK, 'Uniqueness of the Price Level in Monetary Growth Models with Rational Expectations', *Journal of Economic Theory*, Bruges, Belgium, Vol. 7, 1974, pp. 53–65.

G. C. CHOW, *Analysis and Control of Dynamic Economic Systems* (New York: John Wiley, 1975).

J. P. COOPER and S. FISCHER, 'Simulation of Monetary Rules in the FRB-MIT-Penn Model', *Journal of Money, Credit and Banking*, Columbus, Ohio, Vol. 4, May 1972 (a), pp. 384–96.

——'Stabilization Policy and Lags: Summary and Extension', *Annals of Economic and Social Measurement*, New York, Vol. 1, October 1972 (b), pp. 407–18.

——'Stochastic Simulation of Monetary Rules in Two Macro-Econometric Models', *Journal of the American Statistical Association*, Washington, D.C., Vol. 67, December 1972 (c), pp. 750–60.

W. FELLNER, 'On Limited Exchange Rate Flexibility', in W. Fellner *et al.*, *Maintaining and Restoring Balance in International Payments* (Princeton: Princeton Uiversity Press, 1966).

S. FISCHER, 'Stability and Exchange Rate Systems in a Monetarist Model of the Balance of Payments', in R. Z. Aliber (ed.), *The Political Economy of Monetary Reform* (London: Macmillan, 1977a).

——'Long-Term Contracts, Rational Expectations, and the Optimal Money Supply Rule', *Journal of Political Economy*, Vol. 85, February 1977 (b), pp. 191–206.

B. FRIEDMAN, 'Optimal Economic Stabilization Policy: an Extended Framework', *Journal of Political Economy*, Vol. 80, 1972, pp. 1002–22.

——*Methods in Optimization for Economic Stabilization Policy* (Amsterdam: North-Holland, 1973).

M. FRIEDMAN, 'The Case for Flexible Exchange Rates', in *Essays in Positive Economics* (Chicago: University of Chicago Press, 1953).

——'The Role of Monetary Policy', *American Economic Review*, Manasha, Wisconsin, Vol. 58, March 1968, pp. 1–17.

K. D. GARBADE, 'On the Existence and Uniqueness of Solutions to Multi-Period Linear/Quadratic Optimal Control Problems', *International Economic Review*, Osaka, Japan, Vol. 17, October 1976, pp. 719–31.

D. F. GORDON, 'A Neo-Classical Theory of Keynesian Unemployment', *Economic Inquiry*, Los Angeles, California, Vol. 12, December 1974, pp. 431–59.

R. J. GORDON, 'Recent Developments in the Theory of Inflation and Unemployment', *Journal of Monetary Economics*, Vol. 2, April 1976, pp. 185–219.

P. B. KENEN, 'Capital Mobility and Financial Integration: a Survey', *Princeton Studies in International Finance*, No. 39, 1976.

C. P. KINDLEBERGER, 'The Benefits of International Money', *Journal of International Economics*, Amsterdam, Vol. 2, 1972, pp. 425–42.

J. H. LEVIN, 'Reserve Stocks as External Targets and the Stability of Alternative Exchange Rate Systems', *Review of Economic Studies*, Vol. 44, February 1977, pp. 59–69.

R. E. LUCAS, 'Expectations and the Neutrality of Money', *Journal of Economic Theory*, Vol. 4, April 1972 (a), pp. 103–24.

——'Econometric Testing of the Natural Rate Hypothesis', in O. Eckstein (ed.), *The Econometrics of Price Determination*, a Conference sponsored by the Board of Governors of the Federal Reserve System and Social Science Research Council (Washington: Federal Reserve Board, 1972b) pp. 50–9.

——'Some International Evidence on Output-Inflation Trade-Offs', *American Economic Review*, Vol. 63, June 1973, pp. 326–34.

——'An Equilibrium Model of the Business Cycle', *Journal of Political Economy*, Vol. 83, December 1975, pp. 1113–44.

——'Econometric Policy Evaluation: a Critique', in K. Brunner and A. H. Meltzer (eds), *The Phillips Curve and Labour Markets* (Amsterdam and New York: North Holland, 1976).

JAMES E. MEADE, 'The Case for Variable Exchange Rates', *Three Banks Review*, Manchester, September 1955, pp. 3–27.

F. MODIGLIANI and M. H. MILLER, 'The Cost of Capital, Corporation Finance and the Theory of Investment', *American Economic Review*, June 1958, pp. 261–97.

J. F. MUTH, 'Rational Expectations and the Theory of Price Movements', *Econometrica*, London, Vol. 29, July 1961, pp. 315–35.

A. M. OKUN, 'Inflation, its Mechanics and Welfare Costs', *Brookings Papers on Economic Activity*, No. 2, 1975, pp. 351–90.

E. S. PHELPS *et al.*, *Micro-Economic Foundations of Employment and Inflation Theory* (New York: W. W. Norton, 1970).

——and J. B. TAYLOR, 'Stabilizing Powers of Monetary Policy under Rational Expectations', *Journal of Political Economy*, Vol. 85, February 1977, pp. 163–90.

R. S. PINDYCK, *Optimal Planning for Economic Stabilization*, (Amsterdam: North Holland, 1973).

W. POOLE, 'Rational Expectations in the Macro Model', *Brookings Papers on Economic Activity*, No. 2, 1976, pp. 463–514.

T. J. SARGENT, 'A Classical Macro-Econometric Model for the United States', *Journal of Political Economy*, Vol. 84, April 1976, pp. 207–37.

——and N. WALLACE, 'Rational Expectations, the Optimal Monetary Instrument and the Optimal Money Supply Rule', *Journal of Political Economy*, Vol. 83, April 1975, pp. 241–54.

——'Rational Expectations and the Theory of Economic Policy', *Journal of Monetary Economics*, Vol. 2, April 1976, pp. 169–83.

J. TAYLOR, 'Monetary Policy During a Transition to Rational Expectations', *Journal of Political Economy*, Vol. 83, August 1975, pp. 241–47.

——'Conditions for Unique Solutions in Stochastic Macro-Economic Models with Rational Expectations', *Econometrica*, Vol. 45, September 1977, pp. 1377–85.

S. J. TURNOVSKY, 'The Relative Stability of Alternative Exchange Rate Systems in the Presence of Random Disturbances', *Journal of Money, Credit and Banking*, Vol. 7, February 1976, pp. 29–50.

——'Optimal Choice of Monetary Instrument in a Linear Economic Model with Stochastic Coefficients', *Journal of Money, Credit and Banking*, Vol. 6, February 1975, pp. 53–80.

M. L. WEITZMAN, 'Prices versus Quantities', *Review of Economic Studies*, Vol. 41, October 1974, pp. 477–91.

2

Rigid Real Wages and International Economic Policy[1]

BRIAN HINDLEY

For the past forty years, mainstream macro-policy teaching has been based upon Keynes' proposition that money wage rates are sticky or rigid downwards but that real wage rates can be reduced by an upward movement of prices relative to money wage rates. Within the standard closed-economy framework, this property is essential to the restoration of full employment, whether by monetary or fiscal policy.

As a natural extension, the same proposition has been embedded in the theory of macro-policy in an open economy. The pre-monetarist theory of devaluation, although not typically presented as such, was essentially an analysis of the effects of changing the real wage in terms of traded goods via the exchange rate; it being assumed, as Mundell long ago pointed out, that workers were willing to accept real wage cuts through the exchange rate that they were not willing, *ex hypothesi*, to accept through reductions in money wage rates. Similarly, the contention that fiscal policy can restore full employment under fixed exchange rates rests on the assumption that real wages can be reduced by an increase in the money price of non-traded goods or of goods in imperfect international competition.

There have, of course, been numerous attempts to explain why essentially the same real result should be attainable by one means and not by another: not least by Keynes himself. But more recently there has appeared a disposition to question the existence of the paradox itself; and the force of the questioning has been enhanced by widespread experience of simultaneous inflation and unemployment. According to this view, which appears to have supporters in such diverse centres as

Chicago and Cambridge, England, it is real wage rates that are rigid. Empirical evidence can be adduced for at least one country[2].

The new view can be conveniently stylised in the statement that there are two constraints on macro policy, not one, as in the standard view. These are:

(1) $W \geqq W_o$

(2) $\frac{dW}{dt} \cdot \frac{1}{W} = \frac{dP}{dt} \cdot \frac{1}{P} + \beta \left[\frac{W_o}{P_o} - \frac{W}{P} \right] \quad \beta \geqq 0; \qquad \frac{W}{P} \leqq \frac{W_o}{P_o}$

The new constraint (2) would of course be quite acceptable to exponents of the standard model for levels of employment higher than the natural rate; and this raises the issue of defining full employment—some proponents of constraint (2) clearly wish to suggest that it holds while there is yet involuntary unemployment. Fortunately, the issue can be largely ignored for present purposes: the answer to the question of how employment can be increased under constraints (1) and (2) is independent of the relation between the current level of employment and full employment.

If the economy is below the natural level of employment, however, there is obviously a question as to the means by which constraint (2) becomes effective and this, in turn, connects with the rather tricky issue of the appropriate definition of the real wage rate. If the rigidity is imposed by union leadership, the relevant real wage is, as interpreted by union leaders, not necessarily identical with the real wage perceived by workers, which becomes relevant if union leaders are strongly influenced by shop-floor sentiment.

Here I shall define real wages as $\frac{W(1-t)}{P}$ where t is the tax rate, assumed constant; and P is an index of prices such that if p_i is the money price of good i, and $\hat{P} = \frac{dP}{P}$:

(3) $\hat{P} = \sum_{i=1}^{n} a_i \hat{p}_i \quad \text{and} \quad \sum_{i=1}^{n} a_i = 1$

This measure neglects the possible effects of the rate of interest (via housing and consumer durable purchases); implicitly assumes that there is no non-price rationing or that changes in non-price rationing have no effect on real wages; and, perhaps more importantly, supposes that government expenditure is irrelevant to the real wage, while current – and only current – taxes enter with full weight.

My reason for adopting such a theoretically unsatisfactory definition is not simply that it has empirical support, for this is not overwhelming. But it seems preferable, rather than spending a great deal of time on definition, to analyse the consequences of some one firm hypothesis. With the results of such an analysis, the operational consequences of different definitions may become clearer.

Before proceeding to open economies, it is useful to review the consequences of the combined constraints for the standard single good closed-economy model. In that model, the capital stock is always fully employed, so that an increase in the level of employment implies a reduction in the capital–labour ratio and therefore a reduction in the real earnings of labour.

For the well-behaved production function $X = X(K, L)$, homogeneous of degree one, we have

$$X_L > 0$$
$$X_{LL} < 0;$$

and it follows that monetary and government expenditure policies can by themselves have only a transitory effect on income and employment. Any reduction in the real wage produced by them will result in money wage increases in excess of price increases and this process must eventually restore the initial level of employment.

To avoid this, tax rates must be adjusted to maintain constancy of the real disposable wage. We require that

(4) $X_L(1-t) = \text{const.};$

or that

(4′) $$\frac{dL}{dt} = \frac{X_L}{(1-t)X_{LL}} < 0$$

which implies a change of output

(5) $$\frac{dX}{dt} = \frac{dL}{dt} \cdot \frac{dX}{dL} = \frac{X_L^2}{(1-t)X_{LL}} < 0.$$

But the reduction in taxes merely makes possible that expansion of output without any increase in nominal wages. While it will affect demand for output, it will not necessarily do so to the extent required to absorb the change in output given by equation (5).

In the simplest Keynesian terms:

(6) $$X = \frac{I+G}{1-b(1-t)}$$

and we require that the increase in employment made possible by the tax-cut should equal that called for by the increase in aggregate demand; or that

$$(7)\quad \frac{X_L^2\,dt}{(1-t)X_{LL}} = \frac{dG - bX\,dt}{1-b(1-t)}$$

or that

$$(7')\quad \frac{dG}{dt} = \frac{[1-b(1-t)]X_L^2}{(1-t)X_{LL}} + bX$$

where b is the marginal propensity to consume. Thus, government expenditure must rise with the tax-cut if the RHS of equation (7′) is negative, or if

$$(7'')\quad b(1-t) < X_L^2/(X_L^2 - X \,.\, X_{LL}).$$

This condition can be given a somewhat neater form by noting that with given capital stock the elasticity of substitution of labour for capital is

$$\sigma = \frac{\hat{L}}{\hat{X}_K - \hat{X}_L} > 0,$$

and that from $X = KX_K + LX_L$, $(1-\theta)\hat{X}_K + \theta\hat{X}_L = 0$ (where θ is labour's share in output, and where $\hat{X}$ means dX/X).
Thus

$$(8)\quad \frac{X_L}{LX_{LL}} = \frac{\sigma}{\theta - 1},$$

and condition (7″) can be written:

$$(7''')\quad b(1-t) < \frac{\sigma\theta}{1-\theta(1-\sigma)}$$

Hereafter, equation (8) will be used to express results in terms of the elasticity of substitution.

If this condition is satisfied, the expansion in demand could be supplied by a further tax-cut (at the risk of increasing the requisite minimum real wage, the determination of which is here ignored). Only if the expansion in demand implied by the tax-cut is too great does stability require that government expenditure be altered: taxes must be cut by at least the amount indicated by equation (4′), so that if RHS equation (7′) is positive, government expenditure *must* be reduced.

Whether government expenditure rises or not, the budget deficit must.

Tax revenue $R = Xt$ so

$$(9)\quad \frac{dR}{dt} = X + t\frac{dX}{dt} = X + \frac{X\sigma\theta}{(\theta-1)(1-t)}t$$

and $D = G - R$ so

$$(10)\quad \frac{dD}{dt}\cdot\frac{1}{X} = b + \frac{\sigma\theta[1-b(1-t)]}{(\theta-1)(1-t)} - 1 - \frac{\sigma\theta t}{(\theta-1)(1-t)}$$

$$= (b-1)\left(1+\frac{\sigma\theta}{1-\theta}\right) < 0 \text{ if } b < 1.$$

If the change in government expenditure accompanying the tax-cut is less than that given by (7′), so that employment increases by less than the amount given by (4′), the gross real wage will fall, via rising prices as in the standard model, but real disposable wages will rise since the reduction in gross real wages is less than if the full increase in employment made possible by the tax-cut had been obtained. Thus, prices will rise, but by a percentage less than the decrease in the tax-rate. If expenditure increases by more than the amount given by (7′), the result will be an excess demand for goods and services and, in a model without a determinate price level, continuing inflation.

One way of viewing the difference between this and the traditional model is that whereas in the traditional model changes in the budget deficit produce changes in the level of employment regardless of the *level* of taxes and expenditure, in this model the level of employment is determined by the levels of *both* taxes and expenditure. This implies a value of the budget deficit, but there is no necessary relation between changes in the deficit and changes in employment. In the traditional model, an increase in taxes and a sufficiently larger increase in government expenditure will increase employment: in this model, it will simply increase the rate of inflation.

This link is broken, however, if we move from the simple Keynesian world to the opposite extreme of a simple monetarist world with $M = PL(X)$. Fiscal policy now has no effect on the level of employment. The necessary monetary expansion to accompany a tax-cut is given by $\hat{M} = \hat{P} + \varepsilon\hat{X}$ where ε is the output elasticity of demand for real money balances. Recalling that with given money wage rates $\hat{P} = \hat{X}_L$, substitution of equations (4′), (5) and (8) gives:

$$(11)\quad \frac{\hat{M}}{dt} = \frac{(1-\theta)+\sigma\theta\varepsilon}{(\theta-1)(1-t)}.$$

Monetary expansion greater than this will give rise to proportionately increased money wage rates and prices but will not affect employment.

Since in this case there need be no change in government expenditure, the consequent change in the budget deficit is given by equation (9). From the point of view of employment, however, there is now no reason why expenditure should not be changed to match revenue: only the level of taxes is fixed by selection of the level of employment.

I now turn to analysis of the implications of these assumptions for a small open economy in a context of perfect international capital mobility and under the two extreme exchange-rate regimes: fixed and flexible.

AN OPEN ECONOMY MODEL

The model has a now familiar underlying structure: one traded and one non-traded good, with labour fully mobile between sectors but capital specialised to sectors. Real-factor earnings can therefore be derived as a function of the level of employment and the relative price of tradeables.

We have the marginal product condition

$$X_t p_t = W = X_n p_n$$

where X_i is the marginal physical product of labour in sector i; so that for given money wages, equations (3) and (8) imply:

$$(12)\quad \frac{(\theta_t - 1)}{\sigma_t}\hat{L}_t + \hat{p}_t = 0 - \frac{(\theta_n - 1)}{\sigma_n}\hat{L}_n + \hat{p}_n$$

so that $\omega\left(=\frac{W}{P}\right)$ is given by:

$$(13)\quad \hat{P} = -\hat{\omega} = \frac{a(1-\theta_t)\hat{L}_t}{\sigma_t} + \frac{(1-a)(1-\theta_n)\hat{L}_n}{\sigma_n}$$

Note that for a given level of employment ($dL_t = -dL_n$), equation (13) gives no basis for *a priori* presumption as to the direction of change in real wages with respect to a change in relative goods prices.

On this foundation, the basic outlines of the effects of grafting the real wage constraint on to standard models can easily be sketched.

Under *fixed* exchange rates, monetary policy relates only to the payments deficit – not (in comparative static terms) to the level of employment. Fiscal policy affects employment via the output of non-traded goods. Any increase in employment by this means, however, requires a reduction in the real factor earnings of labour and, thus, must be accompanied by a tax-cut to maintain real disposable earnings. As in the closed economy, it is possible that the increase in demand stemming from the tax-cut will be excessive, so that a reduction in government expenditure is required for stability. Nevertheless, to increase employment, the budget deficit must be increased; and via the absorption identity $X - M \equiv S + T - I - G$, this implies a deterioration in the trade balance and, with appropriate monetary policy, a compensating increase in the capital inflow. Alternatively stated, the additional constraint, viewed as a policy goal, uses up a further degree of policy freedom: the government must not only maintain an appropriate budget deficit – there is now an appropriate level of expenditure and taxes taken separately.

Some of these propositions require further comment and quantification. I start with the magnitude of the budget deficit under fixed exchange rates.

Under fixed rates, the small country faces given p_t, and thus given L_t: so that the L_t terms can be eliminated from equation (13). To maintain constant real disposable wages therefore requires that:

$$\frac{W(1-t)}{P} = \text{const.}$$

or that, at constant money wage rates:

$$-\hat{P} - \frac{dt}{1-t} = 0$$

so that

$$(14)\quad \frac{dt}{1-t} = -\frac{(1-a)(1-\theta_n)}{\sigma_n}\hat{L}_n$$

gives the proportional change in employment $\left[\hat{L}_n = \hat{L}\left(1+\frac{L_t}{L_n}\right)\right]$ made possible by a tax-cut dt at constant money wage rates.

Total demand for non-tradeables is the sum of private sector and direct government demand:

$$(15)\quad Q_n = Q'_n + G$$

and we may write

$$(16)\quad Q'_n = Q'_n(p_n, p_t, S)$$

where $S = (p_n Q_n + p_n Q_n)(1-t) = Y(1-t)$ is the disposable money income of the private sector. Differentiating equation (16):

(16′) $\hat{Q}'_n = \eta \hat{p}_n + \varepsilon \hat{S}$

where η is the uncompensated own-price elasticity and ε the income elasticity of demand for non-tradeables.

But $$\hat{S} = \hat{Y} - \frac{dt}{1-t}$$

and $$\hat{Y} = \frac{p_n Q_n}{Y}(\hat{Q}_n + \hat{p}_n)$$

$$= \left(1 - a + \frac{p_n G}{Y}\right)(\hat{Q}_n + \hat{p}_n)$$

and substituting this into equation (16′), the result into the differential of (15), and using (8) and $dQ_n = M_L dL$ to eliminate terms in $\hat{p}_n$ and $\hat{Q}_n$, we derive:

$$(17) \quad -Q'_n \varepsilon \frac{dt}{1-t} + dG$$

$$= \hat{L}_n \left[Q_n \theta_n - Q'_n \eta \frac{(1-\theta_n)}{\sigma_n} - Q'_n \varepsilon \left(a_n + \frac{p_n G}{Y} \right) \left(\theta_n + \frac{(1-\theta_n)}{\theta_n} \right) \right]$$

Define g as the government's share in purchases of the non-traded good $\left(\text{so that } \frac{Q'_n}{Q_n} = 1 - g\right)$; m_n as the private sector marginal propensity to consume non-tradeables $\left(\text{so that } \varepsilon a_n = \frac{\partial \phi_n}{\partial Y} \cdot \frac{Y}{\phi_n} \cdot \frac{\phi_n}{Y} = m_n\right)$; and ϕ as pure price elasticity of demand for non-tradeables (so that $\phi = \eta + m_n = \eta + \varepsilon a_n$). Then (17) simplifies to:

$$(17') \quad -Q'_n \varepsilon \frac{dt}{1-t} + dG = \hat{L}_n Q'_n \left\{ \left[\frac{\theta_n}{1-g} - \frac{(1-\theta_n)}{\sigma n} \phi - m_n \theta_n \right] - \frac{\varepsilon p_n G}{Y} \left[\theta_n + \frac{(1-\theta_n)}{\sigma_n} \right] \right\}$$

The first square bracketed term of (17′) is clearly positive $\left(\frac{1}{1-g} \geqq 1 \geqq m_n\right)$; and the expression takes a much neater form if $G = g = 0$.

To create the correct aggregate demand to absorb the labour available at a constant money wage, $\hat{L}_n$ from (14) must be set equal to $\hat{L}_n$ from (17), yielding:

$$(18)\quad \frac{dG}{dt}\cdot\frac{1}{Q_n'} = \frac{-\sigma_n A}{(1-t)(1-a)(1-\theta)} + \frac{\varepsilon}{1-t}$$

where A represents the expression enclosed in curly brackets in equation (17′). (The conditions under which $\frac{dG}{dt} > 0$ may be obtained from this expression: if $G = 0$, a necessary condition is that $m_n > -\phi$.)

Equation (18) gives the actual number of non-traded goods purchased by the government. Converting into money terms and subtracting tax revenue gives the nominal budget deficit (which, note, is 'real' in terms of traded goods, whose local currency price is fixed):

$$(19)\quad D = Gp_n - Yt$$

Noting that $Y = p_t Q_t + p_n Q_n$, we obtain

$$(19')\quad \frac{dD}{dL_n} = \frac{dp_n}{dL_n}[G - tQ_n] + \frac{dt}{dL}\left[p_n\frac{dG}{dt} - Y\right] - tp_n\frac{dQ_n}{dL}$$

and substituting equations (8), (14) and (18), this becomes

$$(20)\quad \frac{dD}{dL_n} = \theta_n\frac{Q_n p_n}{L_n}\left\{\frac{1-\theta_n}{\sigma_n\theta_n}[g-(1-g)\phi] + mg + [(1-mg)(1-t)-m]\left[\frac{1-\theta_n}{\sigma_n\theta_n}+1\right]\right\}$$

This expression is positive (most easily seen by setting $\phi = 0$ and noting that $g > t$). More interesting is the possible magnitude. The term outside of the brackets on the RHS is the wage rate. But the terms inside the brackets could readily sum to unity or greater. This is most easily seen by assuming that initial $g = t = 0$. Then:

$$(20')\quad \frac{dD}{dL_n} = W\left\{1 + \frac{(1-\theta_n)}{\sigma_n\theta_n}(1-\phi) - m\left[\frac{(1-\theta_n)}{\sigma_n\theta_n}+1\right]\right\}.$$

It follows that under some circumstances, the purchase of employment via fiscal expansion could be very expensive: costing more than the additional output produced. Moreover, equations (20) underestimate the true cost, since it is assumed that all government expenditure is on non-tradeables, and therefore employment producing, whereas governments may have considerable difficulty in confining their purchases to non-tradeables. Finally, the cost is in large part a true social cost, from a national point of view, since the budget deficit will be largely reflected in an increase in foreign indebtedness via an increased trade deficit.

It is not the assumption of real wage rigidity, however, that leads to the order of magnitude of the increase in the budget deficit required to achieve a particular increase in the level of employment. Clearly, the same increment to demand would produce the same change in employment if only nominal wage rates were rigid. The effect of the assumption of real wage rigidity is to fix the appropriate tax-expenditure composition of the boost to demand: were only nominal wage rates rigid, the same effect could be achieved, for example, by an increase in government expenditure alone. (Alternatively, the government then is free to *minimise* the cost of attaining any employment level. This will not, however, typically alter the order of magnitude of the required deficit.)

But not only does the rigid real wage hypothesis require greater precision in the use of budgetary policy and therefore increases the possibility of policy error; it also changes the consequences of errors. A too high tax-rate, for example, will be met by rising nominal money wages whatever the level of expenditure. Before leaving the case of fixed exchange rates, therefore, it is worthwhile to note that in this kind of world the derivative of the price level with respect to money wage rates has an uncertain sign.

To see this, Figure 2.1 is useful. The right-hand quadrant gives indifference curves between traded and non-traded goods: $U_f U_f$ gives the initial level of income and S the initial consumption point. The left-hand quadrant gives the initial supply curve of non-traded goods, OW_o, as a function of their money price (recall that there is a given wage rate and capital stock for non-tradeable production).

An increase in the money wage rate to W_1 shifts this supply curve to OW_1. There is, of course, a similar supply curve for tradeables, but since the money price of these is fixed, the shift of that supply curve immediately translates into a decrease in output to, say, T_w.

It is expositionally convenient to consider the case of internationally immobile capital. In that event, there cannot be in equilibrium a balance of trade deficit or surplus: output of tradeables must be equal to consumption. Thus the new equilibrium is somewhere along $T_w T_w$.

But equilibrium also requires that demand and supply of non-tradeables be equal. Try the hypothesis that the money price of non-tradeables is unchanged, so that relative prices are also unchanged. This

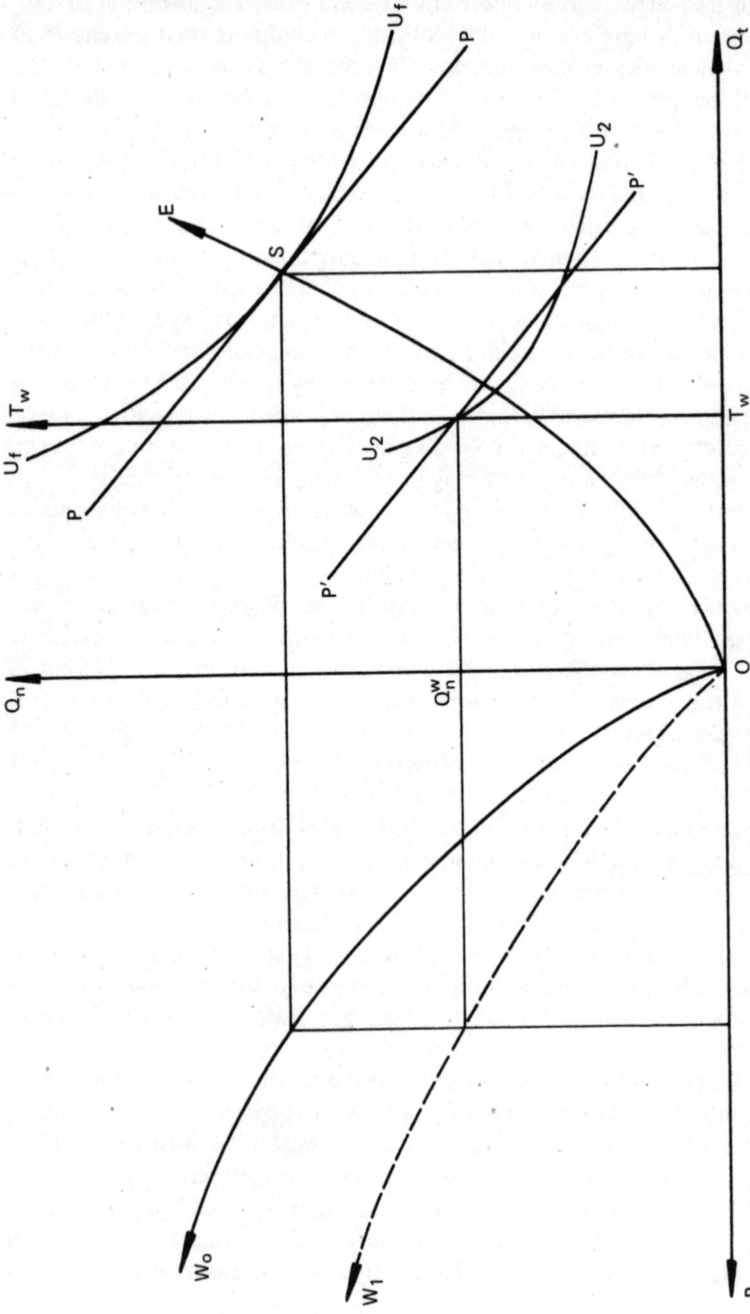

FIGURE 2.1
Money Wage Rate and the Price Level

implies non-tradeable output Q_n^w. If the horizontal through Q_n^w intersects expansion path OE at the intersection of OE and T_wT_w, an unchanged relative price is consistent with both outputs and quantities demanded. If, however, the horizontal through Q_n^w intersects T_wT_w above the intersection of T_wT_w and OE (as drawn in Figure 2.1) unchanged relative prices of goods implies an excess supply of non-tradeables. In that event, non-tradeable output and price must fall further: an increase in money wages causes a *decline* in the price level.

To explore this further, differentiate $Q_np_n = K_np_k + L_nW$ holding constant p_b and K_n, and divide through by K_np_n. The result is:

$$(21)\ \hat{Q}_n = (1-\theta_n)\hat{p}_k + \theta_n\hat{L}_n + \theta_n\hat{W},$$

and using this to eliminate $\hat{p}_k$ and $\hat{Q}_n = \theta_n\hat{L}_n$ to eliminate $\hat{L}_n$, we arrive at:

$$(22)\ \frac{\hat{Q}_n}{\hat{W}} = -\sigma_n\frac{\theta_n}{1-\theta_n}.$$

A similar expression is applicable also to tradeables. Thus, at constant relative prices, an increase in wage rates will cause a diminution in relative quantities supplied of:

$$(23)\ \frac{\hat{Q}_n^s}{\hat{Q}_t^s} = \frac{\sigma_n}{\sigma_t}\cdot\frac{\theta_n}{(1-\theta_n)}\cdot\frac{(1-\theta_t)}{\theta_t}.$$

But on the demand side at constant relative prices,

$$(24)\ \hat{Q}_n = \varepsilon_n\hat{I}_n$$

so the changes in relative quantities demanded are given by

$$(25)\ \frac{\hat{Q}_n^D}{\hat{Q}_t^D} = \frac{\varepsilon_n}{\varepsilon_t}$$

and there is an excess supply of non-tradeables, and therefore a fall in their money price if:

$$(26)\ \frac{\hat{Q}_n^D}{\hat{Q}_t^D} > \frac{\hat{Q}_n^s}{\hat{Q}_t^s}.$$

Thus:

$$(27)\ \frac{\hat{P}}{\hat{W}} \lesseqgtr 0 \text{ as } \frac{\varepsilon_n}{\varepsilon_t} \gtreqless \frac{\sigma_n}{\sigma_t}\frac{\theta_n}{(1-\theta_n)}\frac{(1-\theta_t)}{\theta_t}$$

which gives no particular presumption as to whether the price level rises or falls. (Although if the share of labour in non-tradeable production is greater than that in tradeable production, this would give some basis for a presumption that the price level rises.)

If there is international capital mobility, the outcome depends upon the behaviour of saving relative to investment. Thus, if investment is reduced by less than saving, the economy can in equilibrium finance a trade deficit by the sale of bonds abroad. In that event, consumption of tradeables can exceed output: T_w in Figure 2.1 is further to the right; and the likelihood of $\hat{P} > 0$ is increased. However, although saving is likely to fall with the level of income, the return to capital has been reduced by the same wage-push process. There is no evident reason to suppose that saving will fall by more than investment and, therefore, no basis for a presumption with respect to the direction of the trade balance or the price level.

This proposition, of course, applies to the price level effect of wage push in an open fixed exchange-rate economy whatever the source of the push. From this point of view, the real-wages-rigid hypothesis is one of several supplying an explanation for ostensibly autonomous money wage movements.

The important issue, from the point of view of policy, however, is the means by which the government can escape from the onerous budgetary and capital-account requirements of maintaining a desired level of employment. Obviously, a large number of tax-subsidy schemes is available, but, here, I concentrate on the classic tool of devaluation.

The essential point is that the government's expenditure policy is supporting output of the non-traded good. Thus, devaluation, regarded as a means of increasing the relative price of traded goods, is an alternative means of increasing the quantity of non-traded goods demanded and thus of reducing the government's expenditure requirement. The problem is that if devaluation raises the price level, as by equation (13) it might, then taxes must be reduced if money wage rates are not to rise to an off-setting extent. Thus it appears that tax revenue might fall by more than government expenditure, resulting in an increased budget deficit and, from $X-M \equiv S+T-I-G$, in an increased trade deficit.

To examine this possibility, define the budget deficit D as:

$$(28)\quad D = Gp_n - Yt$$

so that assuming an initially balanced budget:

$$(28')\quad \frac{dD}{\hat{L}_n}\frac{1}{Gp_n} = \frac{\hat{p}_n}{\hat{L}_n} + \frac{\hat{G}}{L_n} - \frac{\hat{t}}{\hat{L}_n} - \frac{\hat{Y}}{\hat{L}_n}$$

Now from equations (15) and (16):

$$(29)\ \hat{G} = \frac{\theta_n}{g}\hat{L}_n - \frac{(1-g)}{g}[\eta\hat{p}_n + \varepsilon_{tn}\hat{p}_t + \varepsilon\hat{S}]$$

$\hat{t}$ is given by equation (13); $\hat{p}_t$ by equation (12); and $S = Y(1-t) = [p_tQ_t + p_nQ_n](1-t)$

Noting that the balanced budget condition $Gp_n = Yt$ may be reformulated as $\dfrac{Gp_n}{Q_np_n} = \dfrac{(1-t)\ Y}{(1-t)Q_np_n}\cdot t\cdot\dfrac{Q'_np_n}{Q'_np_n}$ to give $g = \dfrac{(1-g)t}{(1-a)(1-t)}$[1]

substitution yields:

$$(30)\ \frac{dD}{\hat{L}_n}\cdot\frac{1}{Gp_n} = \frac{\hat{p}_n}{\hat{L}_n}\left\{\left[1-\frac{1-g}{g}\eta\right] + \left[\frac{\sigma_n(1-\theta_t)}{\sigma_t(1-\theta_n)}\cdot\frac{\theta_n(1-a)}{\theta_t(1-g)}\cdot\frac{1}{a}\right]\varepsilon_{tn}\right.$$

$$\left. + \frac{\theta_n\sigma_n}{g(1-\theta_n)} + \left[\frac{\sigma_n\theta_n}{(1-\theta_n)}\right]\left[\frac{1-\theta_t}{\sigma_t\theta_t} - \frac{1-\theta_n}{\sigma_n\theta_n}\right]\left[\frac{1-a}{1-g} - \frac{1-m}{g}\right]\right\}$$

Clearly, the first three terms of the RHS are positive, as is the first term of the final set of square brackets. Necessary (but obviously not sufficient) conditions for $\dfrac{dD}{dL_n} < 0$ are therefore that either

$$\text{(i)}\ \frac{1-a}{1-g} - \frac{1-m}{g} > 0 \quad\text{and}\quad \left(\frac{(1-\theta_t)}{\sigma_t\theta_t} - \frac{(1-\theta_n)}{\sigma_n\theta_n}\right) < 0$$

or

$$\text{(ii)}\ \frac{1-a}{1-g} - \frac{1-m}{g} < 0 \quad\text{and}\quad \left(\frac{(1-\theta_t)}{\sigma_t\theta_t} - \frac{(1-\theta_n)}{\sigma_n\theta_n}\right) > 0.$$

The first possibility occurs if the price level and money income fall, at constant employment, as a result of the shift of labour from non-tradeables to tradeables. In that event, even though the tax rate can be raised, tax revenue might fall. The second, already referred to, arises if the tax rate must be reduced and tax revenue therefore falls.

Neither possibility can be eliminated, in the sense that extreme conditions can be found for which $\dfrac{dD}{dL_n} < 0$. Thus, in case (i), as $\sigma_n \to 0$

$$(31)\ \frac{dD}{Gp_n} \to \frac{\hat{p}_n}{\hat{L}_n}\left\{\left[1-\frac{1-g}{g}\eta\right] - \frac{1-a}{1-g} + \frac{1-m}{g}\right\}$$

The term $\hat{p}n/\hat{L}n \to \infty$, but a sufficiently large g and a sufficiently small a can result in a negative sign for the expression in curly brackets (an outcome that obviously requires $g > a$). Similarly, for case (ii), equation (30) can be reformulated as

$$(30') \quad \frac{dD}{\hat{L}_n} \cdot \frac{1}{Gp_n} = \frac{\hat{p}_n}{\hat{L}_n} \left\{ \left[1 - \frac{(1-g)}{g} \eta \right] + \frac{\sigma_n \theta_n}{(1-\theta_n)} \frac{(1-\theta_n)}{\sigma_t \theta_t} \right.$$

$$\left. \times \left[\frac{1-a}{a} \frac{\sigma_t \theta_t}{1-\theta_t} \cdot \frac{1}{g} + \left(1 - \frac{(1-\theta_n)\,\theta_t \sigma_t}{(1-\theta_t)\,\theta_n \sigma_n} \right) \left(\frac{1-a}{1-g} - \frac{1-m}{g} \right) \right] \right\}$$

so that allowing $\sigma_t \to 0$ and assuming $e_{tn} = 0$ and $\varepsilon = 1$ (so that $1 - a = m$), the second term $\to \infty$ if $a > g$. However, in case (ii) the condition $1 > \frac{(1-\theta_t)}{\sigma_t \theta_t} - \frac{(1-\theta_n)}{\sigma_n \theta_n}$ (which conforms to the popular disposition to regard non-traded goods as labour-intensive) is sufficient (though not necessary) to guarantee $dD/dL > 0$: that is, that the required budget deficit falls with devaluation.

Nevertheless, it remains possible that appropriate use of budgetary policy to maintain a given level of employment with devaluation may require an increased budget deficit, and therefore an increased trade deficit, though it is, perhaps, not very probable. But it would be an error to transfer this 'New Cambridge' result to the movements of a flexible exchange rate. In fact, under flexible exchange rates, the indeterminancy vanishes.

The essential point is that under flexible exchange rates, internal demand is determined by monetary policy, not by the budget deficit. Taxes must still be altered to maintain disposable real wages in the face of changes in relative prices and the level of employment, and therefore tax revenue alters with these variables. But the government is free to determine its expenditure with reference to other objectives than the level of employment. In principle, expenditure could always be adjusted so as to maintain a balanced budget.[3] Adoption of flexible rates substitutes monetary policy for fiscal policy, so that the mechanism that operates under fixed exchange rates, whereby the government must maintain a particular level of both taxes and expenditure to attain its chosen level of employment (and with devaluation may be forced to accept a lower level of taxes but not a similarly reduced level of expenditure) does not apply under flexible rates.

This appears to give flexible exchange rates an advantage over fixed exchange rates in conditions of real wage rigidity. Not only does the movement of the exchange rate insulate the economy from foreign disturbances in the long run[4] – which is of course true whether wage rates are rigid in real or nominal terms – but it frees government expenditure policy from the constraint imposed upon it by maintenance of a fixed exchange rate.

CONCLUDING COMMENT

Much of the drama in discussion of the real wage rigidity hypothesis in fact derives from the typically accompanying proposition that the level of rigidity (or its trend) is non-feasible, in the sense that the full employment wages bill will so squeeze capital income as to reduce growth, or will ultimately exhaust national income. Such problems can only be dealt with by political means. The roughly 10 per cent reduction in the United Kingdom disposable real wages from 1976 to 1977 can be regarded as an example.

Here, I have implicitly assumed that the level or trend is feasible, so that what is at issue is inter-temporal stabilisation of labour earnings, possibly at the cost of destabilising the temporal distribution of other sources of income.

With that very important proviso, the real wage rigidity hypothesis (as real wages are here defined), provides additional problems for economic policy in the sense that it increases the potential for error and also alters the consequences of error. Nevertheless, the indications are that appropriate deployment of the standard tools of economic policy can cope with the alteration: more readily with flexible rates than with fixed.

NOTES

1. I am grateful to John Black, Koichi Hamada and Alasdair Smith for their useful comments – but, none of them is responsible for errors or omissions.
2. R. J. Ball, T. Burns and J. S. E. Laury, 'The Role of Exchange Rate Changes in Balance of Payments Adjustment: the United Kingdom Case' *Economic Journal*, Cambridge, March, 1977.
3. However, in so far as expenditure policy affects the relative price of goods, and therefore the real wage, expenditure policy will have an impact on employment.
4. The qualification 'in the long run' is necessary in view of the monetary magnification hypothesis, which suggests the possibility that a change in the rate of monetary expansion in one country, by causing depreciation of that country's exchange rate in excess of its eventual expected rate of depreciation, will affect other economies. In turn, this implies that governments, believing

themselves confronted by real wage rigidity and unable to quickly change tax rates, will wish to manage their exchange rates – in effect, intervening to maintain constancy of the relative price of traded and non-traded goods. The same comment applies to 'unwarranted' speculation influencing the exchange rate.

3

Asset-market Determination of Exchange Rates: Initial Empirical and Policy Results

WILLIAM H. BRANSON and
HANNU HALTTUNEN

The asset-market approach to short-run determination of the exchange rate, and analysis of the channels of longer-run adjustment, go back to David Hume in the 1700s.[1] This approach has had a recent revival with widespread floating of exchange rates.[2]

Under the system of floating exchange rates existing since 1971, exchange rates have shown substantially more variance than movements in relative price levels. This suggests that, while in the long run the movement of a floating exchange rate will follow roughly the path of relative price levels, the short-run equilibrium value of the rate is determined by other factors. These factors are demand and supply in the markets for financial assets. While in the long run it is useful to view the exchange rate as the relative price of national outputs, in the short run it is more useful to view it as the relative price of national monies.

In this paper, a model of short-run asset-market determination of the exchange rate is outlined. Initial empirical verification of the short-run aspects of the model is also presented.

The plan of the paper is as follows. First, there is an outline of the model which has formed the basis for the empirical work reported later. This model is the one developed by Branson (1976b). It bears a family resemblance to other 'asset-market' models referred to earlier but it also gives an adjustment path towards the long-run equilibrium determined by relative prices. The following section gives the first empirical results so far obtained for the short-run model, relating movements in exchange rate to movements in asset stocks. In the last section we outline a method for presenting and using the initial empirical results for policy.

I THEORETICAL MODEL

For analytical simplicity and clarity, the discussion here will focus on a small country, taking the interest rate on world-traded assets as exogenously determined.

SHORT-RUN DETERMINATION OF THE EXCHANGE RATE

Short-run Asset-market Equilibrium

In the short run, literally at each instant of time, the exchange rate is determined as part of the financial-market system that brings demands for assets in line with predetermined stock supplies. Here we will aggregate earning assets into two categories: domestically-issued assets B with interest rate r and foreign-issued assets F, which earn an interest rate $\bar{r}$ which is fixed on the world market. Domestic portfolio-balancers hold a third asset, domestically-issued money M. We assume B and M are non-traded assets. At each point in time, the stocks of M, B and F in the aggregate portfolio of the domestic private sector are given by history. Since only F is traded, there is no possibility of swapping M or B for F with the rest of the world. F can be accumulated only by running a current-account surplus over time.[3]

At each point of time, the asset–market equilibrium conditions are given by:

Supply = Demand

(1) $M = m(r,\bar{r})\,W;$ (money market)

(2) $B = b(r,\bar{r})\,W;$ (home asset–market)

(3) $eF = f(r,\bar{r})\,W;$ (foreign asset–market)

(4) $W = eF + B + M$ (balance-sheet constraint)

Here e (home currency price of foreign currency) is the exchange rate used to translate F into home currency.[4] Equation (4) is the balance-sheet constraint, which insures that $m+b+f=1$. The three demand functions give the desired distribution of the domestic wealth portfolio W into the three assets.

The balance-sheet constraint (4) plus an assumption of gross substitutability among assets in the portfolio distribution function implies

$$m_r + f_r = -b_r < 0; \quad m_{\bar{r}} + b_{\bar{r}} = -f_{\bar{r}} < 0$$

Here a subscript denotes a partial derivative. The three market equilibrium conditions (1) to (3) contain two independent equations in e and r, given the balance-sheet constraint (4). Any pair of (1) to (3), with W substituted from (4), can be used to determine short-run equilibrium values for e and r.

In Figure 3.1 we show the pairs of interest rate r and exchange rate e that alternatively hold the demand for money equal to its supply (MM), the demand for domestic assets equal to their supply (BB), and the demand for foreign assets equal to their supply (FF). Thus the intersection of these curves is the equilibrium solution for the exchange rate (e_0) and the interest rate (r_0) given M, B, F and $\bar{r}$.

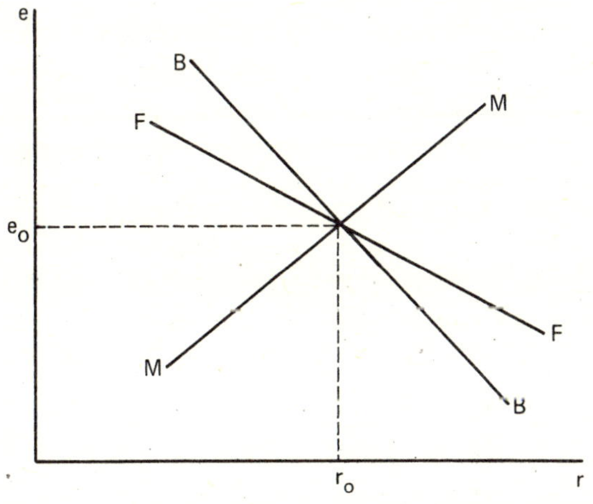

FIGURE 3.1
Equilibrium r and e

Short-run Stability

The first question we ask is: is the short-run equilibrium (r_o, e_o) stable? The short-run dynamic adjustment system for r and e is assumed to be given by equations (5) and (6).

(5) $\dot{r} = \lambda[B - b(r, \bar{r})W]$ (home asset–market)

(6) $\dot{e} = \gamma[f(r, \bar{r})W - eF]$ (foreign asset–market)

Here λ and γ are adjustment coefficients ($0 < \lambda, \gamma < \infty$). Linearising this system around the equilibrium r_0, e_o point (with the wealth definition (4) substituted for W) yields the adjustment equation

$$(7)\quad \begin{pmatrix} \dot{r} \\ \dot{e} \end{pmatrix} = \overset{S}{\begin{bmatrix} -\lambda \overline{W} b_r & -\lambda \bar{b} F \\ \gamma \overline{W} f_r & -\gamma \overline{F}(1-f) \end{bmatrix}} \begin{pmatrix} r_o - r \\ e_o - e \end{pmatrix}.$$

Signs of the elements of the stability matrix S are as indicated. Necessary and sufficient conditions for stability of the r_o, e_o equilibrium are that trace $(S) < 0$ and determinant $(S) > 0$. The trace condition is obviously met. The determinant is

$$\text{Det } (S) = \lambda\gamma WF[b_r(1-f) + f_r b] > 0,$$

since $b_r > -f_r$, and $1 - f > b$. Thus the short-run equilibrium is stable.

Short-run Comparative Statics

The comparative statics of the short-run equilibrium can be obtained by total differentiation of equations (1) and (2), with (4) written in for W:

$$(8)\quad dM = WM_r dr + Wm_{\bar{r}} d\bar{r} + m[dM + dB + edF + F de];$$

(the MM curve)

$$(9)\quad dB = Wb_r dr + Wb_{\bar{r}} d\bar{r} + b[dM + dB + edF + F de]$$

In matrix form, (8) and (9) can be written as

$$(10)\quad \overset{A}{\begin{bmatrix} \overset{-}{Wm_r} & \overset{+}{mF} \\ \overset{+}{Wb_r} & \overset{+}{bF} \end{bmatrix}} \begin{pmatrix} dr \\ de \end{pmatrix} = \overset{B}{\begin{bmatrix} \overset{+}{1-m} & \overset{-}{-m} & \overset{-}{-me} & \overset{+}{-Wm_{\bar{r}}} \\ \overset{-}{-b} & \overset{+}{1-b} & \overset{-}{-be} & \overset{+}{-Wb_{\bar{r}}} \end{bmatrix}} \begin{pmatrix} dM \\ dB \\ dF \\ d\bar{r} \end{pmatrix}$$

The determinant of A is negative. The solution for changes in r and e is given by

$$(11)\quad \begin{pmatrix} dr \\ de \end{pmatrix} = \frac{1}{\text{Det }(A)} \begin{bmatrix} bF & -mF \\ -Wb_r & Wm_r \end{bmatrix} \begin{bmatrix} b_{ij} \end{bmatrix} \begin{pmatrix} dM \\ dB \\ dF \\ d\bar{r} \end{pmatrix}$$

An open-market purchase of B is characterised by setting $dB = -dM$ in (11). An open-market purchase of F sets $edF = -dM$. The expression for $dr/d\bar{r}$ is

$$\frac{dr}{d\bar{r}} = \frac{WF}{\text{Det }(A)}\left[-bm_{\bar{r}} + mb_{\bar{r}}\right] \lesseqgtr 0, \text{ as } (mb_{\bar{r}}) - (bm_{\bar{r}}) \lesseqgtr 0.$$

This can be manipulated to give the condition

$$\frac{dr}{d\bar{r}} \lesseqgtr 0 \text{ as } \frac{b_{\bar{r}}/b}{m_{\bar{r}}/m} \lesseqgtr 1, \text{ or } \frac{E(b/\bar{r})}{E(m/\bar{r})} \lesseqgtr 1,$$

where $E(b/\bar{r})$ is the elasticity of b with respect to $\bar{r}$, *etcetera*. In other words, the condition for $dr/d\bar{r} > 0$ is that demand for home assets be more sensitive to changes in the rate on foreign assets than is the demand for money.[5]

The effects of a change in F (through the current account) on e and r can be solved from (11). It should be apparent from the system (1) to (4) that $E(e/F) = -1$,[6] and $dr/dF = 0$ are the solutions. As F rises, e falls proportionately, holding (eF) constant. This leaves the rest of the system undisturbed, not requiring a change in r.

Finally, the elasticities of e with respect to open-market increases in M are as follows:

$$\frac{M}{e}\frac{de}{dM}\bigg|_{dB=-dM} = \frac{M}{eF}\left[\frac{f_r/b_r}{b(m_r/b_r) - m}\right];$$

(12)

$$\frac{M}{e}\frac{de}{dM}\bigg|_{edF=-dM} = \frac{M}{eF}\left[\frac{-1}{b(m_r/b_r) - m}\right]$$

If the system is completely symmetric, so that $M = eF = B$, and $m_r = f_r = -0.5b_r$, the first elasticity is 1.0 and the second is 2.0. Thus in general a mixed open-market operation could be expected to raise e on impact more than proportionately to the increase in M.

The results of the various accumulation and open-market experiments are summarised in Table 3.1. The signs come directly from equation (11).

The entries in Table 3.1 give the direction of change of the interest rate and the exchange rate following (*a*) an increase in any one of the asset stocks, holding the others constant, in the first three columns, and (*b*) an expansionary open-market operation, with M exchanged for B or for F, in the last two columns. One important implication of Table 3.1 is that an

TABLE 3.1
Effects of Increases in Asset Stocks on Short-run Equilibrium Interest Rate (r) and Exchange Rate (e)

	Effects of accumulation of stocks			*Effects of open-market operations*	
Effects on:	ΔM	ΔB	ΔF	$\Delta B = -\Delta M$	$e\,\Delta F = -\Delta M$
r	−	+	0	−	−
e	+	?	−	+	+

increase in the domestic money stock M, either through a budget deficit or an open-market operation, directly raises the exchange rate e. The increase in e is required for financial market equilibrium, and should come quickly, before any effects on the price level are seen. Thus, in the short run, the exchange rate is determined by financial market equilibrium, not by relative prices. A second important implication of Table 3.1 is that if the country is running a surplus on current account, so that net foreign assets F are increasing, this tends to reduce the exchange rate; a deficit on current account, with F falling, raises the exchange rate. This is the key to dynamic adjustment of the exchange rate as we move from short run to long run.

DYNAMIC ADJUSTMENT OF THE EXCHANGE RATE

In the short run the exchange rate is determined by requirements of asset market equilibrium, given existing stocks of money, domestic assets and foreign assets. But this is not the end of the story. The value of the exchange rate at one point in time, $t(0)$, given income, absorption, the domestic price level and other real variables, may yield a non-zero balance on current account. With flexible exchange markets, the sum of the balances on capital account and current account is identically zero. Thus a non-zero current-account balance implies an equally non-zero capital-account balance of the opposite sign. If the current account shows a surplus, the capital account is in deficit and the private sector is accumulating foreign assets; F is increasing. If the current account is in deficit, F is decreasing. As F changes, the exchange rate changes through the short-run mechanism described above on page 56. Thus if the initial value of the exchange rate $e(0)$ yields a non-zero current-account balance, F is either increasing or decreasing, moving e from $e(0)$. The point of this section is to outline the *dynamic adjustment* through the current account and to show the condition under which it leads to a stable long-run equilibrium value for e where the current-account balance is zero and the stock of net foreign assets is not changing.[7]

Solving the asset market model (equations 1 to 4) yields a *reduced form* equation for the exchange rate:

$$(13)\ e = e(F; M, B, \bar{r});$$

Signs of the partial derivatives are those given in Table 3.1. We can now study dynamic adjustment of the exchange rate over time by combining (13) with the balance of payments equation[8] with a flexible exchange rate,

$$(14)\ 0 = X\left(\frac{e}{p}\right) + \bar{r}F - \dot{F}, \quad \text{or} \quad (14)\ \dot{F} = X\left(\frac{e}{p}\right) + \bar{r}F.$$[9]

Here X is the current account less net investment income, essentially merchandise trade, travel, and tourism – we will call this the trade account; $\bar{r}F$ is net investment income; $\dot{F}$, the rate of accumulation of foreign assets, is the capital account. The current account Z is defined by,

$$(15)\ Z = X\left(\frac{e}{p}\right) + \bar{r}F = \dot{F}$$

If the Marshall–Lerner elasticity conditions holds, $X' > 0$. This is necessary, but not sufficient, for stability.

For a given domestic price level P, consider the case in which the initial equilibrium exchange rate $e(0)$ yields a positive current account $X + \bar{r}F > 0$. In this case, through (14) net foreign assets are accumulating in domestic portfolios: $\dot{F} = Z > 0$. As F increases, the exchange rate falls, via (13). This reduces X, so that $\bar{r}F$ is increasing and X is falling. Using the reduced-form equation (13), we can write the adjustment equation (14) as

$$(16)\ \dot{F} = X[e(F)/P] + \bar{r}F.$$

The stability condition is then

$$(17)\ d\dot{F}/dF = X'e_F + \bar{r} < 0.$$[10]

From equation (13) we have $e_F < 0$ $[E(e/F) = -1$ where $E(e/F)$ is the elasticity of e with respect to $F]$ and the Marshall–Lerner condition gives us $X' > 0$. But for stability, the trade effect of increasing F must outweigh the investment income effect: $X'e_F < \bar{r}$. If this holds, the adjustment process will be stable.

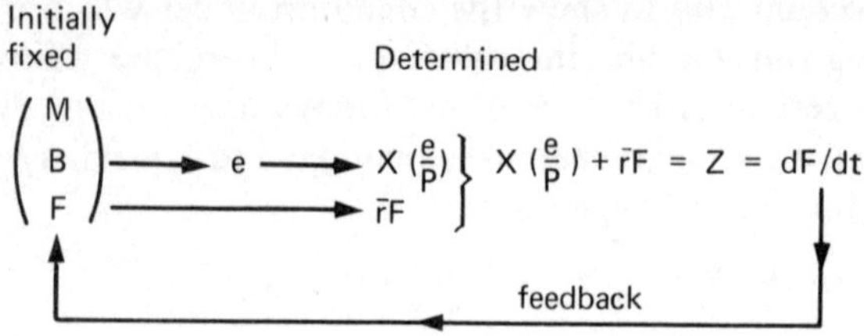

FIGURE 3.2
Exchange-rate Adjustment over Time

An overview of the adjustment mechanism is shown in Figure 3.2. The initial values of M, B, F, determine a value for e as in the first section. This, in turn, yields a value for net exports (X), given the internal price level P. The initial value of net foreign assets F also yields a net income on foreign assets, $\bar{r}F$. Net exports, X, and investment income $\bar{r}F$, sum to the balance on current account Z, which is the rate of accumulation of net foreign assets, dF/dt. This feeds back on F, moving e as shown in Table 3.1. If the initial values of e and F yield a zero balance on current account $Z = 0$, implying $X = -\bar{r}F$, the system will be in equilibrium in the sense that F and e will remain unchanged.

If the adjustment mechanism is stable, then the exchange rate will track movements in P, but only approximately. The adjustment mechanism in this model is movements in F. Thus between long-run equilibrium investment income $\bar{r}F$ changes, and $X\left(\frac{e}{p}\right)$ must show offsetting variations. Thus e will adjust in stock equilibrium to changes in P, but only enough to allow a terms-of-trade effect in e/p that adjusts X to offset changes in transfer income $\bar{r}F$.[11]

II EMPIRICAL VERIFICATION OF THE SHORT-RUN EXCHANGE-RATE MODEL

ESTIMATING EQUATION FOR THE EXCHANGE RATE

In moving from the theoretical formulation of the previous section to an estimating exchange-rate equation for different currencies, we begin by drawing the implications of the theory for prediction of a bilateral rate. Then we go on to details of the estimating equation, and the actual econometric estimates. The theory of the first section focused on one country facing a world market: the problem here is to translate that into an operational theory of determination of one bilateral rate between two countries.

In Table 3.1 we saw the effects of movements in asset stocks on the exchange rate of one country facing a given world financial market summarised by $\bar{r}$. The effects of changes in the domestic money stock M, or the stock of net foreign assets F were clear. The effects of changes in domestic assets B were unclear; the sign depends on relative substitutabilities in portfolio demand functions. Thus the theory gives us clear predictions only of the effects of changing the stock of domestic M and F on e.

If we extend this analysis to a world of two countries, each with J earning assets and a money, with total supplies of each asset fixed in the short run, we have $(2J+2)$ assets, and the interaction of their demands and the fixed supplies determines the $2J$ rates of return plus one exchange rate e. The equilibrium value of the exchange rate is the value at which the two private sectors together are willing to hold the existing stocks of the two national monies.

Further extension of this general equilibrium problem of determination of interest rates and exchange rates to a real world with N countries, each with J earning assets and a money, would give us $NJ+N$ assets in all (NJ earning assets and N monies). The interaction of supply and demand now determines equilibrium values for the NJ interest rates and $(N-1)$ exchange rates.

When we move to a bilateral model for a particular rate – for example the \$/DM rate – the natural extension of the theory is a model that includes movements in both the United States and German money stocks and net foreign assets (= cumulated current account). There are some problems involved when we use both countries' foreign assets stocks in determining the bilateral rate. Due to data limitations we use, however, both countries' total stocks of net foreign assets. This implicitly assumes that third-country assets are perfect subtitutes for German assets for United States portfolio holders, and vice versa. This is clearly unsatisfactory, but an improvement awaits development of reliable bilateral data.

Changes in these variables have clear effects on the \$/DM rate, if the theory holds. These are summarised in Table 3.2 below. Symmetrically, an increase in the United States money stock should raise the \$/DM rate and an increase in the German money stock should lower it; following from Table 3.1, on page 60, the opposite should hold for the two F

variables. These reactions should be rapidly apparent in the data, certainly within a quarter. After all, the asset–market view is about short-run determination of the exchange rate.

Following the model of the first section, where we assumed that tradeable and domestic assets are not perfect substitutes, we might also include domestic assets B in Table 3.2. But there is no *a priori* sign pattern for the effects of changes in these asset stocks on e (\$/DM). So in an initial look at the data, with not many observations since rates began to move in 1971, not much is to be gained by including these variables in the analysis; at this point, we do not even know the signs to expect for their coefficients.

TABLE 3.2

Effects of Changes in United States and West German Money Stock and Net Foreign Assets on \$/DM Rate

Effect of increases on the \$/DM rate (e)	*Money stock (M)* US	*Money stock (M)* W. Germany	*Net foreign assets (F)* US	*Net foreign assets (F)* W. Germany
e(\$/DM)	+	−	−	+

The same line of reasoning extends to the focus on United States and West German money and foreign assets in the empirical analysis, to the exclusion of the other countries' monies as well. As was noted before, short-run equilibrium values of exchange rates and interest rates for N countries are determined by equilibrium conditions in the NJ asset markets. But in operational terms, it is only for the *bilateral* monies and F variables (with the assumption of perfect substitutability between tradeable assets) that we have clear expectations of their effects in determining the bilateral exchange rate. For all other countries' monies, the effect on the particular bilateral rate will depend on the relative substitutability of those monies with the assets of the two countries at hand. For example, if Canadian dollars and US dollars are good substitutes, an increase in the Canadian money stock would drive up the \$/DM rate. But if Canadian dollars and Deutsche marks were better substitutes, the same increases would drive the \$/DM rate down.

Thus the effect of changing third-country money stocks on the exchange rate between two countries is ambiguous, as is the effect of changing domestic non-monetary assets in the two countries under analysis. If we had outside knowledge on the relative substitutability of assets denominated in various currencies, we could contemplate the estimation of a general equilibrium model for all the relevant exchange rates. But in the absence of such information, we begin with a bilateral model for the \$/DM rate e (\$/DM), as a function of measures of the United States and West German stocks of money and net foreign assets:

$$(18)\ e(\$/\text{DM}) = H(M_U, M_G, F_U, F_G)$$

where the subscripts U and G stand for United States and West Germany, respectively.

Equation (18) gives us the general form for the equation to be estimated econometrically. Before it can be estimated to obtain the relevant effects of Ms and Fs on e, we need to specify the particular form of the equation to be estimated, and the particular statistical series to be used for the variables in H.

The equation for estimation will be a log-linear version of equation (18)

$$(19)\ \ln e = \alpha_1 + \alpha_2 \ln M_U + \alpha_3 \ln M_G + \alpha_4 \ln F_U + \alpha_5 \ln F_G + \varepsilon.$$

The coefficients α_2 and α_5 should be positive and α_3 and α_4, negative, as shown in Table 3.2 opposite. We use a log-linear form initially because in that case the parameters α_2 to α_5 are conveniently the elasticities of e with respect to movements in the asset stocks.

THE SAMPLE PERIOD AND DATA

The dollar-Deutschemark (\$/DM) rate has shown the greatest variability among the principal dollar exchange rates since 1971, and the other major currencies have been more or less managed to maintain particular relationships to either the dollar or the Deutschemark. Thus our view of the exchange market is bipolar. In the centre is the \$/DM rate, with other currencies moving either against the US dollar, such as the Canadian dollar and the yen, or the Deutschemark, such as sterling, the French and Swiss francs and the lira. Therefore, equations of the form of (19) were estimated for currencies related either to the dollar or to the Deutschemark. The following classification was used: (\$/domestic currency) rates were used for Germany and Japan; (DM/domestic currency) rates were used for France, Italy, Switzerland and the United Kingdom.

The time period for estimation runs from July 1971, just before the United States suspended dollar convertibility, to June 1976, the latest observation available for certain series at the time of estimation. The \$/DM rate showed substantial movement during the period August

1971–February 1972, as did the other rates, too. From then through January 1973, the Bundesbank stabilised the exchange rate in an attempt to hold to the Smithsonian Agreement of December 1971. After March 1973, the rate has floated under management. Thus, an estimation period beginning after this might be considered more appropriate for a model of floating rates. However, the movements of the rates before early 1973 contain some useful information, and the relation of the predicted movements of the rates from the asset–market model, and the actual movement during 1972 and 1973 may be quite instructive.

In order to see if the structure of the model is dependent on the sample period, equation (19) was estimated for the whole period from July 1971 to June 1976 and also for the sub-period April 1973 to June 1976. There are some exceptions due to lack of data but these are explained in connection with the estimation results.

The data are drawn mainly from the International Monetary Fund's (IMF) *International Financial Statistics* and are monthly observations. The exchange rates are monthly averages, and the stock variables are beginning-of-the-month observations. This formulation implicitly assumes that stock values at the beginning of the month determine the rate during the month. In the regression results report below, the stock variables are defined as follows. The money stocks are the well-known *M*1s. We use *M*1 because the relationship between the base and the money stock is quite loose and because *M*1 often is an independent target variable for monetary policy. Thus, for an initial model of foreign exchange behaviour, we take *M*1 as being (approximately) determined exogenously.[12] The net foreign asset series are cumulations of current-account balances of each country on benchmark observations.[13]

The monthly current-account figures are interpolated using monthly trade-account figures as reference series. This method was used for all countries except Japan and Germany, where monthly data were readily available, and Switzerland, where the interpolation had to be started from annual current accounts because of lack of quarterly figures. These data do not include valuation changes from movements in asset prices, that is capital gains. This is a defect that should be remedied with more extensive empirical work on the model. All data for stock variables are seasonally adjusted. It should be noted also that our first estimated equations use total foreign-asset stocks, which include central bank reserves as well. Instead we should be using private foreign-asset stocks; after all we are dealing with the private sector portfolio behaviour. So implicitly when using total *F*s we assume purely flexible rates with no central bank intervention in foreign exchange markets. There exists also a possibility for a certain type of systematic intervention behaviour, which is consistent with the equation using total Fs. This case is discussed later in connection with possible extensions of the models.

EMPIRICAL RESULTS

Exchange Rates ($/domestic currency)

Table 3.3A and 3.3B give the estimation results of equation (19) for Germany and Japan for the period July 1971 to June 1976 and April 1973 to June 1976, respectively. Since the ordinary least squares (OLS)

TABLE 3.3
($/Domestic Currency)-Rates, Estimated in Logs
A: Sample period 1971:8 to 1976:6

Country	*Con.*	M_D	M_U	F_D	F_U	*RHO*	*DW*	$\bar{R}^2$
Germany	−6.014	−.772	2.220	.215	−.374		.683	.852
	(5.7)	(−4.6)	(7.4)	(3.2)	(−4.6)			
Germany	−2.166	−.622	.260	.418	−.100	.888	1.370	.948
	(−1.3)	(−2.1)	(0.7)	(2.6)	(−1.3)	(16.1)		
Japan	−4.923	.344	−.589	.180	−.123		.578	.772
	(−3.7)	(2.5)	(−1.4)	(7.7)	(−2.1)			
Japan	−7.009	.093	−.058	.169	−.094	.777	1.405	.898
	(−6.2)	(0.9)	(−0.2)	(3.0)	(−1.6)	(8.8)		

B: Sample period 1973:4 to 1976:6

Country	*Con.*	M_D	M_U	F_D	F_U	*RHO*	*DW*	$\bar{R}^2$
Germany	−.834	−.278	.502	.206	−.292		0.671	.297
	(−.3)	(−1.3)	(0.5)	(1.9)	(−2.4)			
Germany	−.061	−.471	.010	.273	−.113	.727	1.314	.647
	(−.0)	(−1.4)	(.0)	(1.6)	(−1.2)	(6.1)		
Japan	−5.662	.137	−.279	.187	−.109		.688	.795
	(−4.1)	(0.8)	(−.7)	(4.9)	(−1.9)			
Japan	−4.480	.097	−.436	.133	−.071	.690	1.405	.885
	(−3.2)	(.7)	(−1.7)	(2.0)	(−1.3)	(4.9)		

estimates showed substantial serial correlation in the error terms, Cochrane–Orcutt estimates are presented as well. The symbols represent:

e	= $ or DM price of domestic currency
con.	= constant term
M	= money stock
F	= foreign asset stock
$\bar{R}^2$	= squared correlation coefficient, adjusted for degrees of freedom

DW = Durbin–Watson statistics, and
RHO = the first-order serial correlation coefficient

t-ratios are given below the coefficients.

Subscript *G* and *U* refer to Germany and the United States respectively and *D* stands for 'domestic' country.[14]

Regressions are reported for the following currencies:
Japan,
France,
Italy,
Switzerland,
the United Kingdom.

All *M*s are in domestic and all *F*s in foreign currency. Because we have two different types of equations for ($/domestic currency) rates and for (DM/domestic currency), we have two different 'foreign' countries. When the United States is treated as a 'foreign' country, all *F*s are in dollars and when Germany is treated as a 'foreign' country all *F*s are in Deutschemarks.

In what follows we discuss the results country by country and then give a brief summary of the results.[15]

Germany

The plot of actual movements in *e*($/DM) and those predicted by the OLS equations for Germany in Table 3.3A for the period August 1971 to June 1976 is shown in Figure 3.3. The coefficients all have the expected signs. The predicted values of the exchange rate follow the general pattern of movement of the actual rate fairly well, but the residuals are highly autocorrelated. The Cochrane–Orcutt equation shows a RHO value of nearly 0.9, with only the German variables retaining significance.

For the shorter sample period (Table 3.3B) the results are not as good as for the longer one. The coefficients still have the right signs but those for money stocks are not significant any more and they are much smaller than those estimated from the longer period. The *F*-elasticities are fairly stable and the most significant. As an initial attempt at estimating the asset market model the results seem mildly encouraging.

Japan

The equations for ($/¥)-rate are roughly similar across estimation periods. *F*-elasticities have the right signs, they are fairly stable and significant. Coefficients for money stock variables are generally insignificant and they have wrong signs. This may be due to the high

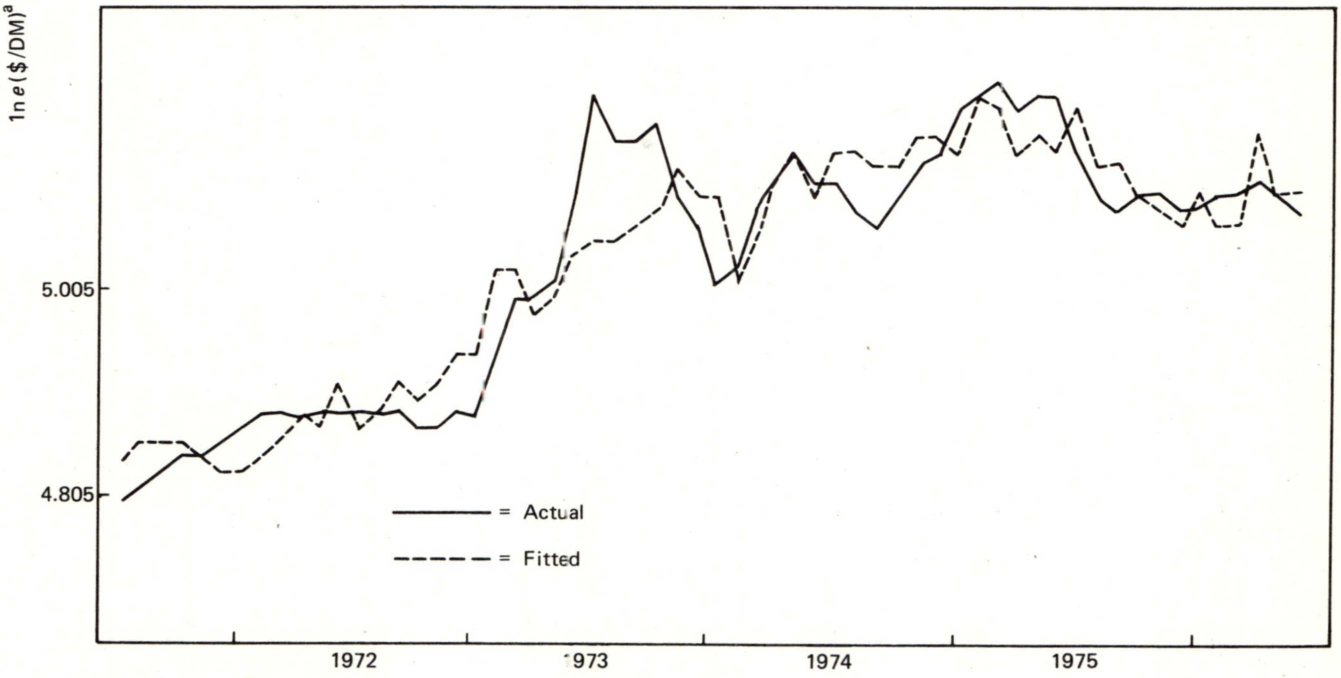

FIGURE 3.3
The ($/DM)-Exchange Rate

[a] e($/DM) is an index rebased for Figure 3.3, 1971:7 = 100 (ln 100 = 4.605).

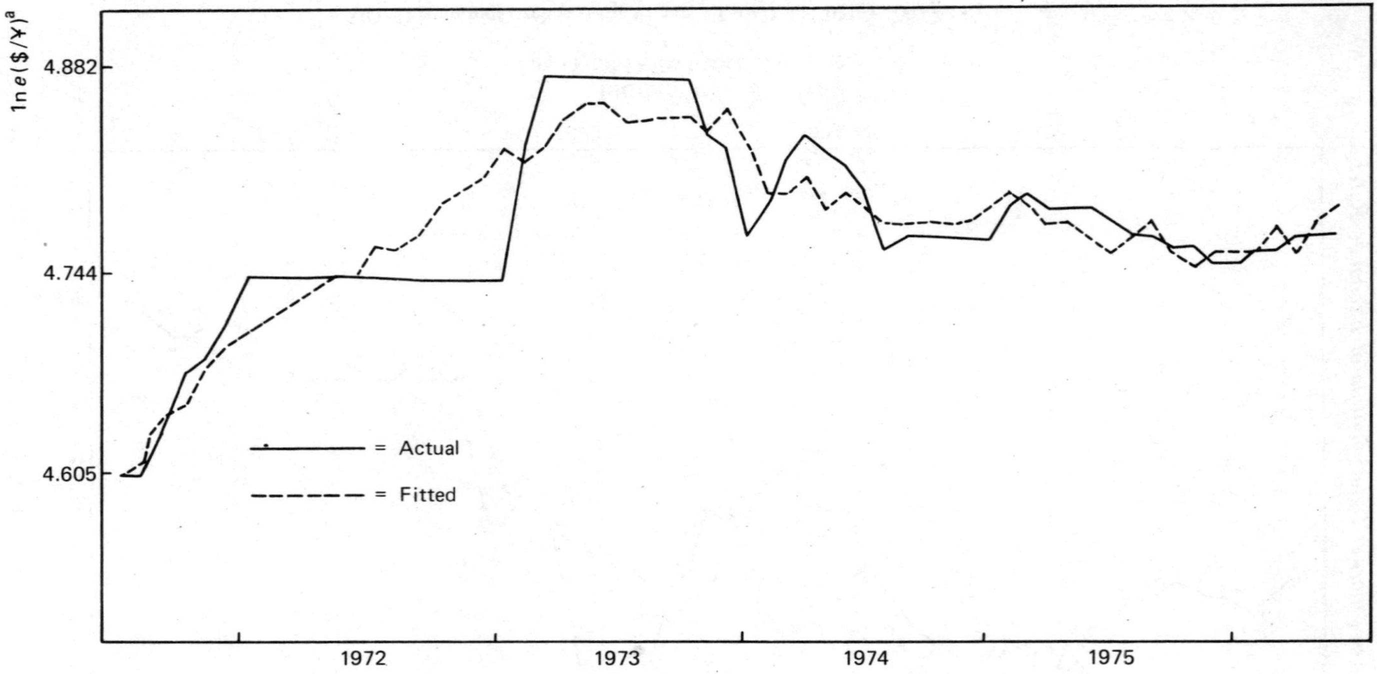

FIGURE 3.4
The ($/¥)-Exchange Rate

[a] $e(\$/¥)$ is an index rebased for Figure 3.4, 1971:7 = 100 (ln 100 = 4.605).

correlation between them (.99). One possibility of taking care of this problem would be to constrain the coefficients to be equal in absolute values. The plot for ($/¥)-rate is shown in Figure 3.4.

Exchange Rates (DM/domestic currency)

Tables 3.4A and 3.4B report the results for France, Italy, Switzerland and the United Kingdom for the periods August 1971 to June 1976 and April 1973 to June 1976, respectively.

TABLE 3.4
(DM/Domestic Currency) Exchange Rate, Estimated in Logs
A: Sample period beginning in 1971

	Con.	M_D	M_G	F_D	F_G	*RHO*	*DW*	$\bar{R}^2$
Sample period 1971:8 to 1976:3								
France 1	−1.257	−1.353	1.639	.024	−.061		1.202	.898
	(−2.4)	(−11.6)	(16.3)	(1.2)	(−.7)			
France 2	−.436	−.555	.739	.031	−.073	.855	1.605	.933
	(−.4)	(−3.4)	(3.0)	(1.2)	(−.5)	(9.0)		
Sample period 1971:8 to 1975:12								
Switzerland	1.171	−.850	.623	.079	−.098		.589	.866
	(1.6)	(−5.5)	(6.0)	(2.8)	(−2.3)			
Switzerland	−3.369	.003	.501	−.015	.071	.853	1.765	.951
	(−2.9)	(.0)	(3.5)	(−.3)	(0.8)	(13.8)		
Sample period 1971:12 to 1976:6								
United Kingdom	21.038	−1.509	.782	−.527	−.905		9.28	.966
	(13.2)	(−9.6)	(3.3)	(−8.8)	(−13.1)			
United Kingdom	22.4	−.749	−.214	−.514	−.912	.800[a]	1.538	.980
	(4.0)	(−3.5)	(−.7)	(−2.5)	(−4.2)			

[a] *RHO*-value estimated by search method because non-linear estimation failed to converge.

B: Sample period beginning in 1973

	Con.	M_D	M_G	F_D	F_G	*RHO*	*DW*	$\bar{R}^2$
Sample period 1973:4 to 1976:3								
France 3	−3.906	−1.121	1.343	.114	.277		1.601	.881
	(−5.8)	(−9.9)	(12.7)	(4.7)	(2.5)			
France 4	−4.010	−1.056	1.269	.119	.295	.180	1.787	.879
	(−4.9)	(−7.6)	(9.1)	(4.1)	(2.2)	(1.0)		
Sample period 1973:8 to 1976:6								
Italy	5.779	−1.915	1.919	−.091	−1.040		1.322	.905
	(3.5)	(−9.7)	(5.3)	(4.0)	(−4.0)			
Italy	.300	−1.228	.749	.034	−.247	.655	1.778	.932
	(.1)	(−4.7)	(1.9)	(.7)	(−.8)	(8.2)		

TABLE 3.4 (*contd*)

B: Sample period beginning in 1973

	Con.	M_D	M_G	F_D	F_G	*RHO*	*DW*	$\bar{R}^2$
Sample period 1973:4 to 1975:12								
Switzerland	−.771	−.671	.874	−.026	−.027		.920	.919
	(−.4)	(−1.7)	(7.1)	(−.6)	(−.5)			
Switzerland	−4.490	.004	.563	−.040	.161	.679	1.926	.953
	(−2.8)	(.0)	(3.3)	(−.8)	(1.5)	(5.6)		
Sample period 1973:4 to 1976:6								
United	6.763	−1.400	1.376	−.041	−.423		1.141	.897
Kingdom	(.8)	(−7.0)	(2.6)	(−.1)	(1.6)			
United	10.445	−.648	.128	−.139	−.413	.800[a]	1.584	.929
Kingdom	(.9)	(−2.3)	(.2)	(−.3)	(−.9)			

[a] *RHO*-value estimated by search method because non-linear estimation failed to converge.

C: Regressions for France

Con.	M_D	M_G	F_D	F_G	*RHO*	*DW*	$\bar{R}^2$
Sample period 1971:8 to 1976:3							
−1.592	−1.406	1.644	.035			1.209	.899
(−9.5)	(−16.8)	(16.5)	(4.3)				
−.827	−.584	.689	.035		.874	1.616	.934
(1.2)	(−4.0)	(3.2)	(1.4)		(11.5)		
−.672	−1.279	1.631		−.161		1.181	.897
(−2.9)	(−12.8)	(16.2)		(−4.1)			
.295	−.512	.636		−.136	.875	1.529	.932
(.3)	(−3.1)	(2.8)		(−.9)	(10.0)		
Sample period 1973:4 to 1976:3							
−2.301	−1.012	1.436	.059			1.370	.861
(−9.8)	(−8.9)	(13.5)	(5.5)				
−2.244	−.862	1.283	.061		.343	1.696	.865
(−6.5)	(−5.4)	(7.7)	(4.0)		(1.8)		
−.849	−1.034	1.511		−.200		1.076	.801
(−3.2)	(−7.1)	(11.8)		(−3.4)			
−1.876	−.576	.583		.092	.846	1.617	.855
(−.8)	(−2.7)	(2.2)		(.3)	(7.3)		

France

The first two equations in Tables 3.4A and 3.4B summarise the results for the (DM/F-France) exchange rate. The plot from equation France 1 is given in Figure 3.5. Both money stocks are quite significant in both OLS and Cochrane–Orcutt equations across both sample periods. The *F*-elasticities have the right signs but are insignificant in Table 3.4A over the longer sample. In Table 3.4B, the *F*-elasticities are significant but the German *F* takes on the wrong sign. This confusion could be due to the high correlation (.94) of the two *F* series.

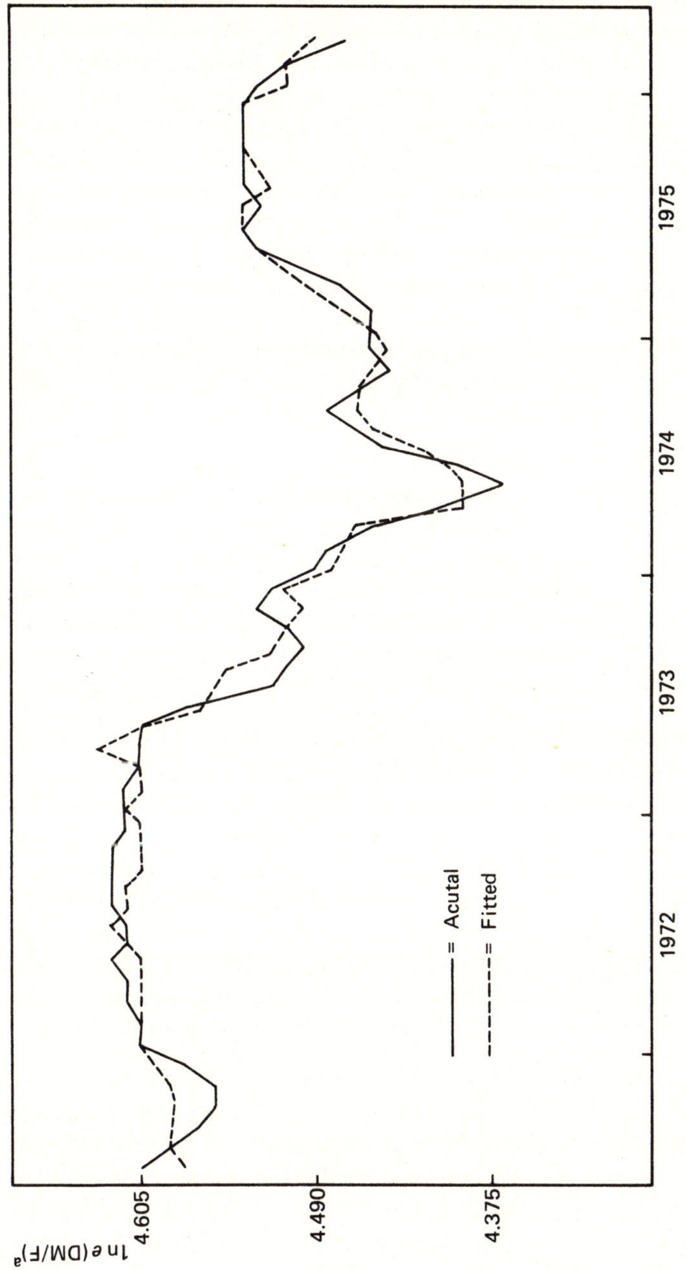

FIGURE 3.5
The (DM/F)-Exchange Rate

[a] *e*(DM/F) is an index rebased for Figure 3.5, 1971:7 = 100 (*ln* 100 = 4.605).

This conjecture is followed up in Table 3.4C which reports regressions for France, including alternative F_F or F_G but not both. These regressions in OLS form generally assign a significant coefficient with the right sign to the F variable included, but in most cases Cochrane–Orcutt estimation makes the coefficient insignificant. It should be noted that, because the French foreign-asset stock is negative through the estimation period, the signs are reversed because of logarithms for the estimation. The signs of the coefficients in Tables 3.4A and 3.4B are reversed back so the expected sign for F_F is positive. Because figures for the second quarter of the current account for France were not available the sample period ends in March 1976. The comparison of the results for different estimation periods shows that the structure has remained fairly stable.

Italy

In Table 3.4B, results for the (DM/Lira)-rate are shown. Because the time series of the Italian foreign asset stock includes both positive and negative values it was possible to start the estimation period only from July 1973, after which it has been negative. The signs of the numbers were reversed for the estimation and thus the same comments apply as in the case of France. The cofficient of F_I in the OLS equation has the wrong sign and is highly significant. This anomaly is eliminated in the Cochrane–Orcutt equation.

Switzerland

For Switzerland the data base of the Swiss foreign-asset stock is very weak. Only annual current-account figures are available and the interpolated monthly figures should be treated with caution. That is why the sample period also ends in 1975 because annual current-account figures for 1976 at the time of estimation were not available. In the equation of Table 3.4A the signs are correct and all the coefficients significant. When the Cochrane–Orcutt correction is applied to this equation, however, all variables except M_G become insignificant. Similarly, over the shorter period of Table 3.4B, only M_G is significant.

United Kingdom

For the (DM/£)-rate all the coefficients are significant but F_E takes on the wrong sign in the OLS estimate for the period November 1971 to June 1976 (Table 3.4A). Re-estimation by the Cochrane–Orcutt method over the longer sample leaves F_E with the wrong sign, and makes M_G insignificantly positive. The problem with F_E remains in the shorter sample of Table 3.4B.

Equations estimated for the (\$/£) rate generally give less satisfactory results than those for the (DM/£) rate shown here. Part of the reason may be that minimum lending rate (MLR) in the United Kingdom seems to be varied to stabilise the (DM/£) rate. A simple linear regression, adjusted for serial correlation, of MLR on the DM/£ rate and a time trend for the period October 1971 to July 1976 gives the following result:

$$\underset{}{\text{MLR}} = \underset{(4.1)}{22.7} - \underset{(3.1)}{2.0e(\text{DM}/£)} - \underset{(0.3)}{0.02t}$$

$$\bar{R}^2 = .92; \quad DW = 1.9; \quad RHO = .87.$$

Summary of the Initial Empirical Results

As a whole the initial estimation results of the asset–market model seem mildly encouraging. In most of the equations, significant coefficients have expected signs and they have reasonable values. The residuals in nearly all the OLS estimates, however, are highly autocorrelated. There may be several reasons for this but we think that this is mainly due to our tentative and fairly rough initial specification of the estimating equation rather than a basic problem with the theory. We hope to improve the results, when we take a more careful look at the estimating equation and introduce reaction functions into the story.

It is perhaps worth noting that the present model is consistent with the model developed by Artus (1976) for Germany. Artus' model is a structural first difference (or flow) version of the model, where ours is a reduced-form, levels (or stock) version. Our empirical results for Germany in qualitative terms are similar to those of Artus. The comparison of the estimated coefficients, however, is difficult because Artus uses percentage changes in his exchange-rate variables and absolute changes in others.

PURCHASING POWER PARITY AND DEMAND FOR MONEY

According to the theoretical model developed in the first section the exchange rate is determined in the long run by equilibrium conditions in international markets for goods and services, that is by relative prices. In the short run the exchange rate is determined by equilibrium conditions in asset markets and that is why relative prices – representing purchasing power parity – do not enter the estimating equation. Several authors, however, formulate their model in such a way that a relative price term shows up in the (reduced form) exchange-rate equation [see, for example, Dornbusch (1976b), Artus (1976)].

As an *ad hoc* exercise we added relative prices to our basic equation (19) and carried out the estimation for all the countries and for the same sample periods as before, all estimates OLS. Tables 3.5A and 3.5B summarise the results for the (\$/domestic currency)-rate for the periods August 1971 to June 1976 and April 1973 to June 1976 respectively. Tables 3.6A and 3.6B give the corresponding results for the (DM/domestic currency)-rates.

TABLE 3.5

(\$/Domestic Currency) Exchange Rate, Estimated in Logs

A: Sample period 1971:8 to 1976:6

Country	*Con.*	M_D	M_U	F_D	F_U	P_U/P_D[a]	$\bar{R}^2$	*DW*
Germany	−.940	−.361	1.222	.670	−.452	−1.673	.876	.576
	(.4)	(−1.8)	(2.8)	(4.2)	(−5.8)	(−3.0)		
Japan	−4.976	.331	−.563	.179	−.123	−.031	.800	.582
	(−3.7)	(2.4)	(−1.3)	(7.9)	(−2.1)	(−.4)		

[a] Price indices (*P*) come from *International Financial Statistics* (Washington: IMF, annual) and are industrial production prices. Subscripts for *P* have the same meaning as before.

B: Sample period 1973:4 to 1976:6

Country	M_D	*Con.*	M_U	F_D	F_U	P_U/P_D	$\bar{R}^2$	*DW*
Germany	−2.571	.017	.084	.559	−.396	−1.387	.379	.756
		(.1)	(.1)	(3.1)	(−3.2)	(−2.4)		
Japan	−4.340	.085	−.567	.156	−.040	.229	.832	.749
	(−3.4)	(.6)	(−1.5)	(4.3)	(−.7)	(2.9)		

In the cases of Germany and the United Kingdom the relative price coefficient is negative and significant (for the longer sample period). This is not the result which might be expected from PPP. For all other countries relative prices enter with positive, and in most cases, significant coefficients.

The negative signs of the price terms, however, are not necessarily inconsistent with the PPP. Here we give one possible interpretation. Following Dornbusch (1976b) we specify a simple model:

(i) $\ln \bar{e} = \ln P - \ln \overset{*}{P}$

(ii) $x = \lambda(\ln e - \ln \bar{e})$

(iii) $\ln M = A - \alpha r + \ln P$

(iv) $\ln \overset{*}{M} = B - \beta \overset{*}{r} + \ln \overset{*}{P}$

(v) $r + x = \overset{*}{r}$

TABLE 3.6

(DM/Domestic Currency) Exchange Rate, Estimated in Logs

A: Sample period beginning in 1971

Country	*Con.*	M_D	M_G	F_D	F_G	P_G/P_D	$\bar{R}^2$	*DW*
France (1) (71:8 – 76:3)	−2.550 (−5.3)	−.744 (−5.4)	.987 (7.6)	.018 (1.1)	−.071 (−1.0)	.360 (6.2)	.934	1.113
France (2) (71:8 – 76:3)	−2.933 (−10.8)	−.810 (−6.8)	.996 (7.7)	.032 (4.8)		.358 (6.2)	.934	1.109
Switzerland (71:8 – 75:12)	−3.631 (−3.8)	−.603 (−5.1)	.607 (7.7)	−.104 (−2.7)	.059 (1.4)	.793 (5.9)	.921	.924
United Kingdom (71:11 – 76:6)	20.428 (13.7)	−1.630 (−9.7)	.832 (3.7)	−.179 (−1.1)	−.824 (−10.9)	−.827 (−2.0)	.968	1.032

B: Sample period beginning in 1973

Country	*Con.*	M_D	M_G	F_D	F_G	P_G/P_D	$\bar{R}^2$	*DW*
France (1) (73:4 – 76:3)	−3.807 (−5.9)	−.907 (−6.0)	1.055 (6.0)	.080 (2.8)	.194 (1.7)	.207 (2.0)	.891	1.517
France (2) (73:4 – 76:3)	−2.807 (−9.9)	−.775 (−5.8)	1.021 (5.7)	.036 (−2.8)		.272 (2.7)	.885	1.352
Italy (73:7 – 76:6)	−.303 (−.1)	−1.250 (−4.4)	1.449 (4.4)	−.098 (7.2)	−.854 (−4.3)	.636 (3.0)	.925	1.365
Switzerland (73:4 – 75:12)	−2.318 (−1.0)	−.676 (−1.8)	.710 (4.2)	−.074 (−1.3)	.042 (.6)	.452 (1.4)	.921	.972
United Kingdom (73:4 – 76:6)	6.420 (.6)	−1.383 (−3.9)	1.378 (2.6)	−.047 (−.1)	−.413 (1.3)	.047 (.1)	.894	1.132

where $\bar{e}$ = long-run equilibrium exchange rate
e = current exchange rate (domestic/foreign)[15]
P = prices
M = money
A, B = terms, which include all other variables in the demand for money functions
r = interest rates
x = expected depreciation of the exchange rate
λ = partial adjustment coefficient of expectation
α, β = interest responses of money
$*$ refers to the foreign country.

Equation (i) is the PPP, equation (ii) says that expected depreciation of the currency is proportional to the difference between $\ln e$ and $\ln \bar{e}$, equations (iii) and (iv) are the demand for money functions and equation (v) gives the interest-rate parity. Solving the system for the $\ln e$ and assuming that $\alpha = \beta$ (that is the interest responses are equal in both countries) and $A = B$, we end up with the following equation:

$$\text{(vi)}\quad \ln e = \frac{1}{\alpha\lambda} \ln \frac{M}{\overset{*}{M}} + \left(1 - \frac{1}{\alpha\lambda}\right) \ln \frac{P}{\overset{*}{P}}$$

As can be seen the sign of the relative price elasticity $\left(1 - \frac{1}{\alpha\lambda}\right)$ depends on the interest response of money α and expectation coefficient λ. If $\alpha < \frac{1}{\lambda}$ the negative sign on the relative price elasticity is expected. If, for example, interest-rate elasticity $\left(\frac{\partial M}{\partial r} \cdot \frac{r}{M} = \alpha r \text{ in the above model}\right)$ is .20 and $r = .10$ all values of $\lambda < .5$ produce negative price elasticities.

Turning back now to the empirical results shown in Table 3.5 and 3.6, some implications on the basis of the above analysis can be drawn. The absolute values of the coefficients of money stocks in the cases of France and Switzerland are not very far from each other and the sum of these and the price elasticities are close to unity for these countries which is in accordance with equation (vi). This could be interpreted to imply that, in very rough terms, the demand for money functions was the same in Germany, France, and Switzerland. Estimated coefficients for other countries do not fill these constraints. On the whole relative prices seem to contribute significantly to the explanation of movements in exchange rates. Unfortunately we cannot be sure which channels their effect comes through. If PPP determines the long-run equilibrium exchange rate in the spirit of the theory developed in the first section (and thus a relative price term does not enter the reduced form exchange-rate equation) then asset demand functions need respecification (for example they might be specified in real terms to allow relative prices to enter the exchange-rate equation). Other possible effects might come through expectations: demands for assets depend on the expected exchange rate which in turn is a function of relative prices.

SOME EXTENSIONS OF THE ESTIMATING EQUATION

In the first empirical estimates of the model reported earlier in this section we used total foreign-asset stocks in the estimating equation. Here we extend the model for the (\$/DM) rate and replace total Fs by private-sector holdings of foreign assets (F^p),[16] superscript p stands for private sector. In Table 3.7 we summarise the estimation results for the period August 1971 to June 1976. All the equations were estimated in linear form by OLS.

TABLE 3.7

(\$/DM)-Exchange Rate with Private Foreign Asset Stocks

Equation	*Con.*	M_G	M_U	F_G	F_U	F_G^p	F_U^p	$\bar{R}^2$	*DW*
Sample period 1971:8–1976:6									
(1)	−.016	−.0023	.0032	.0032	−.0018			.831	.694
	(−1.5)	(−4.5)	(7.8)	(3.1)	(−4.1)				
(2)	−.242	−.0022	.0039			.0011	−.0017	.816	.715
	(−4.7)	(−3.8)	(9.4)			(1.6)	(−3.6)		
(3)	−.249	−.0022	.0040		−.0016	.0011		.810	.710
	(−4.8)	(−3.8)	(9.5)		(−3.3)	(1.6)			

Equation (1) of Table 3.7 is our basic equation in linear form[17] with total foreign asset stocks. As can be seen all the coefficients are significant with right signs. When total Fs are replaced by private foreign-asset stocks (see equations (2) and (3)) F_G^p loses significance, which is not the result we might expect if the theory behind the equation holds. This could be, however, interpreted using a very simple reaction function for intervention as follows.

If intervention by the central bank (ΔF^g) in foreign exchange markets reacts in a systematic way to changes in the exchange rate, we have

(a) $\Delta F^g = \theta \Delta e$ where θ is constant.

Recall that the exchange-rate equation in difference form is given by:
(b) $\Delta e = \alpha \Delta F^p + \text{other terms}$

By definition

(*c*) $\Delta F^p = \Delta F - \Delta F^g$

Solving for Δe, we obtain

(*d*) $$\Delta e = \frac{\alpha}{1+\alpha\theta}\Delta F + \frac{1}{1+\alpha\theta}\text{ (other terms)}$$

Equation (*d*) is our basic equation in difference form with *total* foreign assets. If the above interpretation is at all correct, the problems arising from the simultaneity between the exchange rate and foreign-asset stock could be resolved with careful specification of policy reaction functions and with proper estimation methods.

III USE OF THE MODEL FOR POLICY

The short-run exchange-rate equations of the preceding section provide a convenient vehicle for exposition of the policy problem facing monetary authorities on decisions concerning the exchange rate. To illustrate, let us begin with a linear form of an equation for the \$/DM rate:

(20) $$e(\$/\text{DM}) = \alpha_0 M_G + \alpha_1 F_G{}^p + \alpha_2 Z.$$

Here we include all non-German variables in Z, taken to be exogenous, and focus on the policy trade-off problem for Germany. Equation (20) gives a three-way trade-off between movements in e, M_G, and $F_G{}^p$, given Z.

In (20), $F_G{}^p$ is the accumulation of assets in private-sector portfolios which moves the exchange rate e. The central bank can eliminate this source of pressure by intervening in the exchange market, absorbing this asset flow itself. Using the identity $F \equiv F^p + F^g$, we can introduce intervention directly into equation (20):

(21) $$e = \alpha_0 M_G + \alpha_1 F_G - \alpha_1 F_G{}^g + \alpha_2 Z.$$

Here for a given total accumulation of foreign assets F, movement in the exchange rate depends on the extent of intervention F^g.

The policy problem will generally come to the monetary authorities as follows. Over some interval—perhaps a half-year or year—staff members produce a forecast of the current-account balance at current exchange rates. The integral of this balance is an accumulation ΔF in (21). Given ΔZ and ΔF, the authorities see the three-way trade-off. With no intervention and no change in M, e will move by $\alpha_1 \Delta F$. Intervention will reduce the movement in the proportion $\Delta F^g/\Delta F$. A change in monetary policy will reduce the movement by $\alpha_0 \Delta M$. Thus, given the estimate of ΔF from the current account integral, the policy-maker can consider triples of Δe, ΔM, ΔF^g that are feasible, and choose the target point for policy.

The policy surface just described is shown in Figure 3.6. Taking ΔZ as zero for convenience; without loss of generality, the current account integral over the forecast period fixes the ΔF^g intercept. The parameters of the estimated equation then determine the slope of the feasible policy plane. Intervention with no change in M will move along trade-off AB. Money stock changes trade against intervention along AC. A zero-intervention policy gives a trade-off between changes in M and e along BC. Combination policies move to the interior surface of the plane. There will, of course, be one such plane for each current account forecast.

Figure 3.6 provides a convenient exposition of the policy problem facing the authorities in a floating-rate world. With the current account reacting with a lag to current changes in e, the policy problem is to find

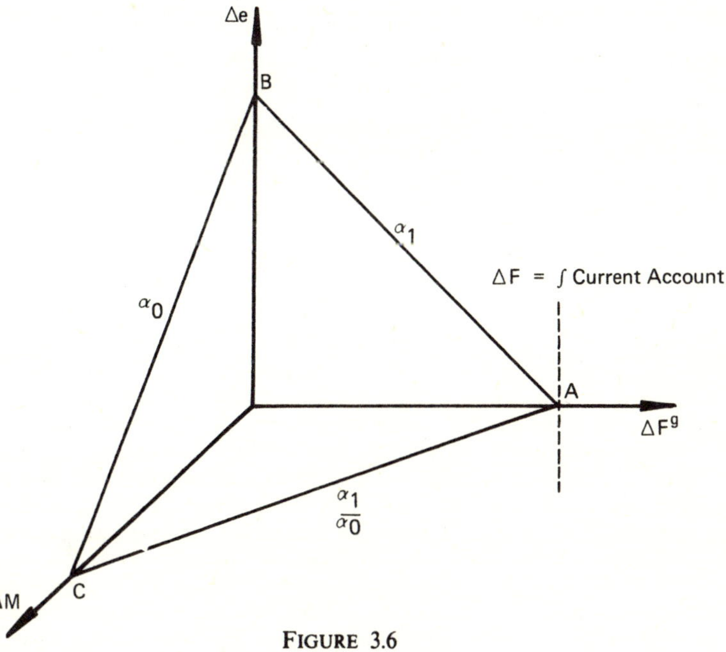

FIGURE 3.6
Feasible Policy Surface

the mix of intervention, monetary policy, in the aggregate sense, and exchange-rate movements, that are most satisfactory in the short run. Figure 3.6 gives the feasible set.

As a numerical illustration from our initial estimates, consider an example from Table 3.7, page 79, equation (3), for the \$/DM-rate (treating Germany as the home country):

$$e(\$/\mathrm{DM}) = -.249 - .00224M_G + .00399M_U + .00106F_G{}^p - .001626F_U.$$

Rewriting for relative changes and calculating elasticities at means, we get:

$$\hat{e}(\$/\mathrm{DM}) = -.810\hat{M}_G + 2.800\hat{M}_U + .007\hat{F}_G{}^{p*} - .314\hat{F}_U.$$

Combining this with the identity $F^p = F - F^g$, also calculated for relative changes at means, we get:

$$\hat{F}^p = 10.80\hat{F} - 9.80\hat{F}^g$$

Substituting, we arrive at:

$$(22)\quad \hat{e}(\$/\mathrm{DM}) = -.81\,\hat{M}_G + 2.80\,\hat{M}_U + .09\,\hat{F}_G - .07\,\hat{F}_G{}^g - .31\,\hat{F}_U.$$

This equation gives estimates for both β_0, the elasticity analog to the linear coefficient α_0 in equation (21) ($\beta_0 = -.81$) and β_1, the analog to α_1 in (21) ($\beta_1 = .07$), and hence provides a basis for calculating all three of the bilateral trade-offs indicated. Of course, given the size of the standard errors shown, the degree of precision in these calculations still leaves much to be desired. Nevertheless, a start has been made in the estimates of the second section, pages 63–80. If these help to clarify the policy problem, they will be worth their opportunity cost.

NOTES

1. See, for example, Hume (1752) in Cooper (1969).
2. An excellent introduction to the literature in the area is the *Scandinavian Journal of Economics*, Stockholm, No. 2, 1976, which contains the papers from an August 1975 seminar on 'Flexible Exchange Rates and Stabilisation Policy', organised by the Institute of International Economic Studies of Stockholm University. Of particular interest in the present context are the historical survey papers by Jacob Frenkel and Johan Myhrman, the original contributions of Rudiger Dornbusch and Pentti Kouri, and the synthesising papers of Richard Cooper and Michael Mussa, all in that volume. In addition, the important unpublished paper by Lance Girton and Dale Henderson (1976) which develops the short-run equilibrium analysis, the

paper by Rudiger Dornbusch (1976b) which gives quite similar results to those developed in the following sections in a model tied to long-run expectations and the paper by Robert Flood (1976) which provides a similar analysis, are also worth mentioning.

3. The following model is an attempt to develop the simplest possible extension of the general equilibrium analysis of Tobin (1969) to include a foreign sector with a flexible exchange rate. For a full exposition of the model, see Branson (1976b).
4. Both B and F are taken to be short-term fixed-price assets to avoid the complications introduced by capital gains resulting from changes in r and $\bar{r}$. These generally do not change the qualitative results in one-country models. See for example, Branson (1972) or Allen and Kenen (1976). For the opposite results in a two-country world, however, see Boyer (1976). For the same specification of asset–market equilibrium, see Flood (1976).
5. This is yet another example of the importance of substitutability in asset markets emphasised by Tobin (1969).
6. The unitary elasticity of e with respect to changes in F follows from the implicit assumption of static expectations. With regressive expectations, the elasticity would be less than unity (in absolute value) and vice versa with extrapolative expectations. See Branson (1976b).
7. The dynamic properties of the model are studied more precisely in Branson (1976b). Since the empirical results of the second section, pages 63–80, relate only to the short-run model, we only outline the dynamics here.
8. Here, and throughout, the balance-of-payments items are stated in terms of foreign exchange. This is simply a matter of analytical convenience; multiplying by e will convert them into home currency.
9. It is interesting to note that the adjustment equation (14) is formally the same as the government budget equation of Blinder and Solow (1974, p. 52). We will find the same formal correspondence in the stability condition (17) below. The duality between the government budget and the current account in the macro-adjustment process is explored in some detail in Branson (1976a).
10. Here P is set at unity for expositional clarity. The analogous expression in Blinder and Solow (1974) is equation (20), p. 55.
11. See Branson (1976b) for a fuller exposition. See also Gale for a different look at the same problem with changing X between equilibria.
12. There is room here for a detailed model of the money-supply process, including also a reaction function for sterilisation behaviour.
13. Benchmark figures come from the *Survey of Current Business*, November 1975, p. 32; and *Bundesbank Monthly Review*, October 1974, p. 14, for the United States and Germany. Benchmarks for other countries are OECD Secretariat estimates, provided by the relevant Country Desks.
14. The theoretical model here is developed for '$\left(\frac{\text{domestic currency}}{\text{foreign currency}}\right)$' exchange rate. The empirical results, however, are for e ($/domestic currency) or e (DM/domestic currency). Thus in order to avoid misunderstanding the United States or Germany should be here interpreted as 'home' countries and others as 'foreign' countries.

15. The reader should note that henceforth e is defined as the $ or DM price of domestic currency rather than (as in the first section, p. 56) the 'domestic' currency price of 'foreign' currency.
16. We use the identity $F^p = F - F^g$ to derive $F^p - F^g$ for the United States and Germany comes from *International Financial Statistics* (Washington: IMF, annal) and is Deutsche Bundesbank's foreign assets (converted into dollars) and Federal Reserves foreign assets, respectively.
17. Logs could not be used because German foreign asset stock has some negative values during the sample period. Moreover, linear equations are easier to handle when we add intervention to the story. Just for a comparison we calculated the elasticities using equation (1) of Table 3.7 at means of the variables. Dots over the variables refer to percentage changes.

$$e(\$/DM) = -.84\dot{M}_G + 2.27\dot{M}_U + .22\dot{F}_G - .35\dot{F}_U$$

The result is very similar to the corresponding equation in Table 3.3A.

REFERENCES

P. R. ALLEN and P. B. KENEN, 'Portfolio Adjustment in Open Economies: a Comparison of Alternative Specifications', *Weltwirtschaftliches Archiv*, Hamburg, Vol. 112, No. 1, 1976.

J. R. ARTUS, 'Exchange Rate Stability and Managed Floating: the Experience of the Federal Republic of Germany', *International Monetary Fund Staff Papers*, Washington, Vol. 23, No. 2, July 1976.

A. S. BLINDER and R. M. SOLOW, 'Analytical Foundations of Fiscal Policy' in *The Economics of Public Finance* (Washington: Brookings Institution, 1974).

R. S. BOYER, 'Net Foreign Assets and the Exchange Rate Regime', unpublished paper dated April 1976.

W. H. BRANSON, 'Macroeconomic Equilibrium with Portfolio Balance in Open Economies', Stockholm Institute for International Economic Studies, Seminar Paper No. 22, 1972.

——'Portfolio Equilibrium and Monetary Policy with Foreign and Non-Trade Assets', in E. Claassen and P. Salin (eds), *Recent Issues in International Monetary Economics* (Amsterdam: North-Holland, 1975).

——'The Dual Roles of the Government Budget and the Balance of Payments in the Movement from Short-Run to Long-Run Equilibrium', *Quarterly Journal of Economics*, Cambridge, Mass., August 1976 (a).

——'Asset Markets and Relative Prices in Exchange Rate Determination', Stockholm Institute for International Economic Studies, Seminar Paper No. 66, 1976 (b).

R. N. COOPER (ed.), *International Finance: Selected Readings* (Baltimore: Penguin Books, 1969).

——'Monetary Theory and Policy in an Open Economy', *Scandinavian Journal of Economics*, Stockholm, No. 2, 1976.

R. DORNBUSCH, 'The Theory of Flexible Exchange Rate Regimes and Macroeconomic Policy', *Scandinavian Journal of Economics*, No. 2, 1976 (a).

——'Expectations and Exchange Rate Dynamics', *Journal of Political Economy*, Chicago, Illinois, December 1976 (b).

R. FLOOD, 'Asset Trading, Exchange Rate Determination and Exchange Rate Dynamics', unpublished paper dated March 1976.

J. A. FRENKEL, 'A Monetary Approach to the Exchange Rate: Doctrinal Aspects and Empirical Evidence', *Scandinavian Journal of Economics*, No. 2, 1976.

D. GALE, 'The Trade Imbalance Story', *Journal of International Economics*, Amsterdam, May 1974.

L. GIRTON and D. W. HENDERSON, *Central Bank Operations in Foreign and Domestic Assets under Fixed and Flexible Exchange Rates*, International Finance Discussion Paper No. 83 (Washington: Federal Reserve Board, 1976).

P. J. K. KOURI, 'The Exchange Rate and the Balance of Payments in the Short Run and in the Long Run: a Monetary Approach', *Scandinavian Journal of Economics*, No. 2, 1976.

M. MUSSA, 'The Exchange Rate, the Balance of Payments, and Monetary and Fiscal Policy under a regime of Controlled Floating', *Scandinavian Journal of Economics*, No. 2, 1976.

J. MYHRMAN, 'Experiences of Flexible Exchange Rates in Earlier Periods: Theories, Evidence and a New View', *Scandinavian Journal of Economics*, No. 2, 1976.

J. TOBIN, 'A general Equilibrium Approach to Monetary Theory', *Journal of Money, Credit and Banking*, Columbus, Ohio, No. 1 1969.

4

Model of an Industrial Country under Fixed and Flexible Exchange Rates

MALCOLM D. KNIGHT and
DONALD J. MATHIESON

The purpose of this paper is to construct and estimate a macro-economic model of an industrial country which is operating in a world of internationally integrated goods and asset markets. In developing the model we have attempted to achieve a trade-off between two conflicting objectives. While we would like a model which is small enough that its theoretical properties can be analysed easily, we also want to incorporate the important, real and monetary factors that influence major economic aggregates such as prices, interest rates, exchange rates, the main components of gross national product, and the balance of payments. Our specification therefore attempts to incorporate the effects of capital and goods market arbitrage as well as international portfolio and spending adjustments. This structure is sufficiently general that it can be applied to different countries with only minor modifications. In this paper parameter estimates are presented for the United States, the United Kingdom, Germany, Canada and Japan.[1]

The model is also designed to take into account the major structural changes that have taken place in the international economy during the 1960s and 1970s. Perhaps the most important of these changes has been the movement away from a system of fixed par values to one of managed floating exchange rates by the major industrial countries. Our specification tries to capture the effects of this change by assuming that a country's exchange regime is reflected in the way its central monetary authorities intervene in the foreign exchange market. Thus in our model the determinants of the reaction function for exchange market intervention are allowed to shift as the country's exchange-rate regime changes from fixed par values to managed or free-floating.

Since the exchange rate plays such a fundamental role in linking economic activity across countries, our analysis places special emphasis on identifying the factors which lead to exchange-rate movements. Both the experience of the past few years and the recent theoretical literature emphasise that the exchange rate should be treated as the relative price of two national monies; that it responds to excess demands in both goods and asset markets; and that the latter markets may actually have a predominant influence on the level of a floating exchange rate in the short run.[2] Our analysis of exchange-rate movements incorporates both arbitrage processes and the effects of disequilibrium in goods and asset markets.

Once our estimation work has been completed,[3] we plan to link the five models together into a single multi-country system which describes the central nexus of the international economy and to use this model for simulation and analysis of national economic policies in an explicitly international framework. Although the theoretical and empirical analysis that is described in the present paper clearly reflects work in progress rather than a finished study, we feel that the estimation results for each country are interesting enough to justify further work on the multi-country system.

The first section of this paper describes the structure of our macroeconomic model for an individual economy, while the effective exchange-rate index and other rest-of-the-world (ROW) indices are considered in Section II. In Section III we present our initial estimates of the model for each country. While the preliminary nature of our empirical research makes it inappropriate to draw any sweeping conclusions, it gives us a great many interesting insights into the relative explanatory power of various hypotheses across countries. Thus the third section contains a summary of our conclusions and a discussion of the avenues for future research that are suggested by our initial results.

I THE BASIC STRUCTURAL MODEL

The model includes domestic and foreign goods, money balances, and bonds. Residents of each country are assumed to produce a homogeneous stream of domestic output that is either consumed at home or exported. Since the countries under consideration are all developed industrial economies, a large proportion of their exports consists of manufactured goods that are sold in a world market which is less than perfectly competitive. In contrast to much of the theoretical literature, we do not assume that the domestic goods which enter foreign trade are perfect substitutes for goods produced abroad. Instead, the degree of substitutability between domestic and foreign goods can be measured empirically from the point estimates of certain demand elasticities in the model. This implies that total (home and foreign) demand for domestic output tends to decrease when the relative price of domestic output rises, and conversely when it falls.

Just as changes in the terms of trade are assumed to eliminate excess demands in the market for goods and services, so financial markets are brought into equilibrium by movements in relative interest rates between the home country and the rest of the world. Nevertheless, the role of interest-rate movements is somewhat different from that of prices. We assume that, in the long run, domestic and foreign securities are perfect substitutes for one another when covered forward.[4] But we do not constrain wealth-owners to adjust their international asset portfolios immediately in response to change. This means that the model allows domestic yields to deviate temporarily from international interest parity.[5]

The general approach outlined above implies several specific assumptions about the overall structure of the model. These are:

(i) Market prices and quantities do not respond instantaneously to exogenous disturbances.

(ii) Walras' Law holds. Since the excess demands of the domestic and foreign private sectors must each sum to zero, the excess demand for money is – in each case – equal to the sum of the excess supplies of goods and securities.

(iii) International interest-rate parity and (relative) purchasing power parity are long-run (that is, steady state) properties of the model, but they need not hold at every instant.

On the above assumptions, the basic model is a system consisting of supply and demand functions, adjustment functions and identities. It is specified in continuous time and estimated using a discrete approximation that has the same structural form as the continuous system. The model contains fourteen equations, including eleven adjustment functions and four identities. Definitions of the variables are given below:

Variables of the Model

E = real expenditure by the domestic private sector
Y = real domestic output
I = real imports of goods and services (National Accounts basis)
X = real exports of goods and services (National Accounts basis)
p = implicit price deflator for domestic output
M = nominal money stock
C = nominal stock of domestic credit
r = domestic interest rate (per cent per quarter)
R = international reserves of gold and foreign exchange
ε = effective exchange rate index (units of domestic currency per unit of foreign currency)
θ = dollar exchange rate (units of domestic currency per US dollar)
DK = capital account of the balance of payments (in domestic currency; inflow = +)
p^* = expected domestic price level
ε^* = expected level of the effective exchange rate
G = real domestic government expenditure on current goods and services
m = domestic money multiplier
θ_0 = par exchange rate (domestic currency per US dollar)
a_i = dummy variable (equals unity in periods when the home country declares a par value for its currency; zero otherwise)
p_f = index of prices in ROW
r_f = index of ROW interest rates (per cent per quarter)
M_f = US dollar value of nominal money stock in ROW
Y_f = US dollar value of real output in ROW
$(E_f + G_f + X_f)$ = total sales of goods and services in ROW valued in US dollars at constant (1970) prices.

In the model, all adjustment functions except that for the interest rate are specified in log-linear form. Demand functions are assumed to be linear in interest rates and log-linear in terms of the other variables. This specification is convenient because interest rates are dimensionally equivalent to logarithms and because it allows either nominal or real interest rates to be specified where appropriate. The real interest rate is defined as $r - D \ln p^*$ where $D \ln p^*$ is the anticipated inflation rate.[6]

Three types of parameter appear in the model: αs are proportions or marginal propensities, γs and δs are adjustment coefficients, and βs refer to demand and supply elasticities. Except where otherwise noted specifically, all equations are so specified that these parameters are expected to be greater than zero. A superscript associated with a variable denotes the following: d represents the *ex ante* demand for a variable and s is the desired supply; an asterisk indicates an expected (as opposed to an actual) value and a circumflex represents the authorities' target level of some quantity that can be influenced by policy action. The letter D is the time differential operator d/dt and 'ln' stands for the natural logarithm. All variables in the model described below are at time t; stochastic disturbance terms are omitted from the equations in the text.

The description of the model begins with the equations that describe the real sector of the domestic economy. Since the basic model is designed to have the simplest structure that meets our objectives, we specify a single adjustment function for total expenditure by the private sector.[7]

$$(1)\quad D \ln E = \gamma_1[\ln E^d - \ln E]$$

$$(1')\quad \ln E^d = \ln \alpha_{11} + \beta_{11} \ln Y - \beta_{12}(r - D \ln p^*)$$

Equation (1) says that domestic residents tend to increase real spending whenever they have an excess demand for goods and services. The desired level of spending (1′) is related positively to the level of domestic real income Y and negatively to the real rate of interest ($r - D \ln p^*$).[8]

The supply of domestic output relative to the trend in potential output also responds to three separate effects: an excess demand effect, a capacity effect, and a Phillips curve effect.

$$(2)\quad D \ln (Y/Y_0 e^{\rho_y t}) = \gamma_{21}[\ln Y^d - \ln Y] + \gamma_{22}[\ln(Y_0 e^{\rho_y t}) - \ln Y] + \gamma_{23}[D \ln p - D \ln p^*]$$

$$(2')\quad \ln Y^d = \ln \alpha_{21} - \beta_{21} \ln\left(\frac{p}{\varepsilon p_f}\right) + \beta_{22} \ln (E + G + X) + \beta_{23} \ln \theta + \beta_{23} \ln (E_f + G_f + X_f)$$

Total demand for domestic output equals the demand for home goods by domestic residents plus that by residents of the rest of the world.

These demands are positively related to the level of total sales in each economy ($E+G+X$ and $E_f+G_f+X_f$, respectively) and negatively to the terms of trade, where β_{21} is a combination of the domestic and foreign price elasticities of demand for home-country output. The first term of equation (2) specifies that if the expected and actual rates of inflation are equal, the rate of growth of output is proportional to the excess demand for home goods. The second term reflects the fact that, over time, firms will attempt to utilise fully their productive capacity. Thus, other things being equal, they will expand current output more rapidly than its trend rate of growth whenever there is a positive gap between potential and actual output.[9] This adjustment may, however, occur much too slowly to maintain the target level of employment desired by the authorities, so its existence does not vitiate the need for counter-cyclical policy. The final term says that if the actual inflation rate is more rapid than the inflation rate that is anticipated by producers, they will interpret this as an increase in the relative price of their products and will increase their supply accordingly.

Having considered the determinants of aggregate demand and supply, we turn next to the current account of the balance of payments. Real imports by domestic residents adjust according to the relation:

$$(3)\quad D\ \ln I = \gamma_3[\ln I^d - \ln I]$$

$$(3')\quad \ln I^d = \ln \alpha_{31} + \beta_{31}\ln\left(\frac{p}{\varepsilon p_f}\right) + \beta_{32}\ln\,(E+G+X)$$

and $\beta_{31} > -1$

This specification assumes that desired real imports are proportional to total sales ($E+G+X$), where the proportion varies directly with the terms of trade.[10] It can be shown that since all real quantities in the model are the corresponding nominal magnitudes divided by the implicit deflator of domestic output, the relative price elasticity of the demand for imports in volume terms is equal to $\beta_{31}+1$. Hence the *a priori* restriction on β_{31} in (3) is that it be greater than minus one.[11]

Expenditure, output and imports are each determined by the recursive processes (1) to (3), while real government expenditure is treated as exogenous. Thus the level of domestic real exports is given by:

$$(4)\quad X = Y - E + I - G$$

This approach, in which actual exports are the residual of the income identity, recognises that the level of exports is affected by the behaviour of domestic producers as well as by the demands of domestic and foreign spenders. It can be shown that the partial derivatives of the real trade balance are:

$$\frac{\partial(\ln X^s - \ln I^d)}{\partial(\ln p - \ln \varepsilon - \ln p_f)} < 0, \qquad \frac{\partial(\ln X^s - \ln I^d)}{\partial r} > 0$$

$$\frac{\partial(\ln X^s - \ln I^d)}{\partial \ln Y} < 0, \qquad \frac{\partial(\ln X^s - \ln I^d)}{\partial(D\ln p^*)} < 0$$

$$\frac{\partial(\ln X^s - \ln I^d)}{\partial \ln (E_f + G_f + X_f)} > 0, \qquad \frac{\partial(\ln X^s - \ln I^d)}{\partial \ln \alpha_{11}} < 0$$

Thus the comparative static properties of the trade balance in our model correspond to standard conclusions in the theoretical literature. It is important to note, however, that the *actual* levels of imports and exports depend on the adjustment parameters of the model as well as on the elasticities of demand and supply. Thus our model admits the empirical possibility that, in the short run, the balance of trade might respond perversely to changes in the terms of trade. Such a 'J-curve' effect might occur, for example, if the level of imports responds to relative price changes more rapidly than does domestic output.

The adjustment function for the domestic price level assumes that the inflation rate may respond to four separate influences: increases in domestic output relative to the capacity level, excess supply in the money market, the departure of the price deflator for domestic output from purchasing power parity equilibrium and the current rate of change in the domestic currency price of foreign output.

$$(5)\ D\ln p = \gamma_{51}[\ln Y - \ln(Y_0 e^{\rho_y t})] + \gamma_{52}[\ln(M/p) - \ln(M/p)^d] - \gamma_{53}[\ln p - \ln \alpha_{51} - \ln \varepsilon - \ln p_f] + \gamma_{54}[D\ln \varepsilon + D\ln p_f]$$

$$(5')\ \ln M^d = \ln \alpha_{12} + \ln p + \beta_{13} \ln Y - \beta_{14} r$$

This adjustment function is based on the assumption that domestic prices are set by a group of firms which operate in conditions of monopolistic competition. The first term implies that each firm will tend to raise its prices more quickly whenever sales of its product are above the level of capacity output that would be sustainable over the long run. If there is generalised excess demand in the economy, all firms will respond in this way more or less simultaneously, so that the aggregate price level rises. The second term in the expression reflects the familiar assumption that monetary disequilibrium may spill over into the goods market and affect the domestic inflation rate. The last two terms reflect the influence of foreign price movements on domestic price formation. Producers are assumed to respond negatively to any rise in domestic prices above the purchasing power parity level and positively to the rate of foreign inflation and the depreciation of the home currency in the exchange market. These responses reflect the underlying assumption that, other things being equal, the pricing behaviour of domestic firms is very closely related to that of their foreign competitors.

Having considered the determinants of domestic output, we now turn to the financial sector of the economy. Our model contains a highly aggregated and simplified monetary system. We begin by noting that the change in high-powered money equals the domestic currency value of the international reserves acquired or given up by the authorities in the course of their intervention on the foreign exchange market ($\varepsilon . DR$),[12] plus the change in net domestic assets held by the central monetary authorities (DC). The determinants of DR will be considered below when we discuss official intervention in the foreign exchange market. Changes in the net domestic assets of the monetary authorities are the main instrument of monetary control. The money supply, however, will be related to the stock of base money via an appropriate money multiplier (m):

$$(6)\quad DM = m(\varepsilon . DR + DC)$$

Thus for simplicity we neglect domestic credit (C) and consider the total money stock. In many studies, the money supply is assumed to be determined exogenously, but such an assumption may be inappropriate if monetary policy responds in a predictable way to variables that are endogenous to the model. The nature of these feedbacks from the private sector to the policy decisions of the monetary authorities probably differs considerably across countries and their effect may change over time. Nevertheless, it seems important to specify at least a simple reaction function for monetary policy in order to remove a potential source of simultaneous equations bias from the model. A possible specification is

$$(7)\quad D \ln M = \rho_m + \gamma_{71}[\ln (Y_0 e^{\rho_y t}) - \ln Y] - \gamma_{72}[\ln p - \ln \alpha_{71} - \ln \varepsilon - \ln p_f] + \gamma_{73}\, Dr + \gamma_{74}[\ln X - \ln I] + \gamma_{75}\, D \ln R$$

Equation (7) assumes that the rate of monetary expansion will exceed the long-run rate (ρ_m) whenever output is below its trend or full employment level ($Y_0 e^{\rho_y t}$); and that it will be reduced if the domestic price level begins to rise above the target level (α_{71}) relative to prices abroad.[13] The third term in (7) posits that the authorities pursue a strategy of leaning against the wind with regard to the interest rate. Finally, the coefficient of $D \ln R$ reflects the degree to which the authorities are able to sterilise the monetary effects of balance-of-payments deficits and surpluses in the short run.[14] A value of unity for γ_{75} would imply that the authorities cannot sterilise balance-of-payments flows even in the short run, while successively smaller values of γ_{75} imply successful sterilisation of a larger proportion of reserve movements. Thus the degree of sterilisation in each country may be determined empirically.

The interest rate equation (8) reflects our assumption that financial markets among the major industrial countries are highly integrated internationally:

$$(8)\ Dr = \gamma_{81}[\alpha_{81}(r_f + D \ln \varepsilon^*) - r] + \gamma_{82}[\ln (M/p)^d - \ln (M/p)]$$

In the absence of monetary disequilibrium, the domestic interest rate adjusts until international interest parity is achieved. Interest parity occurs when the domestic interest rate is proportional to the foreign interest rate plus the expected rate of change in the price of foreign currency.[15] The second term in (8) is designed to catch the short-run effect of monetary disequilibrium on interest rates. Given the price equation (5), an expansionary monetary policy will temporarily increase the real money stock, inducing an excess supply of real cash balances and a fall in the domestic interest rate. Thus the domestic interest rate may deviate from international interest parity in the short run if interest arbitrageurs do not respond instantaneously.

Next we consider the international monetary aspects of the basic model. The exchange-rate regime that a country is operating at any given time is determined by the authorities' intervention strategy in the foreign exchange market.[16] Since most of the major industrial countries have altered their exchange-rate systems during the 1970s, it is important to understand the determinants of official intervention under alternative regimes. Exchange arrangements run in a continuous spectrum from completely flexible to perfectly fixed. We shall briefly consider three variations which correspond broadly to free-floating, managed-floating and fixed par values.

Under free floating, the authorities—if they intervene at all—merely attempt to smooth out short-term or seasonal fluctuations in the exchange rate. In this situation there is no systematic reaction function for exchange reserves. In the case of managed floating, the authorities take a view as to the path of the exchange rate that would be consistent with fundamental trends in the domestic economy and the rest of the world and intervene in the market to resist movements away from this path.

Under a regime of fixed par values, the authorities publish a parity rate θ_o (usually defined in units of domestic currency per US dollar) together with a set of upper and lower bounds (θ_u and θ_L) within which the spot rate is allowed to fluctuate. They then commit themselves to sell official reserves ($DR < 0$) whenever the spot price of foreign currency approaches θ_u and to buy reserves whenever $\theta(t)$ approaches θ_L. θ_u and θ_L are usually referred to as the intervention points. In order to maintain a pegged rate system, the authorities must be prepared to intervene by buying or selling whatever quantity of reserves is necessary to keep the spot rate within these bounds. This implies that the authorities will tend to buy or sell more reserves per unit of time the further $\theta(t)$ is from θ_o. Figure 4.1 depicts a plausible form for the official intervention function (RR) during periods when a pegged exchange rate system is in operation. In Figure 4.1 the rate of change of official reserves, $DR(t)$, is plotted on the vertical axis, while $[\theta_o - \theta(t)]$ (the difference between the par value and the current price of foreign exchange) is plotted horizontally. The

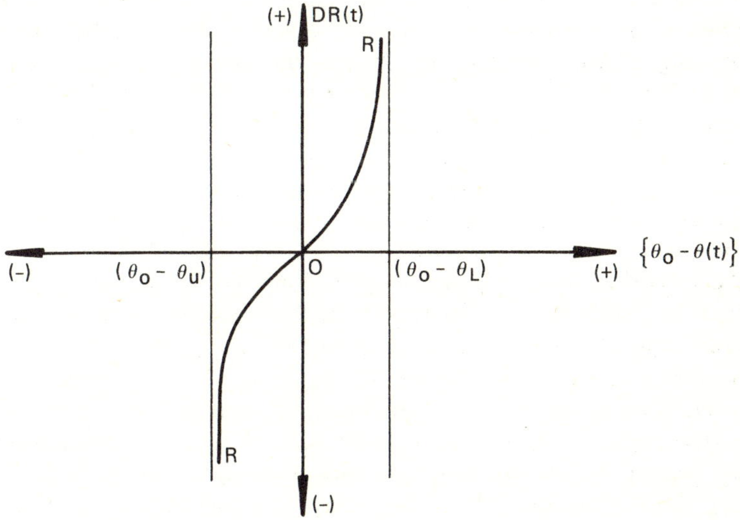

FIGURE 4.1
Official Intervention under Pegged Rates

shape of the *RR* function reflects the assumption that the authorities neither buy nor sell exchange reserves when the current spot rate equals the published parity. As the exchange rate falls, they are willing to buy reserves at a more rapid rate so that as the price of foreign exchange approaches θ_L their rate of reserve accumulation becomes very large. The opposite behaviour occurs when $\theta(t)$ rises above θ_0. This suggests that foreign exchange market intervention by the authorities of a pegged exchange-rate country might reasonably be approximated by a tangent function.

Since all of the countries in our international model have changed their exchange regime on at least one occasion during the time period under consideration,[17] the above analysis helps us to confront the problem of devising an intervention function that is applicable over the whole sample period. Specifically, we propose the following intervention function:

$$(9)\quad D \ln R = a_i.\gamma_{91}\tan[s_1(\ln \theta_o - \ln \theta)] + (1-a_i).\gamma_{92}[\ln p - \ln \alpha_{71} - \ln p_f - \ln \varepsilon] - (1-a_i).\gamma_{93} D \ln \varepsilon$$

In (9), a_i is a dummy variable that has the value unity during periods when the authorities of country *i* are operating a pegged exchange rate system and zero otherwise. Thus the first term of (9) operates when the country has a par value. Here s_1 is a scaling factor that adjusts the tails of the tangent function so that they occur at the intervention points.[18] The second and third terms refer to intervention during periods of managed floating rates. It is, of course, quite possible that for some countries no stable reaction function for exchange reserves exists when the exchange rate is flexible. If the authorities consistently operate a 'managed' float, however, it may be possible to write a function which approximates to their behaviour. An approach suggested in Knight (1976) assumes that the authorities have some notion of the long-run equilibrium terms of trade (α_{71}) and that they intervene in the foreign exchange market more heavily the more the actual exchange rate deviates from this level. This hypothesis is embodied in the second term of (9). The final term reflects a second hypothesis about managed floating, namely that in the post-1971 period central banks have attempted to slow exchange-rate movements by 'leaning against the wind' in their intervention policy.[19] If this hypothesis is correct, then it may give rise to important linkages among monetary aggregates in different countries. Note that, while the part of equation (9) that deals with fixed exchange rates is specified in terms of deviations of the country's dollar exchange rate θ from its dollar par value θ_o, the part that refers to managed floating is specified in terms of the *effective* exchange rate, ε. Thus we also need an equation in the model that relates the dollar exchange rate to the effective exchange-rate index. This equation is:

$$(10) \quad \ln \theta = \ln \varepsilon - \ln \varepsilon'$$

where $\ln \varepsilon'$ (the effective exchange-rate index excluding the dollar component) is derived from the definition of the exchange rate that is given in the next section.

The exchange rate is the outcome of developments in the whole structure of domestic and international markets for goods, securities and money so that, as Isard (1977) has noted, it is not possible to model the exchange-rate determination process unless major simplifications are made. Not surprisingly, the existing literature is somewhat vague on how to specify the exchange-rate determination process in a structural model such as ours, and our problem is compounded by the fact that we need a specification that describes the behaviour of the effective exchange rate across changing exchange-rate regimes.

Our initial approach is based on two propositions. First, in the most general Walrasian system, market prices will move in response to excess demands (or supplies) in all markets. Second, under the assumption that Walras' Law holds, it must be the case that the domestic private sector's excess demand for money equals the sum of its excess supplies of goods and securities; and the same must hold for residents of the rest of the world (that is, the excess demands for goods, money, and securities must sum to zero in each country). It follows that the rate of change in any market price in a three-sector Walrasian model should be expressed as a function of either the sum of the excess supplies of goods and securities in both the domestic and foreign economies, or alternatively as a function of the excess demands for money *both* within the home country and abroad. Since the exchange rate can be viewed as the relative price of two currencies, the above assumptions imply that we can express the rate of change of the exchange rate as a function of the excess demands for money in both the domestic and foreign economies. This formulation can be modified to allow for government intervention to influence the market price of foreign exchange. Thus the rate of change of the exchange rate depends on the excess demand for money by domestic residents, the excess demand for money by foreign residents and the degree of official intervention in the exchange market. Second, exchange-rate movements are also influenced by the fact that economic agents will attempt to arbitrage goods and security prices across economies. As we have already noted, long-run equilibrium in the goods market requires that the domestic price level be proportionate to the domestic currency value of the world price level (that is, relative purchasing-power parity holds). Similarly, long-run equilibrium in the asset market requires that the domestic interest-rate must equal the foreign interest rate plus the anticipated rate of appreciation in the price of foreign currency (that is, interest-rate parity holds). Any departure from either purchasing-power parity or interest-rate parity will naturally lead to arbitrage flows and give rise to movements in the exchange rate.

As a first attempt, we have chosen the following structural form:

$$(11)\ D \ln \varepsilon = \delta_{11} + a_i\delta_{12}[\ln \theta_o - \ln \theta] + (1-a_i)\delta_{13}[\ln p - \ln \alpha_{71} - \ln \varepsilon - \ln p_f] - \delta_{14}[r - \alpha_{81}(r_f - D \ln \varepsilon^*)] + \delta_{15}[\ln (M/p) - \ln (M/p)^d] + \delta_{16}[\ln (M_f/p_f)^d - \ln (M_f/p_f)] + \delta_{17} D \ln R$$

where the domestic demand for money is as given in (5′) above, and the demand for money in the rest of the world is:

$$(11')\ \ln M_f^d = \ln \alpha_{13} + \ln p_f + \beta_{15} \ln Y_f - \beta_{16} r_f$$

This approach assumes that if domestic and foreign markets for goods and securities are simultaneously in equilibrium, and if purchasing-power parity and interest-rate parity are maintained, then exchange-rate movements will reflect only official intervention. An excess supply of domestic money, or purchases of foreign exchange by the authorities, will cause the price of foreign currency to rise; while an excess supply of money on the part of foreign residents will cause it to fall. A domestic interest rate above the corresponding covered foreign yield will stimulate a capital inflow that will appreciate the domestic currency, whereas a domestic price level that is above the equivalent foreign price level will lead to a depreciation of the domestic currency. Thus the exchange rate responds either to differential movements in home and foreign prices or to disequilibrium in the goods and securities markets.

The international sector of the model is completed by the balance-of-payments identity, which determines the nominal value of capital flows between the domestic economy and the rest of the world ($DK > 0$ = inflow):[20]

$$(12)\ DK = pI - pX + \varepsilon . DR$$

In addition to the observable variables, the model (1) to (12) contains the expected inflation rate ($D \ln p^*$) and the anticipated rate of change in the exchange rate ($D \ln \varepsilon^*$), both of which are unobservable. Furthermore, we have argued that the behaviour of the model may depend crucially on the way in which transactors form their expectations of these quantities.

While we plan eventually to test several alternative expectations structures, the present version of our model employs the adaptive mechanism.[21] Thus the expected rate of change of the domestic price level is:

(13) $D \ln p^* = \eta_1[\ln p - \ln p^*]$

Since the exchange rate fluctuated within a narrow band around its parity for much of the sample period covered by the model, we employ a modified adaptive process in which the expected rate responds both to the deviation between actual and expected exchange rates and to movements in the trade balance. The trade balance is used as an indicator of expected exchange-rate movements for two reasons. First, during the Bretton Woods era of adjustable par values, exchange rates were typically 'defended' until the last possible moment. Thus, while the actual effective exchange rate remained virtually unchanged, the country would be experiencing large foreign exchange losses usually accompanied by a deteriorating current-account balance. A purely adaptive process for exchange rates would naturally miss the information available to market participants by these reserve and trade flows. We have therefore adjusted the adaptive structure to incorporate this information. Thus:

(14) $D \ln \varepsilon^* = \eta_2[\ln \varepsilon - \ln \varepsilon^*] - \eta_3[\ln X - \ln I]$

In the case of the United Kingdom, Germany, Canada and Japan, the structure used in our empirical work is essentially that given in (1) to (14). Because of the special role played by the United States as the main reserve currency country in the international monetary system, however, the model is somewhat simpler in the case of the United States. Since the United States authorities do not intervene in the foreign exchange market on a regular basis, the intervention function (9) can be dropped from the United States model along with the identity (6). All terms relating to international reserves are absent from the United States model.

II EFFECTIVE EXCHANGE RATES AND REST-OF-THE-WORLD VARIABLES

As the previous section indicates, the basic model for each country requires that influences arising from all countries, other than the one under consideration, be represented by indices for the effective exchange rate, and for the levels of income, prices, interest rates, and nominal money balances in the rest of the world. The natural question that arises is how these indices are to be constructed. The two most general requirements for any price index are simply that each component of the index must receive a positive weight and that the sum of the weights must be unity (that is, the price index must be homogeneous of degree one in all prices).

Our specification of the effective exchange-rate index for any country *A* satisfies the above general requirements. It is a log-linear formulation of the form:

$$(15)\quad \ln \varepsilon^A = \sum_{j=1}^{n-1} w_j^A \ln \theta_j^A;\ \sum_j w_j^A = 1$$

where ε^A = effective exchange rate of country *A*

θ_j^A = bilateral exchange rate between country *A* and the country *j*.

Once this form has been chosen, the key question concerns the definition of the weights that are to be used. It is clear that in our model it is inappropriate to use trade weights, since we have argued that both real and financial factors affect the level of exchange rates, interest rates and other variables. For our purposes, the most convenient weighting system would seem to involve using Gross National Product (GNP) weights. To construct these weights, we first calculated the dollar value of real GNP in 1970 for each of the countries included in the index, and then derived country *j*'s share of the total GNP of all countries other than *A*. Thus the weights in the effective exchange-rate index for country *A* are:

$$(16)\quad w_j^A = \frac{\text{1970 GNP (country } j)}{\text{1970 GNP (sum of all countries except } A)},\quad j \neq A$$

Time series for the cross-rates required by the effective exchange-rate index are not consistently available throughout our sample period, and in practice the index is calculated from time series published in the International Monetary Fund's (IMF) *International Financial Statistics* using the formula:

$$(17)\ \ln \varepsilon^A = \sum_{\substack{j=1 \\ j \neq A}}^{n} w_j^A \ln \left[\frac{\text{domestic currency/\$ for } A}{\text{domestic currency/\$ for } j} \div \frac{\text{1970 domestic currency/\$ for } A}{\text{1970 domestic currency/\$ for } j} \right]$$

We noted above that one ultimate goal of our research is the construction of a multi-country model for macro-economic analysis and forecasting that explicitly allows for simultaneous interactions among the five included countries. Our effective exchange-rate index is constructed with this objective in mind. Thus instead of including all countries in the world (or all IMF members, *et cetera*), our index incorporates only the five countries estimated in this paper plus France and Australia.[22] It is obvious that in the full five-country model there can be only four independent exchange-rate equations, while the fifth is given implicitly by the identity for the effective exchange rate.[23] In our work, we have chosen the US dollar as the numeraire, so that equations (10) and (11) must also be dropped from the United States model estimated in the next section. In the full multi-country system the effective exchange rate of the United States will be derived from (15).

If the effective exchange rate is calculated as in (15) above, then the index of foreign interest rates must be calculated in an analogous fashion in order to allow for the possibility of interest-rate parity in the long run. Thus, we must have:

$$(18)\ r_f^A = \sum_{\substack{j=1 \\ j \neq A}}^{n} w_i^A r_j$$

where r_j is the nominal interest rate in country j, and the w_j^A are as above.

Similarly, the foreign price level, from the point of view of country A, is:

$$(19)\ p_f = \sum_{\substack{j=1 \\ j \neq A}}^{n} w_j^A \ln p_j$$

where p_j = GNP deflator in country j.

In contrast to the above indices, those for foreign expenditures, the foreign money supply, and the foreign level of income, do not require a weighting scheme, since we only want the sum of expenditures in all the foreign countries. The same will be true for the level of foreign real income and the nominal money stock in the rest of the world. Thus, we must have:

$$(20)\quad E_f^A + G_f^A + X_f^A = \sum_{\substack{j=1 \\ j \neq A}}^{n} (E_j + G_j + X_j)$$

where E_j = real private expenditures
G_j = real government expenditures
X_j = real exports.

$$(21)\quad M_f^A = \sum_{\substack{j=1 \\ j \neq A}}^{n} M_j$$

where M_j = nominal money supply in country j.

$$(22)\quad Y_F^A = \sum_{\substack{j=1 \\ j \neq A}}^{n} Y_j$$

where Y_j = real dollar GNP of country j.

The above indices were calculated for each country during the sample period and used to obtain the estimates for the individual models that are described in the next section.

III ESTIMATION WORK

This section describes the empirical research that is currently under way, and presents some initial parameter estimates for the five countries included in our study. The estimates were obtained from samples of forty-seven quarterly observations for the period February 1964 to April 1975 using the full information maximum likelihood method. As was noted in the first section, pages 94–6, the model attempts to take account of the evolution from fixed par values to managed floating by using an exchange-regime variable a_i that alters the equations which determine the exchange rate and the degree of official intervention in the foreign exchange market. The value of a_i is unity when country i is maintaining a fixed par value and zero otherwise. Since the countries in this study ceased to declare par values on different dates (Canada in 1970, Britain in 1972, Germany and Japan in 1973), the precise definition of a_i for each country is given in the Appendix. In order to retain the property that the stochastic equations of the model are linear in the logarithms of the variables, the effect of the exchange-regime variable a_i has been subsumed into the time series for the par value and the desired exchange rate in such a way that the first terms in equations (9) and (11) are non-zero only at times when a par value is in force, and vice versa for the second term.[24]

Our initial estimation work makes use of several other simplifying assumptions. In the first place, the equation for official intervention in the foreign exchange market has been simplified by approximating the tangent function in (9) with a log-linear relationship. This approximation is satisfactory during normal periods when the market exchange rate would not deviate greatly from its par value, even in the absence of intervention by the authorities. But at times of heavy speculative pressure, such as those which punctuated the final years of the par value system, the log-linear specification is not able to approximate the levels of intervention required to keep the exchange rate within the intervention points (that is, intervention along the tails of the tangent function in [9]). This problem leads us to the general question of the use of dummy variables.

During the sample period, and especially after 1970, there were fundamental changes in the international economic environment that had a strong impact on reserve flows, exchange rates, prices, *et cetera*, in the countries considered in our study. These events included the temporary imposition of wage and price controls, the collapse of the Bretton Woods system of adjustable par values, the shift to managed floating exchange rates among the major industrial countries and the increase in oil prices. In order to reduce the biases in parameter estimates resulting from failure to take account of these exogenous developments, a small number of dummy variables were used in estimating the model for each country. Full descriptions of these variables are provided in the Appendix on pages 113–14.

For purposes of estimation, the continuous model in the first section was approximated using a discrete-time approximation described in Wymer (1972).[25]

Since time series do not exist for expected prices and exchange rates, the parameters of equations (13) and (14) cannot be estimated directly. Our solution was to construct time series for p^* and ε^* using different values of η_1 and η_2. We then re-estimated the models with different combinations of time series for p^* and ε^* representing a coarse grid (0.2, 0.5, 0.8, 1.0, 1.4, 1.7, 2.0, 2.3, 2.5) of values of the adaptive parameters, and chose the η_1 and η_2 that yielded a 'maximum maximorum' for the likelihood function.[26] This procedure gave the following values for η_1 and η_2:[27]

	United States	*United Kingdom*	*Germany*	*Canada*	*Japan*
Prices (η_1)	0.2	0.5	2.5	2.5	0.5
Exchange rate (η_2)	–	0.5	2.5	2.5	0.8

Table 4.1 (pages 106–7) presents the results of the estimation work

undertaken so far. With three exceptions, the same structural model was estimated for each of the five countries in our study. The exceptions are: (i) in the case of the United States, the intervention and exchange-rate equations do not appear; (ii) γ_{81} (which refers to the adjustment of domestic yields to interest parity) has been set to zero in the interest-rate equation for all countries except the United Kingdom and Japan; and (iii) in a few cases other parameters have been set equal to zero.

Several parameters, such as the price and income elasticities in the domestic demand for money, appear in more than one equation of the model. Since we are presently imposing within-equation restrictions only, separate estimates of these parameters are obtained from the price, interest-rate and exchange-rate equations. The second and third estimates of β_{13} and β_{14} are marked with a prime and double prime, respectively. While the point estimates of each parameter are different in each equation, these differences are usually not significant at the 5 per cent level. This result suggests that there might be gains to be had by imposing across-equation restrictions, a refinement which will be attempted in the next round of estimation. The absence of across-equation restrictions also means that it is not possible to identify certain individual behavioural parameters in the exchange-rate equation or (in the case of Britain and Japan) the interest-rate equation. In these cases, Table 4.1 presents estimates of the parameter combinations that can be identified.

In Table 4.1 the point estimate of each parameter listed in the left-hand column is presented for each country, together with its *t*-ratio (in paranthesis). In general, given the way in which the variables are defined to enter each equation, the parameters have positive expected signs. The two compound terms in the exchange-rate equation (marked with an asterisk), however, may be either positive or negative. The constant term in each equation is a non-linear combination of adjustment parameters and basic proportions (for example, the constant term in the expenditure equation is $\gamma_1 \ln \alpha_{11}$ whereas the output and price equations have more complicated constant terms which include the base level of capacity output $\ln Y_o$, *et cetera*). Except in the equation for the money stock, the components of these compond constant terms have not been unscrambled and thus they are unrestricted as to sign.[28]

As has already been emphasised above, the estimation results presented in Table 4.1 reflect only our first probings into the empirical aspects of our problem. We have done little to 'fine tune' the individual models by allowing for significant differences in structure across countries. Nevertheless, these initial results are extremely encouraging:

some of the relationships are quite well estimated, and those that raise problems are generally equations where the theoretical literature has not yet established firm conclusions as to which specification is superior. Of the 211 parameters (excluding constants) that are estimated in the five models, only twenty-four are contrary to their expected sign. On asymptotic tests, 122 of these parameters are significantly different from zero.[29]

Equation (1) for the level of private domestic expenditure is very well determined for all five countries. The income elasticities of domestic spending are significant with plausible values, and the real interest rate has the expected negative sign in all cases except the United Kingdom (though it is only significant in the case of Germany). The mean time lag[30] in the response of domestic spending to its desired level ranges from a high of over ten months in the United States to as little as two-and-a-half months in Britain.

The results for the output equation (2) indicate that the determinants of domestic economic activity vary somewhat among the five countries included in our study. The excess demand effect is significant with the correct sign for Germany and is nearly significant for Japan, while the excess capacity effect is significant for Canada. The 'Phillips Curve' relating actual and expected price changes is significant with the correct sign for the United Kingdom and Japan. In the case of the United States, the estimated Phillips Curve coefficient is significantly negative, a result which may be due to the effects of United States price controls during the period of high domestic economic activity in the early 1970s. It is interesting that in Britain and Japan, which display a significant Phillips Curve trade-off, price expectations adapt relatively slowly to change ($\eta_1 = 0.5$), whereas in Germany and Canada, where the adaptive parameter on price expectations is large ($\eta_1 = 2.5$), no significant trade-off is apparent. Our current specification of the output equation, however, still needs further work and these results can only be regarded as suggestive.

Like the domestic expenditure equation, the level of imports (3) is also well determined for all countries. The mean time lag in the adjustment of imports to an increase in demand for foreign goods ranges from about four quarters in the case of Japan to just over one-and-a-half quarters in Britain and Canada, and less than a quarter for the United States. The point estimates of the elasticity of import demand with respect to the terms of trade are also interesting. In volume terms, the import elasticities ($\beta_{31} + 1$) run from about 0.3 for the United States, and 0.8 in the case of the United Kingdom, to 1.2 and 1.5 in Canada and Germany, and 3.2 in the case of Japan.

TABLE 4.1

Estimation Results[a]

	United States		*United Kingdom*		*Germany*		*Canada*		*Japan*	
(1) *Expenditure*										
γ_1	0.293	(3.34)	1.186	(4.21)	0.476	(3.78)	0.648	(3.84)	0.836	(5.32)
β_{11}	0.800	(7.71)	0.926	(17.12)	0.735	(12.61)	0.843	(24.06)	0.974	(70.63)
β_{12}	1.787	(1.15)	−0.421	(1.29)	2.546	(2.58)	0.835	(1.33)	0.008	(0.02)
Const.	0.339	(1.96)	0.110	(0.44)	0.726	(3.52)	0.342	(2.55)	0.021	(0.44)
(2) *Output*										
γ_{21}	0.082	(0.40)	0.052	(0.19)	0.858	(2.49)	−0.688	(3.57)	0.363	(1.75)
γ_{22}	0.0	—	0.0	—	0.049	(0.73)	0.218	(2.46)	0.0	—
γ_{23}	−0.677	(2.77)	0.805	(3.42)	−0.474	(0.85)	0.005	(0.02)	0.955	(3.00)
β_{21}	0.671	(0.38)	−3.007	(0.20)	−0.138	(2.04)	0.161	(1.08)	0.200	(1.60)
β_{22}	1.400	(1.22)	−10.625	(0.18)	0.751	(11.45)	1.044	(11.55)	0.907	(8.96)
β_{23}	−0.640	(0.41)	4.930	(0.20)	0.231	(2.66)	−0.187	(1.61)	0.462	(1.38)
Const.	−0.233	(1.21)	2.576	(3.53)	1.227	(2.63)	1.131	(2.43)	−0.937	(3.12)
(3) *Imports*										
γ_3	1.068	(4.25)	0.550	(4.16)	0.310	(2.33)	0.660	(3.81)	0.231	(3.77)
$(\beta_{31}+1)$	0.277	1.75	0.803	(2.73)	1.465	(5.64)	1.184	(2.58)	3.182	(6.19)
β_{32}	2.080	(12.52)	2.155	(12.09)	1.065	(4.00)	1.438	(24.73)	0.542	(2.77)
Const.	−11.159	(3.93)	−3.541	(3.67)	−0.668	(0.91)	−2.469	(3.59)	−0.087	(0.43)

(5) *Prices*										
γ_{51}	0.025	(1.52)	−0.862	(4.33)	0.116	(1.86)	0.105	(1.03)	0.149	(4.67)
γ_{52}	0.063	(2.18)	0.243	(4.07)	0.028	(0.68)	0.010	(0.19)	0.322	(5.97)
γ_{53}	−0.006	(0.57)	0.054	(0.91)	0.003	(0.13)	0.178	(3.27)	0.0	—
γ_{54}	0.0	—	0.0	—	0.0	—	0.0	—	0.183	(3.46)
β_{13}	0.824	(4.26)	1.168	(6.01)	0.324	(0.13)	−0.271	(0.03)	1.082	(52.81)
β_{14}	16.133	(2.76)	1.218	(0.36)	6.353	(0.56)	30.050	(0.20)	5.020	(6.19)
Const.	−0.194	(1.83)	3.697	(4.13)	−0.843	(3.62)	−0.483	(1.81)	−0.426	(3.68)
Z11	0.006	(2.49)								
Z12	0.004	(2.08)								
Z13	0.005	(1.71)								
Z14	0.008	(3.35)								
(7) *Money Supply*										
γ_{71}	−0.102	(1.84)	−0.385	(2.28)	0.083	(1.75)	0.300	(1.95)	0.008	(0.26)
γ_{72}	0.043	(1.70)	−0.063	(1.56)	0.018	(1.40)	0.059	(0.64)	0.013	(0.68)
γ_{73}	10.398	(0.98)	16.370	(3.08)	4.294	(1.91)	57.774	(1.32)	2.532	(2.08)
γ_{74}	0.021	(1.01)	−0.136	(1.63)	0.039	(1.48)	−0.033	(0.78)	0.058	(2.55)
γ_{75}	0.0	—	0.190	(3.10)	0.027	(1.86)	0.164	(3.05)	0.0	—
ρ_M	0.038	(3.21)	0.071	(2.66)	0.026	(10.16)	−0.059	(1.37)	0.033	(14.97)
Z51									0.097	(11.84)

[a] Numbers in parentheses are t-ratios. Constant terms and the two compound coefficients marked with an asterisk in the exchange-rate equation may be either positive or negative. All other parameters are expected to be greater than zero.

TABLE 4.1 (*contd*)

	United States		*United Kingdom*		*Germany*		*Canada*		*Japan*	
(8) *Interest Rate*										
$(\gamma_{81}\alpha_{81})$	—		0.092	(6.05)	—		—		0.014	(0.61)
$(\gamma_{81}\alpha_{81}\eta_3)$	—		−0.005	(1.38)	—		—		0.024	(6.28)
$(\gamma_{81}+\gamma_{82}\beta'_{14})$	—		0.291	(5.08)	—		—		0.399	(4.95)
γ_{82}	0.008	(1.42)	−0.021	(5.46)	0.021	(2.39)	0.002	(1.23)	0.013	(1.88)
β'_{13}	1.624	(5.30)	0.930	(6.09)	2.082	(17.77)	2.201	(6.01)	1.324	(12.35)
β'_{14}	15.894	(2.04)	—		10.986	(3.43)	14.445	(1.93)	—	
Const.	−0.039	(1.55)	0.020	(1.49)	−0.161	(2.38)	−0.015	(1.36)	−0.012	(1.77)
(9) *International Reserves*										
γ_{91}	—		13.818	(2.76)	0.008	(0.05)	2.479	(1.03)	4.974	(6.26)
γ_{92}	—		10.009	(2:77)	0.022	(0.51)	0.190	(0.88)	0.0	—
γ_{93}	—		15.937	(2.92)	0.572	(4.05)	1.066	(3.13)	0.279	(0.67)
Const.	—		0.086	(2.28)	(0.008)	(1.53)	0.008	(1.43)	0.017	(7.33)
		Z21	0.140	(0.64)	Z31 0.153	(9.29)	Z41 0.116	(4.05)	Z52 0.222	(6.40)
		Z22	0.255	(2.81)	Z32 0.189	(11.81)	Z42 0.144	(4.72)	Z53 0.129	(3.07)
		Z23	0.069	(2.12)	Z33 0.050	(1.79)	Z43 0.081	(2.75)		
					Z34 0.112	(3.93)				

(10) *Exchange Rate*													
δ_{12}	—			0.902	(8.93)		0.452	(2.89)	1.207	(3.92)		1.446	(5.49)
δ_{13}	—			0.729	(8.32)		0.076	(1.02)	0.374	(9.12)		0.252	(3.79)
$(\delta_{14}-\delta_{15}\beta''_{14})$	—			0.750	(1.75)		−0.321	(0.38)	0.488	(1.40)		2.052	(3.70)
$(\delta_{14}\alpha_{81}-\delta_{16}\beta_{16})$	—			0.580	(1.75)		−5.154	(2.98)	0.174	(0.48)		0.709	(0.72)
$(\delta_{14}\alpha_{81})$	—			0.449	(3.51)		0.654	(5.74)	1.062	(20.79)		0.868	(5.01)
$(\delta_{14}\alpha_{81}\eta'_3)$	—			−0.016	(0.57)		0.072	(1.13)	0.043	(3.08)		0.0003	(0.01)
δ_{15}	—			0.161	(3.93)		0.015	(0.16)	0.046	(1.85)		−0.024	(0.35)
$(\delta_{15}\beta''_{13})$	—			0.156	(1.98)		0.108	(0.72)	0.179	(3.76)		−0.073	(1.21)
δ_{16}	—			0.031	(0.86)		0.124	(0.62)	0.014	(0.40)		0.022	(0.24)
$(\delta_{16}\beta_{15})$	—			−0.008	(0.18)		0.349	(1.01)	0.178	(2.89)		−0.221	(1.20)
δ_{17}	—			—			—		—			—	
Const.				0.155	(0.51)		0.505	(0.74)	0.555	(4.03)		−0.111	(0.84)
			Z21	0.009	(0.72)	Z33	0.029	(2.00)			Z54	0.070	(8.17)
			Z26	0.005	(1.97)	Z35	0.091	(3.63)			Z55	0.054	(6.36)
						Z36	0.015	(1.13)					
Trend Rate of Growth of Output													
ρ_y (per quarter)	0.0084	(30.23)		0.0063	(33.63)		0.0114	(36.38)	0.0126	(69.42)		0.0247	(75.57)

Like the output equation, the results for the price determination process (5) are also somewhat mixed and, as might be expected, the relative influence of the various terms differs across countries. The level of capacity utilisation has the correct sign except (not surprisingly) in the case of the United Kingdom. This effect is highly significant for Japan, less so for Germany. The term representing monetary disequilibrium is always consistent with its *a priori* sign restriction, and is highly significant in the case of the United States, the United Kingdom, and Japan. For Canada, the deviation of domestic prices from international purchasing-power parity is an important determinant of the domestic inflation rate, while Japanese prices appear to respond to current exchange-rate changes and to inflation abroad.

Turning to domestic monetary policy, the estimates of equation (7) yield evidence that, during the sample period, monetary authorities tended to 'lean against the wind' by increasing the money stock more rapidly when nominal interest rates rose (a reaction which is statistically significant in three of the five cases). The estimates of γ_{75} indicate that the authorities in the United Kingdom, Germany and Canada did not completely sterilise the short-run effects of international reserve flows on the domestic money stock, although for Germany the portion sterilised was large. The question of sterilisation of reserve flows does not arise in the case of the United States, while for Japan there is no evidence of a systematic relationship running from international reserves to money, and γ_{75} was eventually set equal to zero. Beyond these effects, the reactions of the monetary authorities are not too consistent either across countries or over time. The underlying long-term quarterly growth rates of domestic money balances ρ_M (the rate that would prevail if output and prices were at their desired levels and there were no reserve flows) are well determined in all countries. Monetary policy seems to have responded to the state of the balance of trade in Japan during the sample period. There is some evidence that excess capacity induced stimulative monetary policy in Germany and Canada, while the relation between domestic and foreign prices may have affected money growth rates in Germany and the United States.

The interest-rate equation (8) assumes that domestic interest rates respond to both deviations from international interest parity and domestic monetary disequilibrium. In the estimation work, the interest parity term was not significant for three countries when both effects were included. Thus the interest parity effect was excluded by setting γ_{81} equal to zero in the case of the United States, Germany and Canada. This simplification was made on grounds of empirical convenience and should not be necessary once across-equation restrictions are imposed on the parameters of the demand for money function in each model. The present restriction corresponds to the assumption that, except in the United Kingdom and Japan, all of the adjustment to international interest parity is borne by the exchange rate, so that nominal interest rates reflect only domestic monetary disequilibrium. The estimates indicate that monetary disequilibrium has a significant effect on the domestic interest rate, and some of the compound terms that result from the interest parity relationship are significant for the United Kingdom and Japan.

In the equation which determines official reserve flows (9), the term representing the authorities' intervention strategy during the fixed-rate period always has the correct sign and is significantly different from zero for the United Kingdom and Japan. Two intervention strategies are considered for the period of managed floating exchange rates: (i) intervention in response to deviations from the authorities' desired level of the exchange rate based on considerations of the relative purchasing power of domestic and foreign currency (γ_{92}), and (ii) intervention to lean against exchange-rate changes (γ_{93}). These parameters always have the correct sign; γ_{92} is significant for the United Kingdom and γ_{93} is significant in all cases except Japan. The dummy variables all enter this equation with the expected sign and, with one exception, they are highly significant.

The results for the exchange-rate equation are very encouraging, especially considering the major changes that occurred during the sample period. Not all parameters are significant at the 5 per cent level, but of the forty-seven parameters in the estimated exchange-rate equation in the four countries, only five violate their *a priori* expected sign, despite the fact that the across-equation restrictions have not yet been imposed. Twenty-three estimated parameters are significant at the 5 per cent level. For the fixed-rate period, the parameter δ_{12} (which reflects the speed at which the exchange rate adapts to its par value) is highly significant for all countries; while the parameter δ_{13}, that reflects the speed at which the rate adjusts to deviations from its long-run equilibrium path under a floating-rate regime, is significant in three cases out of four. Since the compound coefficients associated with domestic and foreign interest rates are combinations of forces that work in opposite directions, one would not necessarily expect them to differ significantly from zero. The coefficient of the adaptive component of the expected exchange rate is highly significant for all countries, although the trade balance term is not.

The estimation results for the five countries that have been discussed in detail above provide support for the overall specification of the model. Nevertheless the present paper is a report on work in progress and it is useful to end by indicating the directions that our research will take from here. First, while our expenditure, import and exchange-rate equations are quite well estimated in all cases, the results for the price and output equations are rather mixed. Since the two equations are closely related, it is natural to wonder if some determinant common to them both has been neglected. One obvious omission is the absence of any variable to reflect the precipitous movements in the prices of primary commodities such as petroleum, metals, *et cetera*, during the 1970s. Since these commodities are important inputs to the production process in the industrialised countries, increases in their relative price tend to depress the base level of capacity output ($ln\ Y_o$), thus raising prices in the industrial countries while at the same time reducing output. We plan to take account of this effect by including the relative price of commodity inputs in our price and output equations.

Secondly, although the estimates of the equation for official intervention in the foreign exchange market are encouraging, we have not yet found a statistically robust specification for the authorities' money-supply reaction function. This may simply reflect the fact that the monetary authorities of the countries included in our study did not always respond in the same way to a given change throughout the whole sample period, but it could also be that our reaction function mis-specifies their behaviour. As a further step, we intend to specify second-order differential equations for international reserves and for the money supply which will allow for considerations of both proportional and integral control in the authorities' responses.

Finally, in order to obtain estimates of the individual parameters in the interest-rate and exchange-rate equations, we intend to impose, during estimation, the across-equation restrictions arising out of the inclusion of the domestic demand for money function in equations (4), (8) and (10). Provided that these restrictions are consistent with the data–and the tests undertaken so far indicate that they are–the additional restrictions should also increase the efficiency of our estimates.

APPENDIX: DUMMY VARIABLES USED IN ESTIMATION

UNITED STATES

Price Equation:

Z11, 1971 Price Freeze (−1.0 in Q3, Q4 1971)
Z12, Post-freeze bulge in prices (1.0 in Q4 1971, Q1 1972)
Z13, Second Price Freeze and Phase IV of Nixon Anti-inflation Program (−1.0 in Q3 1973)
Z14, End of Wage-price Program (1.0 in Q3, Q4 1974)

UNITED KINGDOM

a_1, Exchange-regime Variable (1.0 until Q2 1972; zero thereafter)

Reserves Equation:

Z21, Smithsonian realignment of par values (−1.0 in Q4 1971)
Z22, End of fixed par value for sterling (1.0 in Q2 1972)
Z23, Impact of Q3 1969 revaluation of the Deutsche mark (−1.0 in Q3 1969; +1.0 in Q4 1969)

Exchange-rate Equation:

Z21, Smithsonian Agreement (see above)
Z24, Anticipations associated with 1967 devaluation of sterling (1.0 in Q3 1967)

GERMANY

a_2, Exchange-regime Variable (1.0 until Q1 1973; zero thereafter)

Reserves Equation:

Z31, Reserve flows associated with 1969 Deutsche mark revaluation (1.0 in Q3 1969; −1.0 in Q4 1969, Q1 1970)
Z32, Speculation prior to Q2 1971 revaluation of Deutsche mark (1.0 from Q2 1970 to Q1 1971)
Z33, Smithsonian Agreement (1.0 in Q4 1971)
Z34, Deutsche mark allowed to float (1.0 in Q1 1973)

Exchange-rate Equation:

- Z33, Smithsonian Agreement (see above)
- Z35, Anticipation of 1967 sterling devaluation (−1.0 in Q3 1967)
- Z36, Collapse of Bretton Woods par value system (−1.0 from Q1 to Q3 1973)
- Z37, Oil embargo (1.0 in Q4 1973)

CANADA

a_3, Exchange-regime Variable (1.0 until Q2 1970; zero thereafter)

Reserves Equation:

- Z41, Speculative capital outflow following sterling devaluation (−1.0 in Q1 1968)
- Z42, Re-flux of speculative funds in 1968 (1.0 in Q2 1968)
- Z43, Canadian dollar begins to float (Q2 1970)

JAPAN

a_4, Exchange-regime Variable (1.0 until Q1 1973; zero thereafter)

Money Supply Equation:

- Z51, Impact of 1963 monetary reform on measured money stock in early 1964 (1.0 in Q2 1964)

Reserves Equation:

- Z52, Speculation in favor of yen prior to Smithsonian realignment (1.0 in Q2, Q3 1971)
- Z53, Oil embargo (1.0 in Q4 1973)

Exchange-rate Equation:

- Z54, Speculation on yen associated with Smithsonian realignment (−1.0 in Q3, Q4 1971; +1.0 in Q1, Q2 1972)
- Z55, Collapse of Bretton Woods par value system (−1.0 in Q1 1973)

NOTES

1. This paper represents views of the authors which are not necessarily those of the International Monetary Fund. We gratefully acknowledge comments and criticisms of an earlier draft by Jocelyn Horne, John Black and colleagues on the staff of the IMF. Kellett Hannah and Fernando Santos provided skilled research assistance.

   The choice of the countries used as the starting-point of our research was dictated not only by their relative importance in the international economy, but also by the availability of quarterly data among the International Monetary Fund's monthly *International Financial Statistics*. We are currently gathering data for two more industrial countries.
2. See, for example, Dornbusch (1976), Kouri (1976) and papers appearing in Herin *et al.*, (1977).
3. Simultaneous estimation methods are used throughout, but, for obvious reasons, we must estimate the structural equations for each country on the assumption that the rest of the world variables are exogenous. Thus the estimation procedure reduces the problem of simultaneous equations bias arising from interdependence of variables within each national economy, but it cannot eliminate the bias that arises in the parameter estimates owing to interdependence *across* countries.
4. The model includes the expected future spot exchange rate rather than the current forward rate. The two rates are the same if the behaviour of speculators is risk-neutral and if forward markets operate efficiently.
5. Since the model is specified in continuous time, we allow for the empirical possibility that the mean time lag for the adjustment of domestic yields to interest parity is brief relative to the observation period.
6. Supply and demand functions specified in this way have variable interest-rate elasticities and constant elasticities with respect to all other variables. See Knight (1976).
7. Private domestic expenditure is defined to equal consumption and business fixed capital formation in real terms plus the physical change in inventories. In our model, increases in capacity output which are due to technical change, net investment, or growth in the labour force are subsumed in a trend term ρ_y. Since the level of investment spending does not explicitly feed back on to the capital stock, there is little to be gained by distinguishing between consumption and investment expenditures.
8. Although E^d is desired expenditure on *both* home and foreign goods, it is arguable that it should be a negative function of the terms of trade $(p/\varepsilon p_f)$. This is the case if the substitution effect of a rise in the terms of trade is greater than the income effect; a condition which generally holds so long as home goods are a large proportion of total domestic spending. For the present, however, we omit this complication.
9. In this equation, Y_o represents the level of full employment output in the domestic economy at time o and ρ_y is the long-run average rate of capacity growth.
10. This specification assumes, in effect, that government spending, private spending and gross exports each contain the same proportion of imported inputs.

It should be noted that since the proportion of total sales that is met by domestic production equals one minus the proportion supplied by imports, there are across-equation restrictions between (2′) and (3′). By imposing these restrictions, it would be possible to estimate the price elasticity of the demand for home goods by domestic residents separately from that of foreign residents. However, this restriction has not been imposed in our preliminary estimation work.

11. The physical volume of imports demanded (q^d) is related to I^d by:

$$I^d = \frac{q^d \cdot \varepsilon p_f}{p}$$

from which it follows that:

$$\frac{\partial \ln q^d}{\partial (\ln p - \ln \varepsilon - \ln p_f)} = 1 + \beta_{31}$$

12. Since $\varepsilon . DR$ is defined as the rate of change of international reserves that results from official intervention in the foreign exchange market, its value must be obtained from the balance-of-payments statistics as the total balance settled by official transactions (that is the total currency flow) rather than by first differencing the published reserve stock figures, which include valuation changes and borrowed reserves.
13. In the short run, the authorities' target level of the terms of trade, α_{71}, need not equal the level that private domestic producers regard as the equilibrium price ratio of domestic and foreign goods (α_{51} in equation 5). However, one would expect such a condition to hold in the steady state. Since both the price indices and the effective exchange rate are based in 1970, the estimation results reported in the third section are based on the implicit assumption that $\ln \alpha_{51} = \ln \alpha_{71} = 0$.
14. It seems that, from an empirical point of view, we have everything to gain and little to lose by specifying this function. If a stable reaction function exists, the assumption that the money supply was exogenous would lead to biased estimates of other equations of the model. The difficulty, of course, is that there are many possible specifications of the reaction function and few *a priori* criteria for choosing among them. For a more sophisticated approach which takes account of both proportional and integral control, see Knight and Wymer (1976). Given the money multiplier (m), equation (6) indicates the level of domestic credit that the authorities must maintain in order to achieve the money supply level given by the reaction function (7).
15. This rather loose definition of international interest parity seems appropriate in a highly aggregative econometric model like that specified here. The factor of proportionality, α_{81}, allows for the fact that the particular asset whose interest rate is used in the model may have default risk and other characteristics that differ from those of the assets taken to represent the rest of the world. Also note that we use the approximate interest parity formula, rather than the exact relationship.
16. The authorities can always manipulate the exchange rate by altering restrictions on trade and payments or by inducing capital flows which are not recorded as official monetary movements in the published balance-of-

payments accounts. For the moment, these complications are neglected.

17. Germany altered its par value *vis-à-vis* the US dollar in Q3 1969, Q2 1971 and Q4 1971; and allowed its exchange rate to float in Q1 1973. The United Kingdom made par value changes in Q3 1967 and Q4 1971, and ceased to declare a par value in Q2 1972. Japan adjusted its par value in Q4 1971 and floated in Q1 1973. Canada floated in Q2 1970. In the estimation work the effects of these events on the reserve and exchange-rate equations are caught by dummy variables which have the value unity in the period when they occurred.
18. Specifically, s_1 scales the term in square brackets so that it equals $\pi/2$ when $\theta(t) = \theta_L$ and $-\pi/2$ when $\theta(t) = \theta_u$.
19. Note that the existence of the dummy a_i makes (9) non-linear in variables. The difficulties arising from this non-linearity are considered below.
20. If, given the partial adjustment structure of the model, the flow demands for goods and money are at their desired levels, then the actual flow of capital given by (12) equals that desired by transactors. Since X and I are measured on a national accounts rather than a balance-of-payments basis, DK will differ from published balance-of-payments statistics if there are 'leads' and 'lags' in import payments and export receipts.
21. We would like to test the sensitivity of the model to three alternative assumptions about the nature of the expectations formation process. These are: (1) adaptive expectations; (2) 'rational' expectations; and (3) 'semi-rational' expectations. The rational expectations hypothesis assumes that transactors know the whole underlying structure of the economy to a random term. In contrast, the 'semi-rational' mechanism (proposed in Knight (1976)) assumes that transactors are confident of their knowledge of how major economic aggregates will behave in the long run, but uncertain of the short-run dynamic behaviour of the economy. The theoretical implications of these alternative expectations structures are analysed in Mathieson (1977).
22. The exchange rates of France and Australia are included in the index for two reasons. First, both countries are part of the industrial nexus of the international economy and, secondly, we hope to add them to our multi-country model at a later date.
23. This assumes that the exchange rates of France and Australia are exogenous to the five-country model.
24. Specifically, the time series for θ_o equals the par value during periods of fixed exchange rates and the *market* price of dollars in domestic currency when par values are absent. Similarly, the time series for the authorities' desired level of the effective exchange rate equals the actual effective rate at times when par values are in force.
25. For flow variables, the differential $Dx(t)$ and the level $x(t)$ are obtained by integrating over the observation period and approximating by:

$$\int_{t-1}^{t} Dx(s)ds \approx \Delta x_t, \quad \int_{t-1}^{t} x(s)ds \approx \Gamma x_t$$

where $Lx_t = x_{t-1}$, $\Delta = (1-L)$ and $\Gamma = \frac{1}{2}(1+L)$

Stock variables (which are measured at the end of the period) are integrated twice and approximated by:

$$\int_{t-1}^{t} Dy(s)ds \approx \Delta\Gamma\, y_t, \quad \int_{t-1}^{t} y(s)ds \approx \Gamma^2 y_t$$

Following Wymer (1972), these data were transformed to remove a first-order moving-average process that results from the approximation.

26. This is the set of ηs for which the likelihood ratio test yields the lowest χ^2 value for the estimated model.
27. These parameters correspond to the outer bounds of the grid in 3 cases. Since an adaptive parameter of 2.5 implies a mean time lag of less than two months, it seems likely that extension of the grid to allow for more rapid adjustment of expectations would have little effect on the estimates of other parameters.
28. A word should be said about the interpretation of the parameters in partial equilibrium equations (the β_i). Coefficients of price, income and expenditure variables can be interpreted directly as elasticities, but the model has *variable* interest-rate elasticities. The average elasticity of demand for X with respect to the interest rate r_j is $\beta_{xj} . \bar{r}_j$, where $\bar{r}_j$ is the mean value of this interest rate during the sample period. In the model, all interest rates are in per cent per *quarter*. The average levels for the sample period are: United States $\bar{r} = 0.013$, $\bar{r}_f = 0.017$; United Kingdom $\bar{r} = 0.018$, $\bar{r}_f = 0.015$; Germany $\bar{r} = 0.014$, $\bar{r}_f = 0.015$; Canada $\bar{r} = 0.013$, $\bar{r}_f = 0.015$; Japan $\bar{r} = 0.020$, $\bar{r}_f = 0.014$.
29. The FIML estimator has an asymptotic normal distribution. Thus the term '*t*-ratio' simply refers to the absolute value of the ratio of a parameter estimate to the estimate of its asymptotic standard error, and does not imply that this ratio has a student's *t*-distribution. In a sufficiently large sample this ratio is significantly different from zero at the 5 per cent level if it is greater than 1.96 and significantly different from zero at the 1 per cent level if it is greater than 2.58.
30. The mean time lag is the time required for over 60 per cent of the difference between actual and desired expenditure to be made up. It is measured as the inverse of the adjustment coefficient.

REFERENCES

A. R. BERGSTROM and C. R. WYMER, 'A Model of Disequilibrium Neoclassical Growth in the United Kingdom', in BERGSTROM (ed.), *Statistical Inference in Continuous Time Economic Models* (Amsterdam: North Holland, 1975).

R. DORNBUSCH, 'The Theory of Flexible Exchange Rate Regimes and Macroeconomic Policy', *The Scandinavian Journal of Economics*, Stockholm, Vol. 78, No. 2, 1976(a), pp. 255–75.

——'Expectations and Exchange Rate Dynamics', *Journal of Political Economy*, Chicago, Illinois, Vol. 84, No. 6, December 1976(b), pp. 1161–76.

J. HERIN, A. LINDBECK and J. MYHRMAN (eds), *Flexible Exchange Rates and Stabilization Policy* (London: Macmillan, 1977).

P. ISARD, *The Process of Exchange Rate Determination: a Survey of Important*

Models and Major Issues, Federal Reserve Board International Finance Discussion Paper No. 101 (Washington: Federal Reserve Board, 1977).

HARRY G. JOHNSON, 'Towards a General Theory of the Balance of Payments', in *International Trade and Economic Growth* (London: Allen & Unwin, 1958).

——'The Monetary Approach to Balance of Payments Theory', in *Further Essays in Monetary Economics* (London: Allen & Unwin, 1972).

MALCOLM D. KNIGHT, *Output, Prices and the Floating Exchange Rate in Canada: a Monetary Approach*, Mimeograph No. DM/77/1 (Washington: International Monetary Fund, 1976).

——and C. R. WYMER, 'A Monetary Model of an Open Economy with Particular Reference to the United Kingdom', in M. J. ARTIS and A. R. NOBAY (eds), *Essays in Economic Analysis* (London: Cambridge University Press, 1976).

P. J. K. KOURI, 'The Exchange Rate and the Balance of Payments in the Short Run and the Long Run: a Monetary Approach', *The Scandinavian Journal of Economic*, Vol. 78, No. 2, 1976.

D. J. MATHIESON, 'The Impact of Monetary and Fiscal Policy Under Flexible Exchange Rates and Alternative Expectations Structures', *International Monetary Fund Staff Papers* (Washington: IMF, 1977).

J. R. SHAFAR, 'The Macroeconomic Behavior of a Large Open Economy with a Floating Exchange Rate', unpublished doctoral dissertation, Yale University, 1976.

C. R. WYMER, 'Econometric Estimation of Stochastic Differential Equation Systems', *Econometrica*, Bristol, May 1972.

5

The Sensitivity of Industrial Output and Employment to Exchange-rate Changes

ALAN V. DEARDORFF, ROBERT M. STERN and MARK N. GREENE

Experience with flexible exchange rates has demonstrated that the rates do in fact move substantially when they are allowed to and, as some observers believe, may overshoot their dynamic equilibrium paths. If, in fact, overshooting of an exchange rate does occur, it is a cause for concern to the extent that it gives rise to misleading price signals and thus to unnecessary real adjustments. In order to provide some perspective on this issue, we analyse and attempt to quantify the sensitivity of a country or industry to exchange-rate changes. It will not be possible to give a precise indication of the adjustment costs involved because we lack the knowledge of what equilibrium exchange rates are and of how the various goods and factor markets in fact adjust. Nevertheless, a beginning can be made towards placing some boundaries on these costs by a reasonably realistic modelling of the output and employment effects that may occur when exchange rates change in the major industrialised countries.

The costs associated with exchange-rate fluctuations have been discussed in the literature primarily under the heading of 'false trading'. The concern is that exchange rates may depart from their dynamic equilibrium values and thus cause trade to take place which runs counter to underlying comparative advantage. For example, if 'unwarranted' speculative pressures cause a country's currency to be overvalued compared to its true equilibrium, then that country may find itself importing products from abroad that can be produced more cheaply, in real terms, at home. At the same time, the country's trading partners may be deprived of certain products which the country would normally export, as the real costs of those products are masked by the overvalued currency. As a result, all countries fail to capture a portion of the traditional gains from trade, since these gains require that trade be determined solely by comparative advantage.

Whatever the merits of this argument, however, the phenomenon of false trading cannot be regarded as exclusively the product of a system of flexible exchange rates. False trading may occur whenever exchange rates are misaligned, and government intervention to peg the exchange rate is surely as likely a cause of misalignment as is unwarranted private speculation. To evaluate the alternative systems of pegged versus flexible exchange rates in terms of the false trading that they would induce would therefore require an assessment of the relative abilities of governments and speculators as predictors and enforcers of the equilibrium exchange rate.

This discussion of false trading misses, however, what may be a much more important cost of exchange-rate flexibility. Whenever an exchange rate changes, it alters the structure of prices faced by producers and consumers in all countries and induces them to alter, in turn, the pattern of production and consumption. While these changes are reflected in changes in trade, the costs of adjusting to the new prices will likely be borne by all producers and consumers, whether or not they engage directly in trade.

It is possible, of course, for exchange-rate changes to be caused by internal developments in the underlying economies. Indeed, a principal advantage of flexible exchange rates is the capacity of this system to rapidly reconcile international variations in productivity, inflation, and aggregate demand. Thus, we would not argue that *any* exchange-rate change that we observe is the cause of adjustment costs that should be avoided. But when exchange rates first move one way, then the other, the presumption is that the resulting real adjustments serve no useful purpose. When an industry contracts due to an exchange-rate change, only to expand later when that movement is reversed, it is hard to see how the adjustment costs borne by capital and labour in that industry during the interim can have been offset by benefits elsewhere in the system.

It is in this context, then, that we have chosen in this paper to examine the industry responsiveness to exchange-rate changes in the major industrialised countries. We hope to get an idea not only of the magnitude of these adjustments, but also of how they are distributed across sectors of the economy. This information may then make it possible to form some judgement regarding the costs of adjustment to exchange-rate changes when these changes are not warranted by underlying movements in real economic variables.

Our analysis and estimates will be based upon a large, disaggregated, computational model of world production and trade – a model which we have been in the process of developing for some years. The model is described in some detail below in the following section. Then, in section II, we use the model to compute the percentage change in output that is caused by a 1 per cent change in the exchange rate for each of the twenty-nine industries and eighteen countries that are included in the model. These 'exchange-rate elasticities of output' (EREO) are analysed in terms of various characteristics of the industries and countries in order to see the role that these characteristics play in determining sensitivity to exchange-rate changes.

In Section II we report only the effect on an industry of the exchange rate of the country in which it is located. Yet an industry can also be affected by rates of exchange between pairs of currencies other than its own. To get an idea of the importance of such effects, we calculate the effects of a combination of exchange-rate changes for all countries multilaterally in Section III. For this purpose, we have chosen the combination of exchange-rate changes that actually occurred between 1974 and the first quarter of 1977. This is not an attempt to duplicate the real-world experience of that period, in which many other changes that are not captured in our model undoubtedly took place. On the contrary, our results in this section contrast so noticeably with reality that the role of exchange rates as *endogenous* variables must now be considered.

This is done in Section IV. Here we consider two possible causes of exchange-rate variation, namely an exogenous increase in money wages and an exogenous increase in expenditure. The effects of these changes are analysed under both fixed and flexible exchange rates. The results are compared in order to determine whether exchange-rate flexibility tends to dampen or to magnify the effects of these exogenous disturbances in the context of our model.

The results of the paper are summarised and additional conclusions are drawn in the last section.

I THE MODEL

The model used in this paper is a multi-sector model of the world economy that we developed originally to study the effects of multilateral tariff reductions on disaggregated levels of output and employment.[1] The current version of the model now includes a number of exogenous variables other than tariffs, making it suitable for our purpose in this paper.[2]

The model includes supply and demand functions and market-clearing conditions for twenty-two tradeable industries in world markets, plus markets for these and another seven non-tradeable industries within each of eighteen countries. The size of the model precludes our obtaining a meaningful and general analytical solution. We have, therefore, restricted the functional forms to ones whose parameters are either readily observable from available data or which have been estimated by others using econometric techniques. Within these constraints, however, we have tried to select functional forms which permit a rich variety of behaviour and which experience suggests provide a reasonable description of economic reality.

EQUATIONS OF THE MODEL

The complete model, although without the functional forms, is presented as equations (1) to (12) in Table 5.1. The construction of the functional forms in equations (1 to 4) and (12) will be explained below.

TABLE 5.1
Equations of the Model

Supply functions of products for export

(1) $S_{ij}^X = S_{ij}^X(p_{ij}^X, p_{i1}^H, \ldots, p_{in'}^H, p_{i1}^M, \ldots, p_{in}^M, w_i, K_{ij}^X)$

$i = 1, \ldots, m; j = 1, \ldots, n$

Supply functions of products for home use

(2) $S_{ij}^H = S_{ij}^H(p_{ij}^H, p_{i1}^H, \ldots, p_{in'}^H, p_{i1}^M, \ldots, p_{in}^M, w_i, K_{ij}^H)$

$i = 1, \ldots, m; j = 1, \ldots, n'$

Demand functions for imported goods

(3) $D_{ij}^M = D_{ij}^M(p_{ij}^M, p_{ij}^H, E_i, S_{i1}^H, \ldots, S_{in'}^H, S_{i1}^X, \ldots, S_{in}^X)$

$i = 1, \ldots, m; j = 1, \ldots, n$

Demand functions for home-produced goods

Tradeables:

(4a) $D_{ij}^H = D_{ij}^H(p_{ij}^H, p_{ij}^M, E_i, S_{i1}^H, \ldots, S_{in'}^H, S_{i1}^X, \ldots, S_{in}^X)$

$i = 1, \ldots, m; j = 1, \ldots, n$

TABLE 5.1 (*contd*)

Non-tradeables:

(4b) $D^H_{ij} = D^H_{ij}(p^H_{ij}, E_i, S^H_{i1}, \ldots, S^H_{in'}, S^H_{i1}, \ldots, S^X_{in})$ $\quad i = 1, \ldots, m; j = n+1, \ldots, n'$

Export prices

(5) $p^X_{ij} = R_i p^W_j$ $\quad i = 1, \ldots, m; j = 1, \ldots, n$

Import prices

(6) $p^M_{ij} = t_{ij} R_i p^W_j$ $\quad i = 1, \ldots, m; j = 1, \ldots, n$

Consumer expenditure and tariff revenue

(7) $E_i = E^O_i + \sum_{j=1}^{n} (t_{ij} - 1) R_i p^W_j D^M_{ij}$ $\quad i = 1, \ldots, m$

Market equilibrium for home goods

(8) $S^H_{ij} = D^H_{ij}$ $\quad i = 1, \ldots, m; j = 1, \ldots, n'$

Market equilibrium for traded goods

(9) $\sum_{i=1}^{m} S^X_{ij} = \sum_{i=1}^{m} D^M_{ij}$ $\quad j = 1, \ldots, n$

Trade balance

(10) $B^T_i = \sum_{j=1}^{n} p^W_j (S^X_{ij} - D^M_{ij})$ $\quad i = 1, \ldots, m$

Exchange rates

(11*a*) $R_i = R^O_i$ $\quad$ (Fixed Rates) $i = 1, \ldots, m$

(11b) $B^T_i + B^{KO}_i = 0, R_m = R^0_m$ $\quad$ (Flexible Rates) $i = 1, \ldots, m-1$

Demand functions for labour

Tradeables:

(12a) $L_{ij} = L^X_{ij}(w_i, S^X_{ij}, K^X_{ij},) + L^H_{ij}(w_i, S^H_{ij}, K^H_{ij})$ $\quad i = 1, \ldots, m; j = 1, \ldots, n$

Non-tradeables:

(12b) $L_{ij} = L^H_{ij}(w_i, S^H_{ij}, K^H_{ij})$ $\quad i = 1, \ldots, m; j = n+1, \ldots, n'$

Notation:

Endogenous variables:

S^X_{ij}, S^H_{ij} = Supply of good j by country i, export and home sectors, respectively

D^M_{ij}, D^H_{ij} = Demand for good j in country i, imported and home-produced, respectively

p^X_{ij}, p^M_{ij} = Domestic price of good j in country i, exported and imported, respectively

p^H_{ij} = Home-sector price of good j in country i

p^W_j = World price of good j

E_i = Consumer expenditure in country i

B^T_i = Balance of trade of country i

R_i = Exchange rate of country i (domestic currency per unit of world currency)

L_{ij} = Demand for labour by industry j in country i

Exogenous variables:

K^X_{ij}, K^H_{ij} = Capital stock of industry j in country i, export and home sectors, respectively

w_i = Money wage in country i

t_{ij} = 1 plus the *ad valorem* tariff on imports of good j into country i

E^O_i = Exogenous component of expenditure in country i

R^O_i = Exogenous exchange rate

B^{KO}_i = Exogenous capital inflow into country i

The model includes m countries, $i = 1, \ldots, m$, producing and trading n goods, $j = 1, \ldots, n$, and producing an additional $(n' - n)$ non-tradeable goods, $j = n + 1, \ldots, n'$. A distinguishing characteristic of our model, however, is that both producers and consumers distinguish, within tradeable industries, between goods which are produced and used in the same country, which we will call home goods, and those which are either exported or imported.

Thus, within each country and tradeable industry, producers are separated into two sectors: a home sector which sells only to domestic users, and an export sector which sells only to users in other countries. Each sector has its own supply function, reflecting an assumption that fixed factors of production exist which cannot be transferred between the two sectors in the relevant short run. This non-transferability may be the result of locational requirements or of the need for special product characteristics in the various national markets, although neither of these features is explicit in our model.

Demanders, too, differentiate between home-produced and imported products of a given tradeable industry. In principle, we would like this differentiation to apply among imports from different countries as well as between home-produced and imported goods generally. Data limitations, however, and the difficulty of solving a more general model have led us to permit only the latter kind of differentiation. Thus, consumers, as well as producers in their role as demanders of intermediate inputs, are assumed to regard home-produced and imported goods as imperfect substitutes, but imports from various foreign countries as perfect substitutes. Finally, we assume that demanders are never willing to use the products of their domestic export sectors.

With these assumptions, three separate prices will obtain within each country, i, for each tradeable industry, $j = 1, \ldots, n$. First, a home price, p_{ij}^H, is both paid by users and received by producers in the home sector. It is determined by a purely domestic market which equates home-sector supply, S_{ij}^H, with home demand, D_{ij}^H.

The second and third prices are those of exports and imports. The export price, p_{ij}^X, is received by producers in the export sector and the import price, p_{ij}^M, is paid by users of imports. These prices are determined simultaneously in a single world market in which the sum of all countries' export supplies, S_{ij}^X, is equated to the sum of all countries' import demands, D_{ij}^M. Since demanders regard imports (of industry j) from all countries but their own as perfect substitutes, all countries' export prices must be identical when expressed in a common numeraire (we do not allow for export subsidies). Import prices are then equal to the corresponding export prices augmented by *ad valorem* tariffs. With these relationships only a single world price for each tradeable industry, p_j^W, expressed in units of a numeraire currency, needs to be determined by the world market. Corresponding export and import prices for each country, i, then follow by multiplying p_j^W by exchange rates, R_i (expressed in units of domestic currency per unit of the numeraire) and, for import prices, by one plus the corresponding *ad valorem* tariff, t_{ij}.

The model is completed by specifying markets for foreign exchange with either fixed or flexible exchange rates (as separate cases) and by specifying the determinants of supply and demand. The latter include exogenous nominal wages, w_i, and capital stocks, K_{ij}, as well as appropriate prices and will be explained more fully below. In addition, demands depend also on endogenous levels of consumer expenditure, E_i, which incorporate an assumption that all tariff revenue is redistributed and spent by consumers.

Exchange markets either endogenously determine trade balances, B_i^T (measured in units of the numeraire currency), or, under flexible exchange rates, adjust *via* the exchange rate to maintain these trade balances at constant levels, $-B_i^{K0}$. In the latter case, B_i^{K0} represents an exogenously given inflow of capital into country *i*, which must, for consistency, have the property that the sum for all countries equals zero.

With these remarks, the reasons for most of the equations in Table 5.1 should be clear. Equations (1) and (2) are the supply functions for the export and home sectors, respectively. Both depend on prices of all home and imported goods, reflecting their use as intermediate inputs in production. Equations (3) and (4) are the demand functions for imports and for home goods, respectively. The inclusion of home and export supplies in these functions again reflects the demand for intermediate inputs.

Equations (5) and (6) determine the domestic prices of exports and imports in terms of corresponding world prices, exchange rates, and tariffs. Equation (7) defines expenditure as the sum of an exogenous component, E_i^0, and of the tariff revenue.

Equations (1) to (7) each determine the variable that appears on the left-hand side. The prices of home goods, on the other hand, are determined implicitly by the market-equilibrium condition in equation (8). Likewise, world prices are determined by the market-equilibrium condition in equation (9), which adds up and equates the supplies of exports and the demands for imports from all countries.

Trade balances are defined in equation (10) by adding up net exports for all of a country's tradeable industries, valued at world prices. The exchange regime is represented by either equation (11a) for fixed exchange rates or equation (11b) for flexible exchange rates. In the fixed case, each country's exchange rate, R_i, is set exogenously equal to its pegged value, R_i^0. In the flexible case, on the other hand, we form exchange-market equilibrium conditions for all but one of the countries by setting the sum of their trade balances and their exogenous capital inflows equal to zero. Only $m-1$ of the markets need to be cleared explicitly, since the homogeneity of the system assures that if these are cleared, the omitted market will be cleared as well. However, to remove the indeterminacy of prices and exchange rates that would otherwise arise, we must then specify a numeraire. This is done in the last of equations (11b), where we fix the exchange rate of country *m*.

The selection of the numeraire is not trivial in this model, since exogenous capital flows are specified in units of the numeraire. As exchange rates change, the values of these flows in local currency change, unless it is the numeraire, and this affects the equilibrium that is ultimately reached. In our applications of the model in this paper, we have chosen the United States dollar as the numeraire.

Equations (1) to (11) are together sufficient to determine all of the endogenous variables that they contain. Equation (12) then determines employment in each industry and country as a function of these variables. Employment in this version of the model is entirely demand-determined, the assumption being that labour markets do not clear in the relevant short run and that there is sufficient available unemployed labour to satisfy whatever increases in demand occur. Nominal wages, accordingly, are taken as exogenous, and the employment changes that are implied by the model indicate changes in labour-market disequilibrium.

DERIVATION OF FUNCTIONAL FORMS

Explicit supply and demand functions for use in the model were derived from utility and profit-maximisation behaviour on the part of consumers and firms, assuming explicit utility and production functions. Details of these derivations are contained in a working paper, which can be consulted for further information.[3] Here we will merely report the assumptions that were made and the results.

Since both producers and consumers in our model are demanders of goods, and since each tradeable industry has both imported and home-produced goods available to demanders, it was necessary first to characterise the choice between these two sources of goods. This was accomplished by assuming the existence of functions for each industry that aggregate the services of home and imported goods and which then enter as arguments for the utility and production functions. To assure some flexibility in selecting the degree of substitution between home and imported goods, these aggregation functions were specified as constant elasticity of substitution (CES) functions. The elasticity parameters of these functions for each industry were then inferred from published econometric estimates of import demand elasticities.[4]

To obtain demand functions for consumers, we then specified a Cobb-Douglas utility function. Its arguments were these aggregates of consumption of home and imported tradeable goods plus the consumption levels themselves of non-tradeables. By maximising this utility function subject to the constraint of a given level of expenditure, we obtained the consumers' demand functions for each industry. The differentiated forms of these demand functions appear below as equations (13) for imported goods and (14) for home goods.[5]

$$(13)\quad \hat{C}^M_{ij} = \hat{E}_i + \theta^H_{ij}(\sigma_{ij} - 1)\hat{p}^H_{ij} - (\theta^M_{ij} + \theta^H_{ij}\sigma_{ij})\hat{p}^M_{ij} \qquad i = 1, \ldots, m;\ j = 1, \ldots, n$$

$$(14a)\quad \hat{C}^H_{ij} = \hat{E}_i - (\theta^H_{ij} + \theta^M_{ij}\sigma_{ij})\hat{p}^H_{ij} + \theta^M_{ij}(\sigma_{ij} - 1)\hat{p}^M_{ij} \qquad i = 1, \ldots, m;\ j = 1, \ldots, n \text{ (tradeables)}$$

$$(14b)\quad \hat{C}^H_{ij} = \hat{E}_i - \hat{p}^H_{ij} \qquad i = 1, \ldots, m;\ j = n+1, \ldots, n' \text{ (non-tradeables)}$$

where C^M_{ij}, C^H_{ij} = consumer demand in country i for imported and home-produced products of industry j,

$\theta^M_{ij}, \theta^H_{ij}$ = initial shares of demand in country i for imported and home-produced products of industry j, and

σ_{ij} = elasticity of substitution in country i between imported and home produced products of industry j.

Notice that these demands depend only on expenditure and on the home and import prices of the own industry. Prices of other goods do not appear, since the assumption of a Cobb-Douglas utility function forces all cross-elasticities of demand to be zero.

To derive the behaviour of firms, we assumed in this version of the model that production functions were characterised by fixed coefficients among the home-import aggregates for each industry and between these and an aggregate of primary factors as well.[6] The aggregate function for primary factors (labour and capital) was also specified as CES.[7] For each industry, production functions were assumed to be identical across countries. While the model could easily accommodate different input-output data for each country, we lacked the time and resources to gather and process the requisite data.

By solving the profit-maximisation problem for the firm, subject to the constraints of its production technology and its given capital stock, we obtained the following supply functions for the export and home sectors:

$$(15)\quad \hat{S}^X_{ij} = \varepsilon_j\hat{p}^X_{ij} - \varepsilon_j \sum_{k=1}^{n} b_{kj}[\theta^H_{ik}\hat{p}^H_{ik} + \theta^M_{ik}\hat{p}^M_{ik}] - \varepsilon_j \sum_{k=n+1}^{n'} b_{kj}\hat{p}^H_{ik} - \varepsilon_j b^0_j \hat{w}_i + \hat{K}^X_{ij} \qquad i = 1, \ldots, m;\ j = 1, \ldots, n$$

$$(16)\quad \hat{S}^H_{ij} = \varepsilon_j\hat{p}^H_{ij} - \varepsilon_j \sum_{k=1}^{n} b_{kj}[\theta^H_{ik}\hat{p}^H_{ik} + \theta^M_{ik}\hat{p}^H_{ik}] - \varepsilon_j \sum_{k=n+1}^{n'} b_{kj}\hat{p}^H_{ik} - \varepsilon_j b^0_j \hat{w}_i + \hat{K}^H_{ij} \qquad i = 1, \ldots, m;\ j = 1, \ldots, n'$$

where ε_j = supply elasticity of industry j,
b_{kj} = input-output coefficient for use of good k as input in industry j, and
b_j^0 = value-added share of industry j.

The same problem also yields the following demand functions for imported and home-produced intermediate inputs:

(17) $\hat{Z}_{ij}^M = \hat{Q}_i - \theta_{ij}^H \sigma_{ij} [\hat{p}_{ij}^M - \hat{p}_{ij}^H]$ $\quad i = 1, \ldots, m; j = 1, \ldots, n$

(18a) $\hat{Z}_{ij}^H = \hat{Q}_i + \theta_{ij}^M \sigma_{ij} [\hat{p}_{ij}^M - \hat{p}_{ij}^H]$
$i = 1, \ldots, m;\ j = 1, \ldots, n$ (tradeable)

(18b) $\hat{Z}_{ij}^H = \hat{Q}_i$ $\quad i = 1, \ldots, m; j = n+1, \ldots, n'$ (non-tradeable)

where Z_{ij}^M, Z_{ij}^H = demand for imported and home-produced inputs of good j by an arbitrary sector of country i, and
Q_i = supply of the demanding sector ($Q_i = S_{ik}^X$, $k = 1, \ldots, n$ and S_{ik}^H, $k = 1, \ldots, n'$).

Unlike the consumers' demand functions, the firms' supply functions do depend on prices in all industries, since all potentially provide intermediate inputs. Also, while the firms' demand functions do not directly involve cross-price effects, they do have such effects indirectly, since they depend on supplies, which in turn depend on all prices. Thus, the markets in our model turn out to be very interconnected.

Finally, the firms' demands for labour were also derived from the maximisation problem as follows:

(19a) $$\hat{L}_{ij} = \gamma_{ij}^X \left[\frac{1}{\theta_{ij}^L} \hat{S}_{ij}^X + \frac{\theta_{ij}^K}{\theta_{ij}^L} \hat{K}_{ij}^X \right] + \left(1 - \gamma_{ij}^X \right) \left[\frac{1}{\theta_{ij}^L} \hat{S}_{ij}^H + \frac{\theta_{ij}^K}{\theta_{ij}^L} \hat{K}_{ij}^H \right]$$

$i = 1, \ldots, m; j = 1, \ldots, n$ (tradeable)

(19b) $\hat{L}_{ij} = \frac{1}{\theta_{ij}^L} \hat{S}_{ij}^H + \frac{\theta_{ij}^K}{\theta_{ij}^L} \hat{K}_{ij}^H$ $\quad i = 1, \ldots, m; j = n+1, \ldots, n'$ (non-tradeable)

where γ_{ij}^X = share of exports in total production of industry j, country i, and
θ_{ij}^L, θ_{ij}^K = labour and capital shares of value-added in industry j, country i.

Note that these labour-demand functions, like the supply functions on which they are based, do depend indirectly on wages, both nominal and real. The index of real wages in each industry is different, however, based upon the coefficients of the various price terms that enter the supply functions.

All of these supply and demand functions were derived at the level of the individual firm and consumer and had to be aggregated to obtain the corresponding functions for the economy as a whole. Aggregation of supplies was trivial, given our assumption of linearly homogeneous technologies. Aggregation of demand, however, was more difficult, since demanders of a given good include all other industries as well as consumers, each with a different demand function. Adding these up and differentiating, we obtained the following demand functions for the country as a whole:

$$(20)\quad \hat{D}^M_{ij} = -[v_{ijo} + \theta^H_{ij}(\sigma_{ij} - v_{ijo})]\hat{p}^M_{ij} + \theta^H_{ij}(\sigma_{ij} - v_{ijo})\hat{p}^H_{ij} + v_{ijo}\hat{E}_i + \sum_{k=1}^{n} v_{ijk}\left[\gamma^X_{ik}\hat{S}^X_{ik} + \left(1 - \gamma^X_{ik}\right)\hat{S}^H_{ik}\right] + \sum_{k=n+1}^{n'} v_{ijk}\hat{S}^H_{ik} \qquad i = 1, \ldots, m;\ j = 1, \ldots, n$$

$$(21a)\quad \hat{D}^H_{ij} = -[v_{ijo} + \theta^M_{ij}(\sigma_{ij} - v_{ijo})]\hat{p}^H_{ij} + \theta^M_{ij}(\sigma_{ij} - v_{ijo})\hat{p}^M_{ij} + v_{ijo}\hat{E}_i + \sum_{k=1}^{n} v_{ijk}[\gamma^X_{ik}\hat{S}^X_{ik} + (1 - \gamma^X_{ik})\hat{S}^H_{ik}] + \sum_{k=n+1}^{n'} v_{ijk}\hat{S}^H_{ik} \qquad i = 1, \ldots, m;\ j = 1, \ldots, n \text{ (tradeable)}$$

$$(21b)\quad \hat{D}^H_{ij} = -v_{ijo}\hat{p}^H_{ij} + v_{ijo}\hat{E}_i + \sum_{k=1}^{n} v_{ijk}[\gamma^X_{ik}\hat{S}^X_{ik} + (1 - \gamma^X_{ik})\hat{S}^H_{ik}] + \sum_{k=n+1}^{n'} v_{ijk}\hat{S}^H_{ik} \qquad i = 1, \ldots, m;\ j = n+1, \ldots, n' \text{ (non-tradeable)}$$

where v_{ijo} = share of consumer demand in total demand for good j in country i, and

v_{ijk} = demand by industry k for good j as a share of total demand for good j in country i.

Once the unspecified functions in equations (1) to (4) and (12) to (13) are replaced with appropriately indexed versions of equations (15), (16), (20), (21) and (19), the model is complete. In addition to the elasticity parameters and input-output coefficients already discussed, its solution requires information on exports, imports, total production, and tariffs for each country and industry to be included. We turn now to a description of the selection of countries and industries used for the current application of the model.

APPLICATION OF THE MODEL

The model we have just described is designed to take into account as many as possible of the interconnections among industries and countries at the micro-economic level. The benefit of this, as we shall see, is that it enables us to examine a variety of economic issues that other models cannot address, either because they are too highly aggregated, or because they are specified only in partial equilibrium terms. The cost, on the other hand, is that our model is far too large to be able to say anything concrete without further specification of its parameters. Thus, to use the model, we must apply it to a realistic selection of countries and industries using, as far as possible, actual data to generate the parameters.

We therefore selected eighteen of the world's major industrialised countries as our focus for analysis and proceeded to treat them as though they constituted a closed economic system. The reason for this choice was the compilation of detailed information on *ad valorem* tariffs and imports for these countries, in both printed and machine-readable form by the General Agreement on Tariffs and Trade (GATT).[8] From this source we obtained data on trade for 1970 together with post-Kennedy Round of multilateral trade negotiation (1972) tariffs. We used the trade data for 1970 to conform to that year's output and employment data, which were the latest available at the time that our initial data base was being constructed.[9] The eighteen countries covered were as follows:

Australia	Italy
Austria	Japan
Belgium–Luxembourg	Netherlands
Canada	New Zealand
Denmark	Norway
Finland	Sweden
France	Switzerland
West Germany	United Kingdom
Ireland	United States

Information on output and employment was obtained directly or otherwise estimated from the United Nations and from the OECD publications on national accounts and labour statistics.[10] We used a classification of industries based upon the International Standard Industrial Classification (ISIC), broken down into tradeables and non-tradeables. For manufacturing industries we used the three-digit ISIC data, while for the remaining industries, mostly non-tradeable, we remained at the more aggregated one-digit level. The twenty-nine industries were as follows:

TRADEABLES

ISIC Group	*Description*
1	Agriculture, hunting, forestry and fishing
310	Food, beverages and tobacco
321	Textiles
322	Wearing apparel excluding footwear
323	Leather and leather and fur products
324	Footwear
331	Wood products excluding furniture
332	Furniture and fixtures excluding metal
341	Paper and paper products
342	Printing, publishing
35A	Industrial chemicals (351); other chemical products (352)
35B	Petroleum refineries (353); miscellaneous products of petroleum and coal (354)
355	Rubber products
36A	Pottery, china and earthenware (361); other non-metallic mineral products (369)
362	Glass and glass products
371	Iron and steel basic industries
372	Non-ferrous metal basic industries
381	Metal products excluding machinery, *et cetera*
382	Machinery excluding electrical
383	Electrical machinery, apparatus, *et cetera*
384	Transport equipment
38A	Plastic products, n.e.c. (356); professional, photographic goods, *et cetera* (385); other manufacturing industries (390)

NON-TRADEABLES

ISIC Group	*Description*
2	Mining and quarrying
4	Electricity, gas and water
5	Construction
6	Wholesale and retail trade, restaurants, and hotels
7	Transport, storage and communication
8	Finance, insurance, real estate *et cetera*
9	Community, social and personal services

Given appropriate data for the above countries and industries, solution of the model should, in principle, be straightforward. By differentiating all of the equations of the model, we obtained a system of linear equations relating changes in all of the variables of the system. The coefficients in each of these linear equations were evaluated using the data and elasticity information we had collected. All that remained was to solve the system. Since the system was linear, it could, in principle, be solved by any of a variety of means.

In fact, however, the size of the model made this difficult. With 18 countries and 29 industries, what we have represented here as single equations each become a large number of separate equations to be solved. Depending on how many of these equations are first eliminated by substitution, the number of equations in the model could be as large as 6000. Such a large system strains the capacity of even high-speed computers. And while the number of equations can be reduced substantially by prior substitutions, the substitutions themselves involve a tremendous amount of computation. It was to avoid these difficulties that, in earlier applications of the model, we introduced a number of approximations to reduce the amount of simultaneity in the system.[11]

For this paper, however, we were able to obtain exact solutions. To do so, we first devised a computer program that processes large partitioned matrices in which many of the partitioned blocks contain only zeros and which avoids costly but meaningless computations involving these zeros. Second, we used a Fortran programming technique known as dynamic dimensioning to avoid wasting computer memory space on these empty blocks, even though the contents of all blocks change during the course of the solution. And finally, we applied these techniques first to each of the eighteen countries separately, using only equations (1) to (8) and (10) to solve for their supplies and demands of traded goods in terms of world prices, exchange rates and exogenous variables, and then used equations (9) and (11) to complete the solution. The resulting computer program is costly, but within reason.

The results reported in the remaining sections of this paper, then, were obtained from successive runs of this solution program, each with different values chosen for the exogenous variables. Several of the problems to be dealt with involve analysing the effects of a change in a particular exogenous variable, such as the exchange rate, occurring in only one of the countries. But we also wished to compare the effects of such changes for each country, suggesting the need for eighteen separate runs of the program. To avoid the high cost of such a large number of runs, we adapted the program to handle such problems in a single run. The adaptation required, however, that we not compute the cross-effects of an exogenous change in one country on variables in another. Thus, for example, we report below the effects of exchange-rate changes in each country on output in the same country, but have not computed the effects on variables in other countries, even though these would be available from our model at additional cost.

With the exception just mentioned, the solution program computes the changes in all of the endogenous variables of the model for all countries and industries. This, of course, is far more information than we are able to make use of in this paper. Readers who are interested in additional details of the solutions may obtain them from us at cost.

II EFFECTS OF EXOGENOUS EXCHANGE-RATE CHANGES

Our model suggests, and its solution confirms, a number of channels through which industries can be affected by changes in the exchange rate of the country in which they operate. These will be discussed below, but first let us report what these effects turned out to be, as calculated from our model.

We ran our solution program with positive exchange-rate changes for each country separately. As defined, an exchange-rate increase represents a devaluation of the currency in question. From the solution, we took the ratio of the percentage change in output, by industry, to the percentage change in the exchange rate. These ratios are reported for each country and industry in Table 5.2, as the exchange-rate elasticity of output (EREO). Each column represents the solution of the model for a devaluation of the currency of the country indicated, with all other exchange rates held fixed.

It is clear from the table that the vast majority of industries are affected positively by a devaluation of their countries' currencies, but there is also considerable variation across both countries and industries in the size of this response. In a few cases, the expansion is considerably larger than the exchange-rate change that causes it (the elasticity is larger than one), but the responses vary all the way down to zero and a few are even negative.

It will be recalled that a primary objective of this paper is to determine what it is about a country and industry that determines the size of the exchange-rate response. To do so, we will look at the problem first in theoretical terms, within the context of our model. Then, we will examine the numerical results to see to what extent they confirm our theoretical expectations.[12]

THE EXPORT EFFECT

The most obvious effect of a devaluation of a country's currency is that it raises the domestic prices of both exported and imported goods.

TABLE 5.2

Exchange-rate Elasticities of Output by Industry and Country

	Australia	*Austria*	*Belgium-Luxemburg*	*Canada*	*Denmark*	*Finland*
1	0.18	0.10	0.15	0.11	0.16	0.11
310	0.31	−0.03	0.11	0.05	0.19	−0.05
321	2.55	2.33	2.56	0.53	2.11	1.98
322	−0.04	2.84	4.31	0.21	4.21	3.33
323	5.78	4.36	5.39	3.83	5.85	6.24
324	−0.01	3.08	3.58	0.54	3.39	2.54
331	0.18	2.60	1.92	1.42	1.09	1.94
332	−0.04	0.26	0.72	0.34	1.71	0.48
341	0.56	2.04	2.74	2.34	1.54	3.18
342	0.24	0.75	0.92	0.36	0.34	0.35
35A	0.79	0.99	1.69	0.87	1.29	1.09
35B	4.14	0.26	0.70	1.81	1.40	0.51
355	0.88	2.12	3.36	1.30	2.43	1.80
36A	0.38	1.10	1.60	1.20	0.85	0.70
362	0.53	1.51	2.70	0.58	1.39	1.16
371	0.86	2.52	3.86	1.54	3.04	2.66
372	2.87	1.78	2.42	2.41	1.55	1.63
381	0.30	0.99	1.67	0.61	0.97	0.92
382	0.19	1.21	1.67	0.93	1.46	0.75
383	0.18	0.75	1.37	0.45	1.19	0.64
384	0.20	0.47	1.26	0.40	0.52	0.62
38A	0.61	2.90	2.33	0.78	2.41	1.27
2	1.17	0.80	1.38	1.17	0.30	0.71
4	0.09	0.22	0.29	0.13	0.07	0.27
5	−0.11	−0.12	−0.18	−0.12	−0.18	−0.14
6	0.02	0.08	0.10	0.03	0.02	0.10
7	0.14	0.28	0.38	0.21	0.12	0.36
8	0.07	0.12	0.16	0.09	0.05	0.12
9	−0.05	−0.05	−0.05	−0.05	−0.04	−0.05

	France	*Germany*	*Ireland*	*Italy*	*Japan*	*Netherlands*
1	0.09	0.07	0.22	0.12	0.07	0.18
310	0.09	−0.02	0.22	0.09	−0.03	0.14
321	1.38	1.51	2.52	2.15	0.97	2.42
322	1.26	1.10	4.18	4.05	1.59	2.91
323	3.24	2.44	5.21	5.11	3.05	5.37
324	1.29	0.96	2.40	5.07	3.50	1.71
331	0.38	0.52	0.92	0.68	0.37	0.79
332	0.23	0.49	0.26	0.87	0.07	1.14
341	0.86	1.10	1.80	0.90	0.31	2.24
342	0.19	0.38	0.63	0.46	0.10	0.45
35A	0.94	0.86	1.28	0.81	0.43	1.43

TABLE 5.2 (*contd*)

	France	*Germany*	*Ireland*	*Italy*	*Japan*	*Netherlands*
35B	0.22	0.97	2.19	1.85	0.32	1.52
355	1.89	1.21	2.91	1.56	0.59	2.14
36A	0.41	0.61	2.25	0.73	0.26	1.17
362	0.89	0.90	1.75	0.82	0.35	1.82
371	2.24	1.65	1.59	1.23	0.94	2.97
372	1.30	1.46	2.63	1.16	0.63	2.12
381	0.43	0.78	1.78	0.71	0.34	1.02
382	0.55	1.07	2.48	1.27	0.31	1.41
383	0.48	0.56	1.19	0.55	0.30	1.07
384	0.53	0.71	0.39	0.53	0.22	0.66
38A	0.66	1.51	2.61	1.19	0.72	3.37
2	0.28	0.82	1.29	0.95	0.40	1.29
4	0.11	0.14	0.13	0.10	0.09	0.20
5	−0.08	−0.09	−0.21	−0.12	−0.05	−0.16
6	0.03	0.05	0.08	0.04	0.04	0.08
7	0.14	0.20	0.23	0.16	0.12	0.29
8	0.06	0.10	0.11	0.08	0.06	0.14
9	−0.03	−0.04	−0.04	−0.04	−0.02	−0.05

	New Zealand	*Norway*	*Sweden*	*Switzerland*	*UK*	*US*
1	0.39	0.13	0.08	0.11	0.08	0.03
310	0.64	0.11	−0.07	0.03	0.01	0.01
321	2.84	1.43	1.58	2.31	1.50	0.31
322	−0.03	1.37	1.94	1.56	1.07	0.18
323	5.87	5.87	5.28	2.93	3.36	1.05
324	−0.01	1.36	2.42	1.50	0.98	0.22
331	1.09	0.97	1.52	0.55	0.54	0.35
332	−0.08	0.55	0.94	0.47	0.18	0.05
341	1.56	2.80	3.00	1.41	0.97	0.34
342	0.36	0.22	0.30	0.62	0.26	0.08
35A	0.91	1.34	1.13	1.50	1.10	0.25
35B	0.32	0.97	0.97	7.79	3.58	0.45
355	0.79	2.11	2.02	2.04	1.50	0.36
36A	0.44	1.45	0.71	0.61	0.82	0.20
362	0.80	0.91	1.54	1.17	0.84	0.22
371	0.90	3.81	2.98	1.98	2.30	0.51
372	1.58	2.66	2.52	1.86	2.43	0.56
381	0.43	1.05	1.04	0.89	0.78	0.18
382	0.20	1.09	1.43	1.65	0.83	0.32
383	0.26	0.78	0.93	0.85	0.41	0.16
384	0.30	0.66	0.81	0.53	0.37	0.17
38A	1.71	1.45	1.99	2.61	1.32	0.31
2	0.25	1.09	1.03	0.69	1.01	0.30
4	0.10	0.20	0.20	0.12	0.07	0.03

TABLE 5.2 (*contd*)

	New Zealand	*Norway*	*Sweden*	*Switzerland*	*UK*	*US*
5	−0.13	−0.17	−0.14	−0.17	−0.13	−0.03
6	0.04	0.06	0.06	0.05	0.03	0.01
7	0.15	0.27	0.28	0.17	0.12	0.05
8	0.05	0.11	0.11	0.10	0.06	0.02
9	−0.05	−0.05	−0.05	−0.05	−0.04	−0.01

Thus, the first channel through which a devaluation would be expected to affect output is via the price responsiveness of the export sector of each tradeable industry. Assuming, for the moment, that a devaluation causes export prices to rise by the same percentage as the exchange rate, the effect on the export sector of each industry will depend upon its elasticity of supply. In addition, this effect on the export sector will be reflected in an increase in output for the entire industry that will be larger, in percentage terms, the larger is the export sector as compared to the home sector. *These considerations, then, suggest that the EREO of each industry should be positively related to both the elasticity of supply of the industry and the share of exports in total production.*

THE IMPORT SUBSTITUTION EFFECT

The rise in import prices also should have an effect on output, though it is somewhat less direct. As the import price rises, demanders will substitute away from imports and towards domestically produced goods. As they do so, they will bid up the home price in the industry and thus stimulate production in the home sector as well. This effect is limited, both by the importance of imports in demand and by the willingness of demanders to substitute between imports and home goods. *We would therefore expect two additional determinants of the EREO to be the share of imports in total demand and the elasticity of substitution between imported and home-produced goods.*[13]

THE WORLD PRICE EFFECT

Both the export effect and the import substitution effect depend on the devaluation raising the domestic prices of exports and imports. However, to the extent that these prices do rise, the increased supply of exports and the reduced demand for imports will both tend to depress the world price in the industry. This fall in the world price will to some extent offset both of the direct effects previously mentioned and thus reduce the size of the EREO. Now the decline in the world price will be greater, the greater are the country's exports and imports in the industry as shares of the corresponding world supply and demand. Thus, we would expect the EREO to be negatively related to these shares. *In addition, since both of these shares are likely to depend heavily on the size of the industry as a whole, we would expect the EREO to be negatively related to the value of production.*

THE INTER-INDUSTRY SALES EFFECT

So far we have considered each industry in isolation, without taking into account the roles that might be played by interactions among industries via the input-output structure of the economy. One such role arises from the difference between the responses to a devaluation on the part of consumers and firms as demanders. By causing prices and outputs generally to rise, a devaluation will cause an increase in demands for intermediate inputs, whether or not they happen to be tradable. No such increase is likely, however, on the part of consumers, whose total expenditure is more or less held fixed.[14] Thus, we would expect an additional stimulation to output even in non-tradeable industries, to the extent that they sell a large part of their product to intermediate users. *The EREO, then, should depend negatively on the share of final demand in total demand for an industry.*

THE INTER-INDUSTRY PURCHASES EFFECT

Just as an industry will benefit, under a devaluation, from sales to other industries, it will also be harmed by the need to purchase inputs itself from these industries. For as the prices of goods generally rise, industries which rely heavily on produced, as opposed to primary, inputs will experience an increase in costs. As long as the wage remains fixed, on the other hand, industries with a low dependence on produced inputs will experience very little increase in costs. *Thus, we would expect the EREO to depend positively on the labour share of the industry.*

THE EXPENDITURE EFFECT

In general one might expect consumer expenditure to change as a result of a devaluation, so that the inter-country differences in EREOs would depend on the size and direction of that change. However, since our model does not allow for such expenditure effects as they are usually specified, we cannot explore this issue in any detail.[15] What our model does contain is a dependence of expenditure on the economy's tariff revenue. Given the level of tariffs, this revenue depends on import prices and on the quantity of imports, both of which change, but in opposite directions, with a devaluation. It is not clear, *a priori*, what the net effect on tariff revenue will be. But it should be kept in mind as a possible source of explanation for results of the model which might otherwise be incomprehensible.

Now that we have seen a variety of channels through which exchange rates can affect outputs, it remains to examine the results computed by our model to determine, if possible, which of these channels are most important. Mere inspection of Table 5.2 is clearly inadequate for this purpose. Instead, we have tested for the presence of these effects by computing correlations between the results reported in Table 5.2 and the exogenous variables that we found, in the discussion above, to be likely determinants of the EREO. These correlations are reported in Table 5.3. It should be made clear that, in spite of their appearance, these correlations are *not* the equivalent of estimating a multiple regression equation, which would be inappropriate here since there was nothing stochastic about the generation of the EREO. They are presented merely as a convenient means of describing how our complicated model works.

TABLE 5.3

Correlations of Exogenous Variables with the Exchange-rate Elasticity of Output

Exogenous variable	*Correlation with EREO*
Supply elasticity	.40[a]
Share of industry output exported	.82[a]
Substitution elasticity between imports and home goods	.27[a]
Share of imports in demand	.65[a]
Value of production	−.21[a]
Consumers' share of total demand	−.30[a]
Labour's share	.02

[a] Significant at the .99 level.

All of the correlations reported in Table 5.3 have the expected sign and are, with the exception of the labour share, significant. The largest correlations are clearly with the export and import shares, but correlations with the two elasticities and the consumers' share of total demand are also highly significant, confirming our insights into the workings of the model.

The small correlation for the labour-share variable suggests, however, that our understanding of the model is by no means perfect. We experimented with several other variables which we thought would capture the inter-industry purchases effect, but without success. At this point, we can only say that we are unable to comprehend fully the significance of inter-industry interactions.

III MULTILATERAL EXCHANGE-RATE CHANGES

So far we have confined our attention to the own-country effects of exchange-rate changes, and have incidentally also examined only relative and percentage changes rather than absolute magnitudes. To put these results into perspective, we report, briefly, in this section on a run of the model in which all exchange rates were assumed to change simultaneously.

The exchange-rate changes that we used were those that occurred from the end of the fourth quarter of 1973 to the end of the first quarter of 1977, using the United States dollar as the numeraire currency. The changes are reported as part of Table 5.4. It is evident that quite substantial changes in fact occurred during this period.

We solved the model with these exchange-rate movements as the only exogenous changes.[16] Space does not permit a very complete reporting of the results of this run. We present only the results of the model for total employment in each country, both in thousands of man-years and as a percentage of total employment. These are reported also in Table 5.4. It will be recalled that these employment changes were obtained on the basis of the estimated changes in output by industry, using equation (12). The most notable feature of these results is their lack of correspondence with the actual employment experience of these countries over the last few years. By and large, those countries which have been relatively weak over this period, such as Italy and the United Kingdom, also had depreciating currencies and are calculated as gaining substantial amounts of employment. Likewise, other countries whose general economic performance has been more favourable, such as Germany and Japan, are shown as losing employment.

The reason, of course, is that, in running our model, the only

TABLE 5.4

Actual Exchange-rate Changes, 1973:4 to 1977:1 and Computed Total Employment Changes by Country

Country	*Exchange-rate change (per cent)*[a]	*Employment change*[b] *Thousands of man-years*	*Per cent*
Australia	−25.9	587	11.4
Austria	17.1	−407	−14.7
Belgium-Luxembourg	12.9	−686	−18.4
Canada	−5.8	77	1.0
Denmark	7.5	−136	−6.6
Finland	1.2	−85	−4.1
France	−5.2	−42	−0.2
West Germany	13.2	−2598	−10.9
Ireland	−26.0	232	22.6
Italy	−31.5	4142	26.0
Japan	0.9	−910	−1.9
Netherlands	13.3	−534	−11.8
New Zealand	−32.7	263	26.2
Norway	9.4	−115	−7.9
Sweden	9.3	−263	−7.1
Switzerland	27.6	−560	−20.1
United Kingdom	−26.0	4079	17.2
United States	0.0	−465	−0.6

SOURCE *International Financial Statistics* (Washington: International Monetary Fund, 1977).

[a] Percentage change in United States dollar price of local currency.

[b] Calculated from model with exchange-rate changes in all countries simultaneously.

exogenous changes we included were the changes in exchange rates. It is obvious from our results that the observed exchange-rate changes must in large part have been the consequences of changes in other of the variables that we have taken as exogenous and held constant. Our calculations are therefore very far from capturing reality. They should be viewed only as indicating the strength of the influence of exchange rates, rather than as an attempt to explain recent economic performance. Note in particular that our calculations assume both that money wages are constant and aggregate nominal expenditure is (almost) constant. These are only two of the variables that an attempt to duplicate the real-world experience of the period would have to take into account.

The strength of the employment effects of exchange-rate changes, as calculated, is substantial. The exchange-rate changes that were used in the calculations are, of course, very large. But they are changes that actually occurred. If they had occurred in isolation, they would have resulted in changes in employment in the millions of workers in several countries.

Not surprisingly, there is in Table 5.4 a rough negative correspondence between the changes in exchange rates and employment. Those countries whose currencies depreciated the most tended to be calculated as experiencing the greatest gains in employment, and vice versa. This correspondence is, however, by no means perfect. The French franc, for example, depreciated against the dollar, but the effect on French employment was negative. Similarly, Austria experienced a greater appreciation than Belgium–Luxembourg, but the Austrian loss of employment was smaller. Such differences illustrate the general equilibrium character of our model, where it is impossible to infer with certainty the effects on any one country from its own exchange rate alone. Changes among other currencies also must be taken into account.

These results, together with our previous calculations, thus suggest that exchange-rate changes are capable of causing substantial dislocation. But, of course, this is not necessarily a valid objection to flexible exchange rates if fluctuations occur in response to other real changes in the national economies. Since these other changes appear to have been very important, it strongly indicates the need for a better understanding of their causes.

IV OTHER EXOGENOUS CHANGES

We have just seen from our results in the preceding section the importance of considering the causes of exchange-rate changes rather than taking these changes to be exogenous. In this section, we take a step in this direction by using our model to examine the effects of exogenous changes other than exchange rates and compare the solutions under both fixed and flexible exchange-rate regimes. We consider two such changes: a 1 per cent increase in consumer expenditure and a 1 per cent increase in the money wage. Again our model generates far more information than we can report here, and we will have to confine ourselves to a limited summary of the results.

In Table 5.5, we present the percentage changes in total employment calculated, using our model for each of these changes and for each of the eighteen countries. Each line of the table represents the results for the indicated country of an increase in wages or expenditure for that country

TABLE 5.5

Percentage Changes in Total Employment by Country Caused by Increases in Wages and Expenditure

	Effects of 1% increase in money wage		*Effects of 1% increase in expenditure*	
Country	*Fixed exchange rates*	*Flexible exchange rates*	*Fixed exchange rates*	*Flexible exchange rates*
Australia	−1.46	−1.20	0.88	1.06
Austria	−1.88	−1.35	0.87	1.15
Belgium-Luxembourg	−2.03	−1.15	0.64	1.01
Canada	−1.49	−1.20	0.89	1.07
Denmark	−1.55	−1.30	0.87	1.14
Finland	−1.88	−1.34	0.89	1.14
France	−1.54	−1.27	0.94	1.11
Germany	−1.65	−1.20	0.85	1.05
Ireland	−1.94	−1.47	0.78	1.23
Italy	−1.75	−1.32	0.89	1.12
Japan	−1.49	−1.30	1.02	1.12
Netherlands	−1.68	−1.24	0.79	1.09
New Zealand	−1.64	−1.19	0.76	1.05
Norway	−1.67	−1.28	0.82	1.11
Sweden	−1.64	−1.19	0.85	1.06
Switzerland	−1.77	−1.30	0.80	1.14
United Kingdom	−1.55	−1.18	0.83	1.05
United States	−1.29	−1.21	1.03	1.08

alone, all exogenous variables in all other countries remaining constant. It is evident that the exogenous wage increase has a negative overall effect on employment because production costs rise, which in turn depresses output. The exogenous increase in expenditure has a positive overall effect on employment because it increases aggregate demand and therefore prices and output.

The first thing to notice about the results in Table 5.5 is the small amount of variation among countries. This is not too surprising when we recall that the usual Keynesian macro-economic determinants of employment are excluded from our model. Thus our employment results reflect only micro-economic considerations of supply and demand. Since we have assumed all countries to share identical technologies, we have not allowed very much scope for inter-country variations in response to a given kind of exogenous change.

There are, however, several differences among the countries that are worth noting. Most striking, perhaps, is the apparent dependence, under fixed exchange rates, of the effects of both wage and expenditure increases on country size. In the case of the wage increase, the greatest losses were posted by the smallest countries, such as Belgium and Ireland, and the smallest loss occurred in the United States. A similar (but positive) pattern appears, under fixed rates, for the expenditure increase, with Japan and the United States expanding the most.

The reason for both of these results would seem to be that domestic expenditure in a large country is more readily contained within that country than it would be in a small country, for any effort by residents of a large country to divert expenditure abroad will be met by rising world prices. Thus, when wages rise in any country, this tends to raise domestic prices and cause substitution towards imports. In a small country, this is the end of the story and output and employment simply decline. But in a large country, the increased demand for imports puts upward pressure on world prices which then diverts a part of the demand back home again. Similarly, an increase in expenditure in any country will raise demand for both domestic and imported goods. The resulting upward pressure on the prices of domestic goods will divert additional demand toward imports. But this diversion of demand will be lessened for a large country, again, by a rise in world prices.[17]

These patterns of response under fixed exchange rates do not appear under flexible exchange rates. While there is still a small amount of inter-country variation in the two columns of Table 5.5 that refer to flexible exchange rates, that variation does not appear to be correlated with country size. The reason is that exchange-rate flexibility gives even a small country a mechanism to prevent demand from being diverted abroad. Increases in either wages or expenditure in a country cause its currency to be devalued, with the result that while world prices are not affected, the prices paid by importers and received by exporters are.

This, incidentally, also explains another result that is evident in Table 5.5. Exchange-rate flexibility has a favourable effect on employment for both exogenous changes. When wages increase, employment falls less in all countries under flexible rates than under fixed rates. And when expenditure increases, the increase in employment is greater under flexible exchange rates. Also, for reasons already explained, this advantage is most pronounced for the smaller countries.

Space has prevented us, in this section, from reporting any detailed results by industry, even though such results were generated by our model. But the question might arise as to whether what has been seen here to hold in the aggregate is also true of every individual industry. Naturally, not too many industries can behave differently from the economy as a whole, without altering aggregate behaviour. But it is conceivable for a minority of industries to respond differently. Did this happen?

The answer is that it did, in several ways. First, the aggregate expansion that was caused by an increase in expenditure under fixed exchange rates did not extend to every industry in every country. Instead, in every country except the United States, there were several industries whose outputs fell, the greatest numbers of these being in the smallest countries. For most of these, the reason for the decline appears to be that they were heavily dependent on export sales. As a result, they failed to capture much of the increase in domestic demand, but none the less had to pay higher prices for their inputs, as the expenditure increase caused domestic prices to rise.

On the other hand, with flexible exchange rates, every industry in every country was found to expand as a result of the increase in domestic expenditure. For then, even the export sectors could benefit from the resulting depreciation.

This phenomenon did not arise for the increase in wages. Here all industries in all countries, almost without exception, suffered loss of output under both fixed and flexible exchange rates. The reason of course is that a wage increase acts on the cost side of an industry's operations. It therefore affects all industries similarly, regardless of whether they produce for home or export markets.

Finally, we attempted to determine whether the benefit from exchange-rate flexibility that we noted in the aggregate extended to all separate industries. We computed, for both the wage and expenditure increases, the difference between the changes in industry outputs under flexible and under fixed rates. These differences were positive for the majority of industries, but there was also a substantial minority for which the differences were negative. Thus, there were a number of industries, mostly again in the smaller countries, which expanded more or contracted less, in response to the exogenous changes, under fixed rather than flexible exchange rates.

To determine why these industries were hurt, we correlated the differences, between output responses under fixed and flexible rates, with all of the exogenous parameters of the model. The strongest correlations by far were found with the export and import shares (of supply and demand, respectively) of the industries. These correlations were positive, indicating that the industries which lose from exchange-rate flexibility are probably those in which there is little trade.

Our initial motivation in this section was to evaluate the adjustments necessitated by exchange-rate movements, taking into account the causes of these movements under a regime of flexible rates. The results on this issue are mixed. When the initial shock is an increase in wages, then the exchange rate moves so as to reduce the changes in output and employment caused by the shock. But when the shock is an increase in expenditure, then the exchange-rate moves so as to confine the increase within the country where it originated, and thus, for that country, increases the amount of adjustment that must be accomplished. Thus, the adjustment costs associated with a system of flexible exchange rates seem to depend on the nature of the shocks to which the economy is subject.

We should reiterate at this point that our model and results by no means mirror what the actual effects of exchange-rate changes have been in the past few years. None the less, we have established that exchange-rate changes cannot be looked at meaningfully in isolation from the important underlying changes in domestic exogenous variables that may be the proximate cause of exchange-market variations. Unfortunately, this complicates greatly the task of identifying the relevant adjustment costs. The most we can say on the basis of our results is that such costs can be plausibly large. If we were able to determine the magnitude and time pattern of the disequilibrium exchange rates, our EREO measures would be useful in estimating the adjustment costs. But this will have to await further research that is well beyond the scope of the present effort.

V CONCLUSION

In this paper, we have investigated the implications of exchange-rate changes for levels of output and employment in a disaggregated world economy. The first thing that we learned was that the sensitivity of industrial output to an exchange-rate change can be substantial. In a significant minority of industries, the percentage response of output was greater than the percentage change in the exchange rate itself.

More important, however, is the fact that there is considerable variation across industries and countries in the size of this response. There are even a number of industries in which output falls. The variations in response thus make it difficult to offset possible dislocations caused by exchange-rate changes. If all industries of a country were affected identically, then it might be feasible to use macroeconomic policies to anticipate exchange-rate movements and thus to prevent them from having any effect at all. But, in fact, it is likely to be difficult to find a policy that would affect each industry by just the right amount.

Our numerical results gave us more detail than was usable as to which particular industries would be most sensitive to exchange-rate changes. Accordingly, we tried to make some sense of the mass of results by identifying those characteristics of industries and countries which determine that sensitivity. We were able to identify, on theoretical grounds, six different channels through which exchange rates may affect output. Of these, the first five suggested observable characteristics of industries which we expected to be correlated, positively or negatively, with output changes. When we calculated these correlations, we found all to be of the expected sign and all but one to be highly significant. The only one of the effects which failed to be confirmed was the inter-industry purchases effect. The strongest effect by far appeared to be the direct effect of the exchange rate as a stimulant to exports, as reflected in the high correlation between output changes and export shares. But most of the less direct effects, which take into account general equilibrium interactions among sectors, industries, and countries, were also confirmed by the correlations. We therefore conclude that the complications introduced by a many-industry, many-country model, such as the one used here, do make a difference. A proper understanding of industrial sensitivity to exchange rates would not be possible in a purely partial-equilibrium context.

When we applied our model to the exchange-rate changes that have actually occurred since 1973, we found that, had they occurred in isolation from other exogenous changes, they would have caused tremendous dislocations. These dislocations would have followed a pattern, across countries, that is quite different from what actually occurred during this period. Our conclusion is that the exchange-rate changes that were observed were not in fact purely exogenous or the results of speculative or other non-real considerations. Instead, they must largely have been the result of real underlying changes in the economies involved.

Finally, we used the model to calculate the effects of two other exogenous changes under both fixed and flexible exchange rates. The purpose here was to learn whether floating exchange rates mitigate or exacerbate the dislocations caused by other exogenous shocks. For the case of an exogenous wage increase, we found that the exchange-rate changes caused under flexible exchange rates do tend to offset the effects of the wage increase itself. For an exogenous increase in expenditure, however, we found the exchange rate to have a reinforcing effect, so that the dislocations caused by the shock are larger under floating rates than under fixed rates. Thus, on grounds of adjustment costs alone, the relative desirability of fixed versus flexible exchange rates depends on the kinds of shocks to which the economy is subject.

NOTES

1. See Deardorff, Stern and Baum (1977), where an approximate solution of the current model was used for this purpose.
2. In addition, we have now succeeded in computing the exact solution of the model, so that the approximations used in the earlier paper are no longer necessary.
3. Deardorff, Stern and Baum (1976).
4. These elasticities are surveyed in Stern *et al.* (1976). To infer elasticities of substitution from these estimates, we first used our model to derive import-demand elasticities in terms of substitution elasticities and measurable parameters such as import shares. The result was then solved for the substitution elasticities. Details are contained in Deardorff *et al.* (1976).
5. In these and subsequent equations, we use the proportional form of the total differential. For any variable, X, the notation $\hat{X}$ represents dX/X, and stands for the (infinitesimal) proportional change in the variable.
6. We have developed a version of the model using a Cobb-Douglas production function instead, but have not yet adapted our solution program to use it for calculations.
7. The elasticities of substitution between capital and labour were obtained directly from published estimates in Zarembka and Chernicoff (1971). The fixed coefficients between value added and intermediate inputs were obtained from the input-output table of the United States as published by the Bureau of Economic Analysis (1967).
8. *Basic Documentation for the Tariff Study* (Geneva: GATT Secretariat, 1974).
9. As noted in Deardorff *et al.* (1977), the GATT data had to be adapted in three respects for our use. First, there were frequently several entries under individual four-digit Brussels Tariff Nomenclature (BTN) headings. To save on computational expense, we aggregated all of these entries for the relevant headings, Second, intra-European Community trade was not broken down completely by importing country. An allocation among the nine member countries was made based upon two-digit SITC imports, as reported in OECD foreign trade statistical bulletins. Third, Canada's imports from the European Community were reported in total and had to be allocated to the individual source countries. This was done on the same basis just noted. It may be noted, finally, that imports for the United States and two other countries were reported only on an f.o.b. rather than a c.i.f. basis. No adjustment was made to correct for the c.i.f. differential in these cases.
10. *The Growth of World Industry* (New York: United Nations, 1974).

11. These approximations consisted primarily of using exogenous tariff changes to approximate the change in both expenditure and the prices of intermediate goods, and of ignoring demands for intermediate goods in the demand functions, at certain stages of the solution. While we still feel that these approximations were appropriate in the analysis of multilateral tariff reductions, they are clearly not appropriate here for the analysis of other exogenous changes. Thus, we were forced, for this paper, to seek a method for obtaining an exact solution.
12. This, of course, is not a test of theoretical hypotheses, since the numbers we are using were derived from the model rather than observed in the real world. Our purpose is rather to evaluate the quantitative importance of various theoretical mechanisms by which exchange rates can affect output and employment.
13. Regarding the determinants of the EREO that were mentioned in the preceding paragraph, it is clear that they can also influence, in a more limited way, the extent to which the exchange rate can affect output through the home sector. A large supply elasticity will again contribute positively to the effect, while a large export share of production will limit the influence of the home sector on the total industry. The second of these effects can be neglected, however, since the expansion of the home sector can never be greater, in percentage terms, than the expansion of the export sector. Thus we continue to expect both the supply elasticity and the export share to play positive roles in determining the EREO.
14. Actually, expenditure, in our model, does depend slightly on the exchange rate through the redistribution of tariff revenue, the amount of which changes in response to a devaluation. See the 'expenditure effect' discussed below. Tariffs are too small for this expenditure effect to upset the conclusion that intermediate demands are more responsive than final demands to a devaluation.
15. The possibility that the exchange rate may affect expenditure, through its effect on the terms of trade, has been discussed extensively in the literature of international macro-economics, beginning with the classic papers of Laursen and Metzler (1950) and Harberger (1950). The evidence for this effect, both theoretical and econometric, is limited and mixed. See Deardorff and Stern (1978).
16. Actually, we used the corresponding changes in the reciprocals of these exchange rates, since this is what our model calls for.
17. These descriptions of the adjustment mechanisms are confirmed, incidentally, by the (unreported) results of our model for other variables, such as world prices.

REFERENCES

Basic Documentation for the Tariff Study (Geneva: GATT Secretariat, 1974).

BUREAU OF ECONOMIC ANALYSIS, 'The Input-Output Structure of the US Economy: 1967', *Survey of Current Business* (Washington: US Government Printing Office, for the US Department of Commerce, February 1974).

ALAN V. DEARDORFF and ROBERT M. STERN, 'The Terms-of-Trade Effect on Expenditure: Some Evidence from Econometric Models', *Journal of International Economics*, Amsterdam, Vol. 8, August 1978 pp. 409–14.

ALAN V. DEARDORFF, ROBERT M. STERN and CHRISTOPHER F. BAUM, 'A Simulation Model of World Trade and Production', unpublished manuscript, University of Michigan, 1976.

——'A Multi-Country Simulation of the Employment and Exchange-Rate Effects of Post-Kennedy Round Tariff Reductions', in N. AKRASANEE, S. NAYA and V. VICHIT-VADAKAN (eds), *Trade and Employment in Asia and the Pacific* (Honolulu: The University Press of Hawaii, 1977) pp. 36–66.

C. HARBERGER, 'Currency Depreciation, Income and the Balance of Trade', *Journal of Political Economy*, Chicago, Illinois, Vol. 58, February 1950 pp. 47–60.

SVEND LAURSEN and LLOYD A. METZLER, 'Flexible Exchange Rates and the Theory of Employment', *Review of Economics and Statistics*, Cambridge, Mass., November 1950 pp. 281–99.

ROBERT M. STERN *et al.*, *Price Elasticities in International Trade: an Annotated Bibliography* (London: Macmillan, for the Trade Policy Research Centre, 1976).

The Growth of World Industry (New York: United Nations, 1974).

P. ZAREMBKA and H. B. CHERNICOFF, 'Further Results on the Empirical Relevance of the CES Production Function', *Review of Economics and Statistics*, Vol. 53, February 1971, pp. 106–10.

6

A Two-parameter Purchasing-power-parity Measure of Arbitrage in International Goods Markets

STEPHEN P. MAGEE

An extensive literature exists on the efficiency of securities markets.[1] One efficiency criterion in domestic security markets is the statistical independence of security price changes through time. This approach has been extended to foreign exchange markets under floating exchange rates.[2] Similarly, there have been investigations of the efficiency properties of goods markets with many buyers and sellers. An early paper in this literature by George J. Stigler[3] investigated the statistical distribution of minimum prices in a local market and the economic determinants of price dispersion for different goods. He suggested that dispersion would decrease the more important a commodity was in a buyer's total expenditure, the larger the fraction of repetitive buyers, the larger the amount of accumulated market search and the larger the geographical size of the market. A rich literature has followed this paper on the economics of information.

It is surprising that more has not been written examining the efficiency of goods markets in international trade. There is an extensive discussion of large and persistent deviations from the law of one price between pairs of countries—deviations from purchasing power parity (PPP)—but explicit statistical definitions of efficiency have not been developed. The measurement in these studies is a comparison of the price in one of the economies with the exchange-rate-adjusted price in the other economy.

Many of the PPP studies are macro-economic: they compare national or sectoral (traded goods) inflation rates, adjusted for exchange-rate changes. But there are some interesting exceptions, with micro-economic data.[4] Peter Isard found substantial deviations from PPP for tradeable goods between the United States and Germany for the period 1968–73. Hans Genberg found that there was no significant difference in the variance of inflation rates among fifteen United States cities and the variance of inflation rates among the OECD countries.

If we observe non-zero deviations between prices in two international markets in the same good, we cannot conclude that the international market in these goods is 'inefficient', because we cannot empirically separate unexploited profit opportunities from unmeasured real barriers to full arbitrage. But we can measure the *ex post* deviations in prices and infer the extent to which arbitrage has or has not occurred (regardless of the reason). A two-parameter measure of the extent to which arbitrage occurred is the *variance* in deviations from purchasing power parity and the *periodicity* of these deviations. There is greater arbitrage between two geographically separate markets in the same good, the smaller the average (squared) deviations in the prices between them and the shorter the average time period required for the elimination of such deviations. The definition of arbitrage and its properties are discussed in the next section of the paper. In the third section, we examine how arbitrage has varied between fixed and flexible exchange-rate regimes. Illustrations of the measure using United States-Japanese wholesale price data yield some interesting conclusions: inter-country price differences increase under a floating regime, but the average amount of time they remain away from zero is reduced (greater variance but shorter periodicity). Thus we cannot say whether international arbitrage of goods prices between economies is more effective under fixed or floating rates.

The measurement of differences in (transport and exchange-rate-adjusted) prices between two economies is, in my judgement, more than an arbitrage measure: it also facilitates our understanding of the adjustment mechanism. The more pronounced the differences, on average, the further apart are two economies (in the sense of autarky versus free trade); the smaller the differences, the more integrated are the economies. Similarly, rapid elimination of price differences will be positively correlated with more efficient international adjustment mechanisms. We have discussed politically determined institutional factors that affect the mechanisms of adjustment for years, but these evaluations were usually without rigorous empirical measures. This paper provides one statistical standard by which alternative institutional rules can be tested.

I A TWO-PARAMETER DEFINITION OF INTERNATIONAL MARKET ARBITRAGE

This paper is an extension of the existing literature on purchasing power parity:[5] PPP has a long history in the theory of exchange-rate determination. We are not concerned here with the causation relating product-price ratios between two international markets to exchange rates or vice versa but simply the statistical properties of price differences between two economies. Richard J. Rogalski and Joseph D. Vinso analysed the floating rates of seven countries in the 1920–24 period using monthly data and found no tendency for exchange rates or country price ratios to lead each other for four out of the seven countries: the only observed causation was between contemporary observations. Their study did not focus on the size of the deviations from PPP, which is one measure used here for the degree of market arbitrage.[6]

More recent statistical estimates of the effects of exchange rates on product price ratios between economies range from the totally insignificant effects of the Canadian floating rate on United States-Canadian trade[7] to large effects found between the London and New York cocoa futures market.[8] The Dunn study was addressed explicitly at oligopolistic product markets while the Dominguez study focused on a futures market. Dominguez found that the anticipated devaluation of the British pound in November 1967 was reflected as early as September in the dollar prices in New York relative to the London prices in pounds of cocoa. These two studies suggest that any definition of market efficiency will yield substantial variation across product markets in the degree and timing of international goods market arbitrage.

Consider any two markets, such as the United States and Japan, between which goods are continually traded. Let p be the dollar price of the good, e be the dollar cost of the yen, and p^* be the yen price of the good, inclusive of transport costs, tariffs, and other barriers. Complete arbitrage occurs when identical price quotations occur in the two markets at identical points in time for delivery at identical future dates with all non-price variables identical:

(1) $p = ep^*$

In this case, e is the appropriate forward exchange rate. Divide both sides of the equation by p^* and subtract e from the left hand side, yielding:

(2) $d = p/p^* - e$

where d is defined as the deviation from perfect arbitrage, expressed in units of home currency per unit of foreign currency. If exchange rates are normalixed to equal one over the period under consideration, then the deviations in (2) are also proportional deviations for the prices between the two markets (the United States and Japan). We expect that in the long run, $d = 0$.

Figure 6.1 represents two hypothetical products in the case in which the deviations, d, cycle through time. Notice that the figure has been drawn such that the deviations have a mean of 0; they reach maxima and minima of equal amplitude; and they have fairly constant periodicities. As constructed, the deviations for the second product have both greater variance and longer periodicity than for the first. The deviations shown in Figure 6.1 suggest that there are two reasons why international arbitrage for the second product is less perfect than for the first: its average deviations from zero tend to be larger and it stays away from zero for longer periods of time. We turn now to the two measures of arbitrage efficiency.

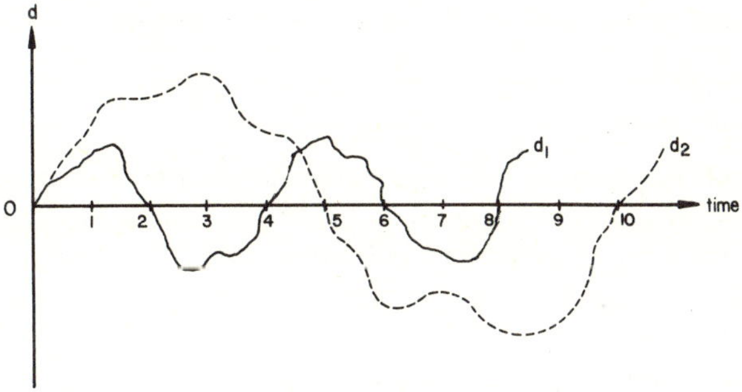

FIGURE 6.1
Hypothetical Deviations from PPP for Two Products

MEASURE 1: VARIANCE IN THE INTERNATIONAL PRICE DEVIATIONS

The first measure of arbitrage efficiency in the market for a single good between two international markets is the variance of the price differences:

$$(3)\quad \begin{aligned} \mathrm{Var}(d) &= \mathrm{Var}(p/p^*) + \mathrm{Var}(e) - 2\,\mathrm{Cov}(p/p^*, e) \\ &= \sigma^2_{p/p^*} + \sigma_e^{\,2} - 2\,\mathrm{Cov}(p/p^*, e) \\ &= \sigma_d^{\,2} \end{aligned}$$

(We ignore variance within each of the two geographic markets: that is, within the United States and within Japan.) We could have used the average absolute deviation as the measure. However, the average squared deviation, the variance, has some desirable properties not possessed by the average absolute deviation. For example, it might be desirable to have large deviations carry a more than proportionately larger weight than the sum of two smaller ones. A 10 per cent deviation has four times the weight in the variance formula that a 5 per cent deviation has.

Since the costs of tariff, monopoly and other market inefficiencies with linear demand are a function of the square of price distortions, there is a linear relationship between our variance measure and the social cost of market price differences. An international product with twice the variance in *d* of another has economic inefficiency costs which are twice as great. There are good economic reasons why less arbitrage occurs in some product markets than in others. Some of these are not amenable to public policy changes (the costs of information, the nature of production, and the costs of changing list prices) while others are (commercial policy and the choice of the exchange-rate system).

MEASURE 2: PERIODICITY IN THE DEVIATIONS

The second measure of arbitrage inefficiency is the periodicity of the deviations: this is the minimum number of time units, on average, required for a sequence of positive and negative deviations to sum to zero. We posit that arbitrage inefficiency increases with (statistically significant) periodicity. According to the second parameter of market efficiency, market 2 in Figure 6.1 is more inefficient than market 1 by this measure since it requires ten periods for market 2 to show no deviations from the law of one price but only four periods for market 1. Once a difference in prices in two markets is opened, how long does it take arbitrage to restore equality? The answer is half the periodicity of the cycles. In Figure 6.1, this is two periods for good 1 and five periods for good 2.

What can generate periodicity? First, long periods over which unrealised expectations occur generate capital gains for one party (pure rents) and capital losses for the other party. While capital gains and losses should affect no real variables, they do affect corporate cash flow. If capital losses occur for long periods at a time (persistent 'overvaluation' of a currency), the cost equals the interest on the increased working capital required to finance such periods.[9] Second, information costs can cause persistent deviations: the more sampling which is required by participants in the market, the longer it will take for price deviations between markets to be arbitraged. Third, we might expect long deviations when there are high costs of making price-list changes and high costs of deviating from list prices. Fourth, stock adjustment models can generate inter-country price deviations when gaps between desired and actual quantities are adjusted gradually. Fifth, inter-country macro-economic policy influences have been shown by Pieter Korteweg and Allen Meltzer to have lagged effects on national price levels.[10]

There are several spurious reasons why long and persistent deviations from purchasing power parity might occur. First, if transactions prices are used in the price statistics rather than spot prices, then spurious cycles are generated which can describe the type of cycle shown in Figure 6.1.[11] These emanate from today's prices being averages of past contracts, whose forecast errors of today's exchange rate are correlated. If we know the statistical distribution of order to import lags, then we can generate substantial periodicity of deviations from time-independent changes in exchange rates.[12] A second reason is that the goods being compared statistically may not be perfect substitutes. We would not expect the differences in prices of different goods to show no deviations through time. A third consideration is that changes in exchange rates plus currency contract effects can generate J-curves and inverted J-curves.[13] These will not, however, generate deviations from PPP, but exactly the contrary: if import contracts are fixed in foreign currency, import prices in home currency will rise by the amount of a devaluation, in the absence of hedging.

The existence of statistically significant periodicity can be detected using spectral analysis. We discuss first the concept of spectral analysis and then turn to its determination of periodicity. There have been many economic applications of spectral analysis.[14]

Spectral analysis allows us to decompose a time series into a sum of cyclical functions, each of which has constant periodicity and amplitude. Consider the empirical time series d in Figure 6.2A. Deviations from purchasing power parity are given on the vertical axis and time in months is shown on the horizontal axis. In Figure 6.2B, we show deterministic functions a and b. Notice that the function a has the same general periodicity as d in Figure 6.2A and series b captures the small fluctuations around this series. The a series has a periodicity of twenty months, while series b has a periodicity of four months. The empirical time series d can be well explained by a linear combination of the two periodic functions a

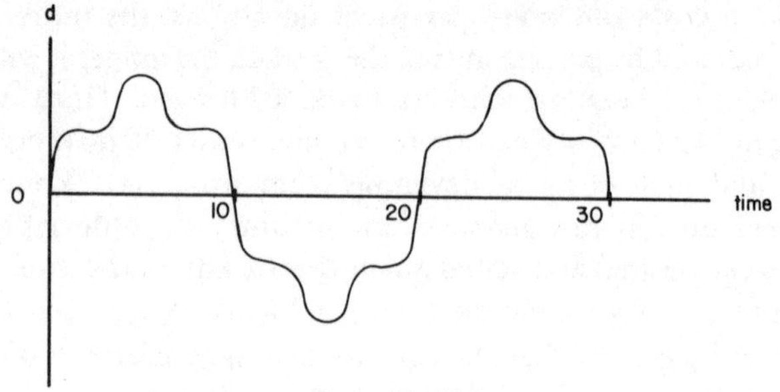

FIGURE 6.2A
Summation of Two Periodic Series

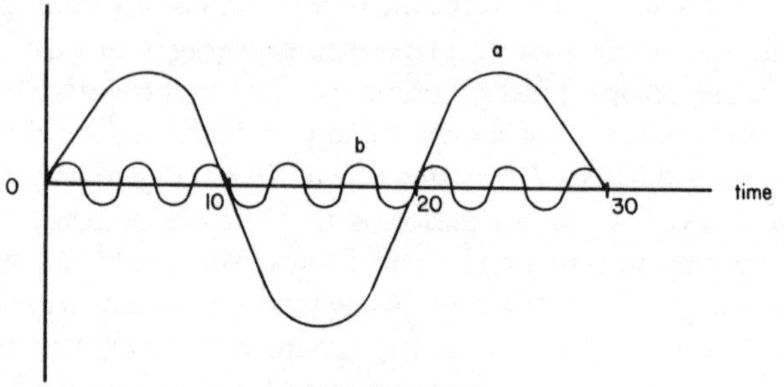

FIGURE 6.2B
Two Periodic Series

and *b*, since the latter are independent. Notice that most of the total variation in time series *d* is explained by the long cycle *a*, and only a small portion by the short cycle *b*.

More importantly, spectral analysis allows us to rank the importance of long and short cycles in explaining the variance in *d* (which, it should be recalled, is our first measure of arbitrage inefficiency). If, in Figures 6.2A and 6.2B the 'power' (to be defined) of the twenty-period cycle *a* is forty, and the four-period cycle *b* is five, then cycle *a* explains eight times as much of the variance in *d* as does *b*. This provides a measure of the statistical significance of long versus short cycles in describing any economic time series. We turn now to a formal definition of the periodicity of a cycle in assessing the arbitrage efficiency of the market. Since much of the variance in time series *d* is dominated by twenty period cycles, then the periodicity is defined as twenty months (if the observations taken were monthly).

The 'power spectrum' allows us to determine the contribution of cycles of all lengths (2, 3, . . . , 50, . . .) to the variance in the time series under investigation. The power spectrum is defined as a density function showing the contribution of each frequency (to be defined) to the total variance of the time series. The sum of the contribution of each cycle length exhausts the total variance in the time series so that the area under the density function in Figure 6.3 equals the total variance in *d* in Figure 6.2A. This explanation of Figure 6.3 is stylised, but it represents the basic idea. One potentially confusing aspect of Figure 6.3 is the definition of the horizontal axis. For the 'power spectral density

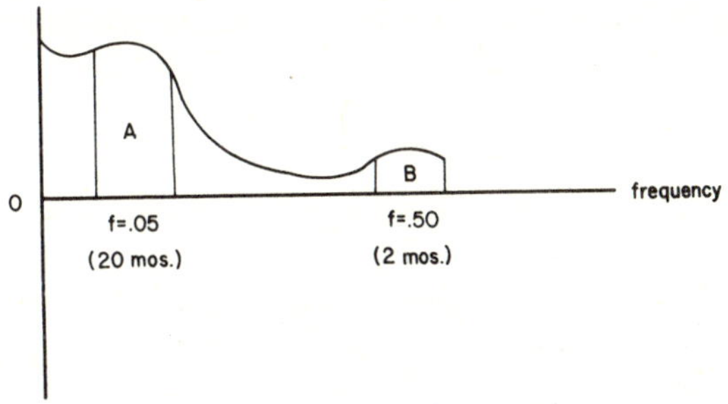

FIGURE 6.3
A Power Spectrum Density Function

function' (hereafter, the 'power spectrum'), the horizontal axis is a linear function of the frequency of each cycle: frequency equals the number of cycles per unit of time. Thus, a function such as *d* in Figures 6.2A and 6.2B with a dominant periodicity of twenty months has a dominant frequency of .05 cycles per month. Since it requires twenty months to complete an entire cycle, the number of cycles completed in any given month (that is, the frequency) is .05 cycles. The important thing to remember about power spectra plots is that cycles with long periods are associated with portions of the horizontal axis near the origin and cycles with short periods are associated with values further to the right. Most statistical time series will not exhibit such clean-cut properties. Notice that the density function in Figure 6.3 has positive amounts of variance being explained by periods of other lengths, which would be the case if random terms of different periodicities were added to *d* in Figure 6.2A.

There are some non-trivial difficulties in the relative efficiency of international market arbitrage using the spectral measure. It is clear that markets with significantly long periodicities are less arbitraged than those with significant short periodicities. But is a market with significantly short periodicity (that is, rapid elimination of deviations from PPP) less efficient than one with no significant periodicity (that is, a market in which both long and short cycles contribute to the variance)? A case can be developed on both sides. Working capital requirements might be lower with significantly short periodicity (because an unanticipated shortfall in prices could be expected to reverse itself sooner) but the failure of apparently profitable arbitrage to occur in the face of predictable (non-seasonal) price movements is unexplained. My own feeling is that the absence of significant periodicity is the most efficient case. Since there is a direct relationship between autocovariation in the time series examined and in the power spectrum, we turn now to some examples.[15]

CASE 1: PERFECT AND NEAR-PERFECT ARBITRAGE

If there were 'perfect' arbitrage between two international markets, then there would be no deviations in the price series (if there were also perfect measurement). Thus, a plot of *d* against time would coincide with the horizontal axis. In this situation, there would be no variance and no measurable periodicity.

Consider, next, near-perfect cases with trendless deviations in prices which are white noise:

(4) $d_t = \varepsilon_t$

A plot of this time series is shown in Figure 6.4A. The corresponding power spectrum for this time series is flat (Figure 6.4B), so that there would be complete efficiency with respect to periodicity. The two-parameter arbitrage efficiency measure would be $A(\sigma_\varepsilon^2, 0)$. The first term is the variance in the deviations and the second is the number of months for which a significant cycle exists. Since no significant periodicity is detectable, we set the second term equal to zero.

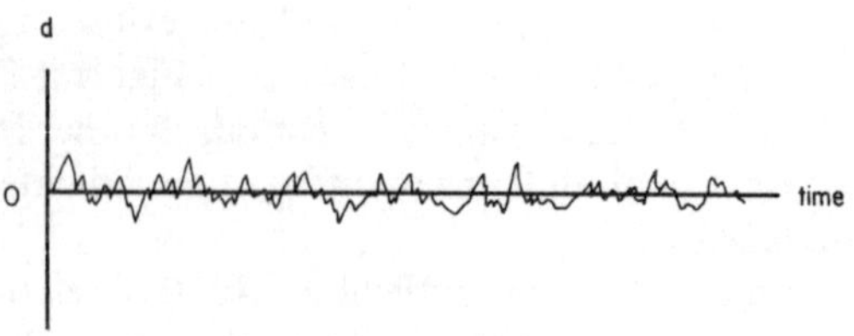

FIGURE 6.4A
White Noise Price Deviations

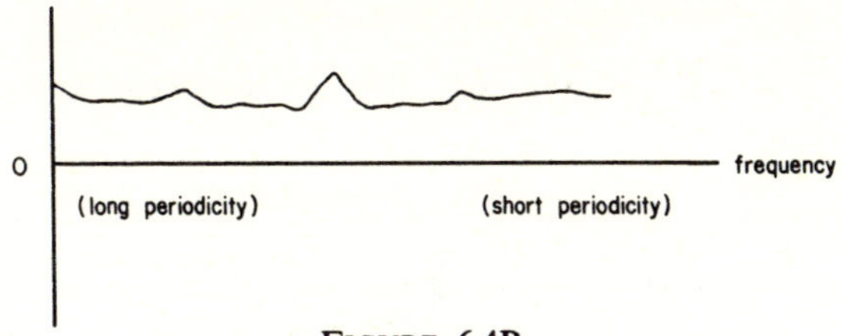

FIGURE 6.4B
The Power Spectrum of White Noise

CASE 2: TREND IN *d*

A series in which *d* exhibits noticeable trend indicates that there is no tendency for full arbitrage within the time period investigated. One interpretation is that a long cycle is present which is longer than the data available. Even though no accurate measure exists for its periodicity, we know that it would be longer than the time series in hand. Figure 6.5A shows such a series. The resulting power spectrum from such a trend (Figure 6.5B) shows a high peak at very long periodicities indicating an absence of arbitrage and hence extreme inefficiency for this commodity. A second interpretation is that there is error in the price series. A third is that the two markets may not be comparable, indicating that non-competing products are being compared.

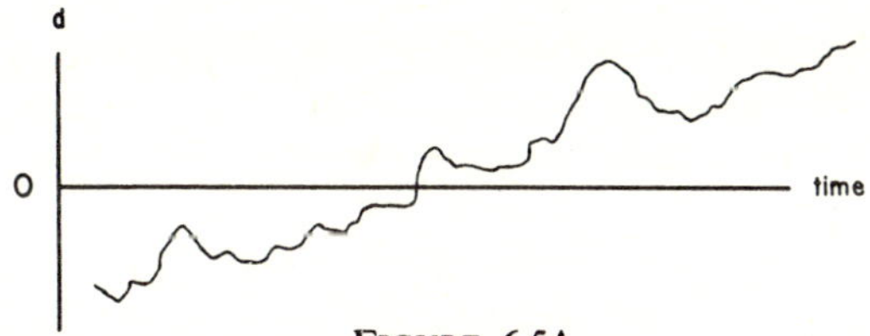

FIGURE 6.5A
Price Deviations with Trend

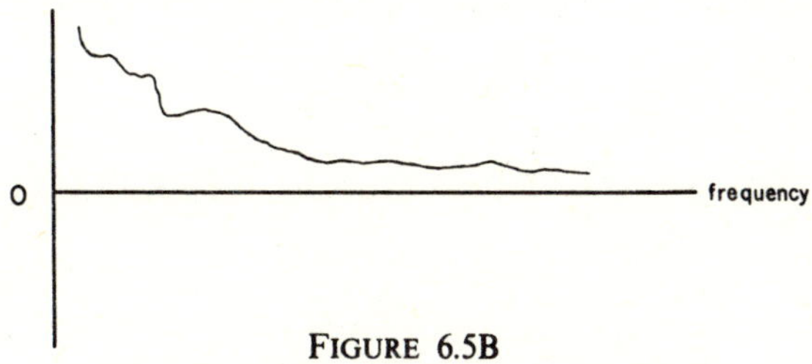

FIGURE 6.5B
The Power Spectrum of Trend Deviations

CASE 3: AN AR(1) PROCESS

Consider a first-order autoregressive process describing deviations of the following type:

(5) $d_t = ad_{t-1} + \varepsilon_t$

When a is positive, as we might expect with many goods markets, the long-period components dominate the series, making it smoother than white noise. Such a process might well describe the deviations of product 1 in Figure 6.1, yielding the power spectrum shown in Fig. 6.6. For $a < 0$, positive deviations in one period tend to be followed by negative ones next period. While this case is not shown, a plot of d on time would be even more ragged than white noise and the power spectrum would be positively sloped, indicating that the variance in d is dominated by short-period influences. The hog cycle (with time periods defined suitably long) or a cyclically unstable adjustment process between two markets might generate such a series.

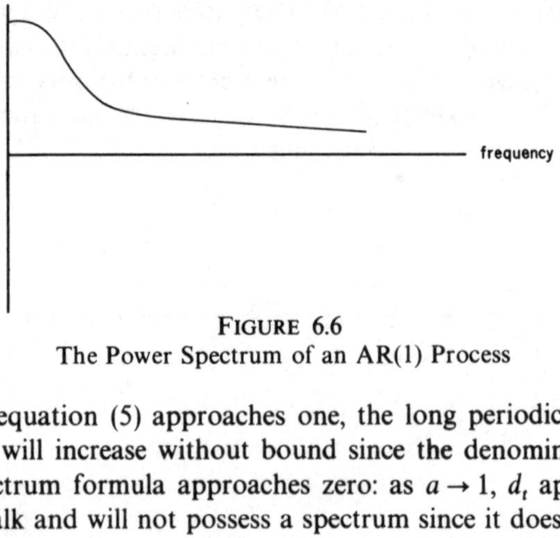

FIGURE 6.6
The Power Spectrum of an AR(1) Process

As a in equation (5) approaches one, the long periodicity peak in Figure 6.5 will increase without bound since the denominator in the power spectrum formula approaches zero: as $a \rightarrow 1$, d_t approaches a random walk and will not possess a spectrum since it does not have a finite variance.

II ARBITRAGE AND ADJUSTMENT UNDER FIXED AND FLOATING RATES

To illustrate these measures of international arbitrage, we apply them to 204 monthly observations of United States and Japanese wholesale prices in the period from January 1959 to December 1975 for four commodities imported into the United States from Japan: tyres, plywood, steel and autos. In 1971, by the four-digit SITC classification of these items, tyres and plywood were each about 1 per cent of the United States imports from Japan, steel was 8 per cent and autos were 14 per cent: the items accounted for nearly one fourth of the United States imports from Japan. With continuous trading, absolute as well as relative purchasing power parity should hold – if one of the prices includes the costs of barriers such as transport costs and tariffs. ('Absolute PPP' holds when there is equality of the exchange-rate and barrier-adjusted prices between the two economies, while 'relative PPP' holds when there is equality of the changes in the same prices through time.)

We assume that PPP holds for the seventeen-year period as a whole. This assumption is required to construct a statistical price series for absolute PPP, since p and p^* (the United States and Japanese prices) are indexes. Once we set $d = 0$ for the whole period, the values for p/p^* in equation (2) are determined. Figure 6.7 to 6.10 show plots of d over the

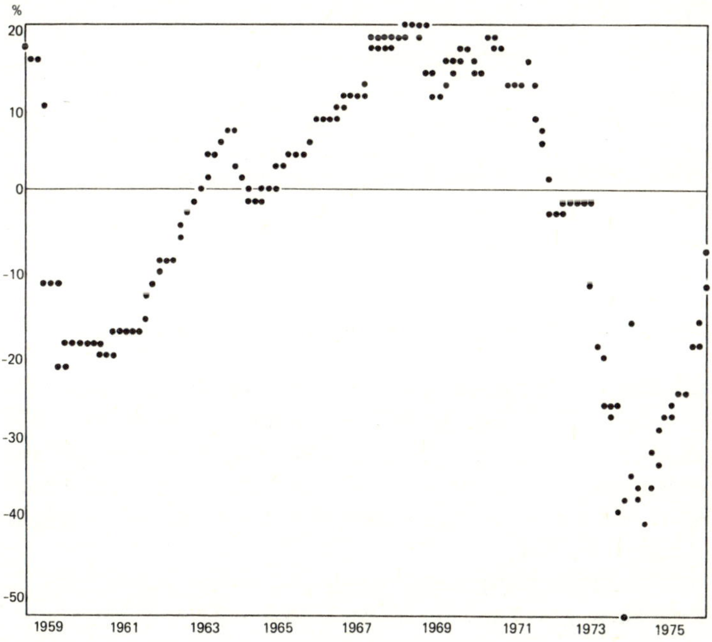

FIGURE 6.7
Percentage Excess of US over Japanese Prices: Tyres

period for the four commodities. The values shown are normalised so that *d* is expressed as a percentage of p/p^*. Positive values indicate the calculated percentage excess of United States prices over Japanese prices, assuming that the average value of *d* equals zero for 1959 to 1975.

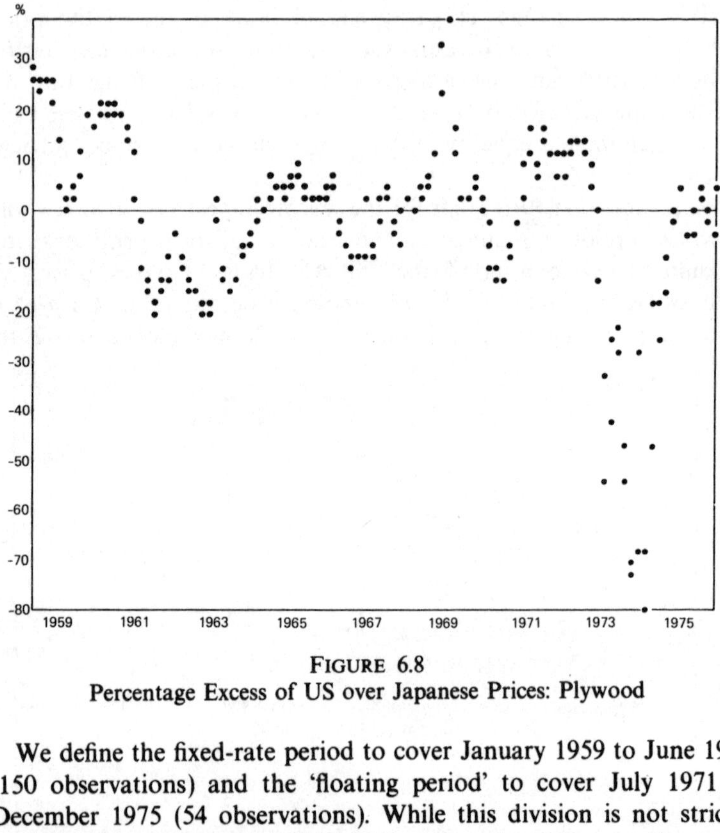

FIGURE 6.8
Percentage Excess of US over Japanese Prices: Plywood

We define the fixed-rate period to cover January 1959 to June 1971 (150 observations) and the 'floating period' to cover July 1971 to December 1975 (54 observations). While this division is not strictly correct, since July 1971, all of 1972 and early 1973 were fixed-rate periods, such a division was necessary to obtain enough observations for the spectral analysis.

All four series display substantial deviations between United States and Japanese prices and three (tyres, steel and autos) show a steady growth of United States relative to Japanese prices over the fixed period. The trough to peak percentage-point increases in United States prices relative to Japanese prices were 34 per cent for autos, 36 per cent for steel

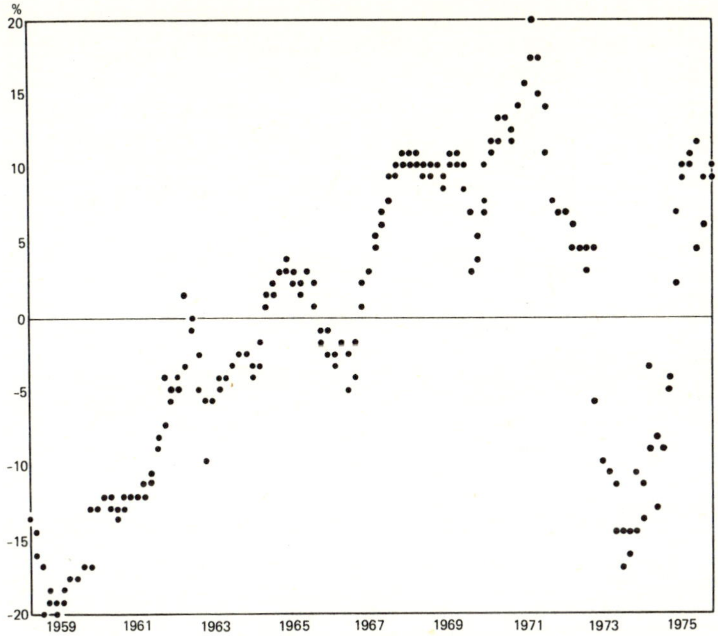

FIGURE 6.9
Percentage Excess of US over Japanese Prices: Steel Plates

and 40 per cent for tyres. Plywood is the one product which shows no relative price trend over the period and to the naked eye, shorter periodicity.

FIXED VERSUS FLEXIBLE RATES, EFFICIENCY AND TRADE ADJUSTMENT

Is a fixed or floating system more efficient in assisting firms to arbitrage away price differences between economies? The data over this period does not permit a complete answer to this question since we cannot remeasure *d* either in the 1960s under a floating rate experiment or in the 1970s under a fixed rate experiment. Robert Z. Aliber has argued correctly that comparisons of systems *per se* should be done with both subject to the same shocks.[16] If fixed rate systems are characteristic of comparative stable periods and floating systems emerge in periods of large monetary and/or real disturbances, then we should not forget that a comparison of the two using actual data is a joint description of the exchange-rate systems and the attendant disturbances.

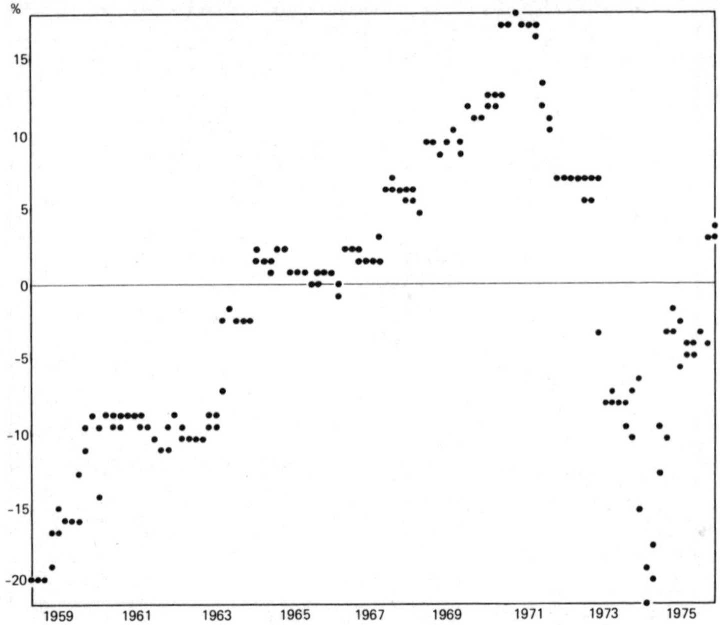

FIGURE 6.10
Percentage Excess of US over Japanese Prices: Autos

Table 6.1 shows the first of the two arbitrage efficiency measures. In all cases except automobiles, the squared deviations in prices between the United States and Japan increased in the floating period. The root-mean-squared deviation for plywood increased from 13 to 26 per cent. As just

TABLE 6.1
Variance in the percentage Wholesale Price Deviations for Four Products Imported into the United States from Japan

	Fixed-rate period Jan. 1959 to June 1971 (150 observations)	*Floating-rate period July 1971 to Dec. 1975 (54 observations)*
	Variance (and root-mean-squared deviation)	
Automobile tyres	174 (13)	274 (17)
Plywood	162 (13)	699 (26)
Steel plates	99 (10)	115 (11)
Automobiles	98 (10)	86 (9)

noted, we cannot generally establish the extent to which the increases were due to the failure of floating rates to facilitate adjustment in individual product markets versus greater underlying macro- and micro-economic period specific disturbances. On the other hand, Figures 6.7, 6.9 and 6.10 are all consistent with considerable 'trend disequilibrium' in the fixed period which is not evident in the floating period. Even this trend effect, however, did not cause the fixed period to show greater variance than the floating period.

TABLE 6.2

Spectral Estimates of the Periodicity of United States–Japan Price Deviations
Relative Power Spectra ($>64 = 1$)

	Periodicity (in months)	*Fixed rates (1959–71)*	*Floating rates (1971–75)*
Automobile Tyres	$\geqslant 64$	1.00	1.00
	32	.49	.59
	16	.05	.11
	11	.01	.02
Plywood	$\geqslant 64$	1.00	1.00
	32	.68	.78
	16	.26	.22
	11	.10	.03
Steel plates	$\geqslant 64$	1.00	1.00
	32	.48	.71
	16	.04	.19
	11	.01	.03
Automobiles	$\geqslant 64$	1.00	1.00
	32	.48	.61
	16	.04	.16
	11	.01	.07

Consider now the second measure of efficiency: the decomposition of the variances in Table 6.1 into their periodicities. The power spectra estimates for both periods are shown in Table 6.2. For three out of four products, the floating-rate period has relatively larger shares of the variance in price deviations explained by cycles of shorter length. The power spectra ratios of the eleven, sixteen and thirty-two-month cycles increased from .55 to .72 for automobile tyres, from .53 to .93 for steel plates and from .53 to .84 for automobiles. For plywood, the importance of these ratios was virtually constant between the two periods. We conclude that there are perceptible, though weak, reductions in the length of time required for purchasing power parity to be restored in the floating-rate period.

Second, note that half or more of the variation in *d* is associated with cycles of sixty-four months and longer in *both* periods. Thus, the spectral density functions are anything but flat and confirm our visual inspection of Figures 6.7 to 6.10 in that these markets exhibit prolonged trips away from price equality. The movement to floating rates reduced the weights of long cycles, but not by much.

Third, we cannot conclude from Tables 6.1 and 6.2 that international goods arbitrage is performed better under fixed or floating rates. *The prices in the two markets tended to get further apart in the floating-rate period (greater variance) but they stayed apart for relatively shorter periods of time.* Only when we can assess the welfare effects of each type of inefficiency can we unambiguously rank the two periods using this data.

COMPARATIVE GOODS-MARKET EFFICIENCY

Assume that the squared differences in the country prices is an appropriate measure of the gross welfare costs of non-arbitrage (a net measure would subtract from gross the amount of the variance explained by non-policy-imposed real economic costs, such as information costs). In this case, the markets between the United States and Japan for tyres and plywood are 'less efficient' than in steel plates and autos in the fixed-exchange-rate period (see Table 6.1). The differences become more pronounced in the floating-rate period, especially with plywood: the gross economic cost of deviations in plywood increased over four-fold in the floating-rate period. Whatever the cause, the effects of the deviations are comparable to non-tariff barriers (recall that transport costs and tariffs, assumed constant, are implicit in one of the prices in the presence of continuous trade). The root-mean-squared deviations in Table 6.1 are the 'tariff equivalents' of the price differences: they range from 10 to 13 per cent in the fixed period and from 9 to 26 per cent in the floating period.

With respect to the periodicity of price deviations, tyres, steel plates and automobiles have similarly shaped power spectra for the fixed and for the floating period. The spectrum for plywood, however, is relatively flatter than the rest, indicating less of a tendency for long forays away from purchasing power parity and therefore greater efficiency.

HISTORICAL ARGUMENTS OVER FIXED VERSUS FLOATING RATES

It is ironical that these statistical results are consistent with the historical arguments of both the opponents and proponents of flexible exchange rates. The opponents have argued that fluctuations in exchange rates would increase trade risk. Table 6.1 shows that, in three out of the four commodities, national markets become more separated with floating rates. On the other hand, proponents of floating rates have argued that market-determined rates would facilitate more rapid adjustment of product market disequilibria. While the evidence is less strong, this, too, occurred in the recent floating period since price deviations were of shorter duration between the countries. The data vindicate both positions.

WHY DID THE DEVIATIONS INCREASE IN THE FLOATING PERIOD?

We address this question by examining the components of the variance in the deviations in Table 6.3. (The units used for the calculations for this table differ from the percentages used in Table 6.1.) In all cases, the deviations increased with the move to floating rates. In the fixed-rate period, the deviations, by construction, are exclusively due to movement in the ratio of United States to Japanese prices, p/p^*. In the floating-rate period, the price ratio variance fell for three of the four products. But the increased deviations from PPP are more explained by the surprising negative covariance between the exchange rate and the price ratios than

TABLE 6.3

A Decomposition of the Variance of Deviations from Purchasing Power Parity during the Floating-rate Period (units are US cents per yen)

	Fixed rates Jan. 1959 to June 1971 (150 observations)	*Floating rates* July 1971 to Dec. 1975 (54 observations)			
	$V(d) = V(p/p^*)$	$V(d) =$	$V(p/p^*)$	$+V(e)$	$-2\,\mathrm{Cov}(p/p^*, e)$
Automobile tyres	1450	2014	855	558	602
Plywood	1680	4241	2415	558	1268
Steel plates	730	1317	505	558	254
Automobiles	780	916	298	558	60

NOTE: The values were multiplied by 10^6 for clarity of presentation.

by variation in the exchange rate itself. The correlation coefficients between p/p^* and e were $-.44$ for tyres, $-.55$ for plywood and $-.24$ for steel, indicating that increases in the dollar cost of the yen coincided with *declines* in the ratio of United States to Japanese prices of all of these goods (for autos the correlation coefficient was near zero).

FLOATING RATES AND MONETARY INDEPENDENCE

The long upward trends in the ratios of United States to Japanese prices in the fixed rate period for tyres, steel and autos are consistent with the stylised facts that the dollar was 'undervalued' in the late 1950s to early 1960s and 'overvalued' in the late 1960s. While these terms are anathema to the many micro-economists who share my own belief in market efficiency, the data in Figures 6.7, 6.9 and 6.10 do not contradict this view. Government trade policy can be used to maintain such price differences but the duration of these deviations is surprising.

In fact, the increases in United States prices relative to Japan for these three commodities in the fixed period are consistent with the view that the United States had a higher 'desired rate of inflation' than Japan.[17] If this were the case, the move to floating rates would remove the balance-of-payments constraint on this price trend, and the United States could follow an 'independent monetary policy'. Further increases in p/p^* would be permitted by increases in the dollar cost of the yen, e. This did not occur, however, in the floating period. Plots of p/p^* (not shown) for the four commodities have no noticeable trend between 1972 and 1975 and they all show a major dip in 1974.[18] Thus it is not clear what forces were at work.

A formal statistical test can be devised of the hypothesis that governments, in fact, exploit their ability to pursue different desired rates of inflation with flexible rates. While there can be occasional changes during fixed-rate periods, p/p^* is continually pushed toward e. This introduces cyclicity in p/p^* which is not imposed by a floating system. To summarise, trends in p/p^* should be more in evidence in floating-rate periods (sharply negatively sloped power spectra) and cycles in p/p^* more apparent during truly fixed-rate periods (shorter periodicity and flatter spectra). We do not test this hypothesis here.

Another interpretation of 'monetary independence' is that random fits and starts (in both directions) by the monetary authorities are more likely in floating periods. Thus, effectively exercised monetary independence implies that country relative prices, p/p^*, will exhibit more variance in floating periods. This hypothesis is not supported by the United

States-Japanese evidence in Table 6.3: for all of the goods except plywood, the variance in p/p^* falls from the fixed to the floating period.

NOTES

The author would like to thank Lalatendu Misra for outstanding research assistance and Thomas K. Lamb for the diagrams. He also wishes to thank Alan Winters, Larry Cooper and Kee Kim for helpful comments and Nanneska Magee and Susan Lisk for editorial comments and typing. The data used in the paper appear in Magee and Thompson (1977).

1. See the references in Fama (1970).
2. See Giddy and Dufey (1975).
3. Stigler (1961).
4. Isard (1977) and Genberg (1976).
5. The existing literature on purchasing power parity includes Lee (1976), Officer (1976a, 1976b) and Hekman (1977).
6. Rogalski and Vinso (1977).
7. Dunn (1970).
8. Dominguez (1972).
9. *Ceteris paribus*, pressures to change prices and reduce both deviations and periodicity should be *lower* on the trading partner taking the arbitrage loss during periods of *low* interest rates.
10. Korteweg and Meltzer (1977).
11. See Magee (1977).
12. This result assumes that traders hedge all foreign exchange risk.
13. Magee (1973) and Magee (1974).
14. See, *inter alia*, Hymans (1973) and the work discussed in Granger and Hatanaka (1964).
15. Granger and Newbold (1977) is the source for most of these cases.
16. Aliber (1975).
17. See Corden (1977) p. 75, for a discussion of this concept.
18. In the Corden (1977) framework, these results are consistent with a reduced desired rate of United States relative inflation in the floating period.

REFERENCES

ROBERT Z. ALIBER, 'Monetary Independence Under Pegged and Floating Exchange Rates', presented at the Conference on Monetary Mechanisms in Open Economies, Helsinki, Finland: 4–9 August 1975.

RICHARD E. CAVES *et al.*, *The International Adjustment Mechanism*, (Boston: Federal Reserve Bank of Boston, 1970).

C. CHATFIELD, *The Analysis of Time Series: Theory and Practice*, (London: Chapman & Hall, 1975).

W. M. CORDEN, *Inflation, Exchange Rates and the World Economy*, (London: Oxford University Press, 1977).

PHOEBUS J. DHRYMES, *Econometrics: Statistical Foundations and Applications* (New York: Harper & Row, 1970).

JOHN R. DOMINGUEZ, *Devaluation and Futures Markets* (Lexington, Mass.: D. C. Heath, 1972).

ROBERT M., DUNN JR., 'Flexible Exchange Rates and Oligopoly Pricing: A study of Canadian Markets', *Journal of Political Economy*, Chicago, Illinois, Vol. 78 January–February 1970, pp. 140–51.

EUGENE F. FAMA, 'Efficient Capital Markets: A Review of Theory and Empirical Work', *Journal of Finance*, New York, Vol. 35, May 1970, pp. 383–417.

JACOB A. FRENKEL and HARRY G. JOHNSON (eds), *The Monetary Approach to the Balance of Payments* (Buffalo, New York: University of Toronto Press, 1976).

Hans Genberg, 'Aspects of the Monetary Approach to Balance of Payments Theory: an Empirical Study of Sweden', in Frenkel and Johnson (1976).

I. GIDDY and G. DUFEY, 'The Random Behavior of Flexible Exchange Rates: Implications for Forecasting', *Journal of International Business Studies*, Vol. 6, Spring 1975, pp. 1–32.

C. W. J. GRANGER and M. HATANAKA, *Spectral Analysis of Economic Time Series* (Princeton, New Jersey: Princeton University Press, 1964).

—— and PAUL NEWBOLD, *Forecasting Economic Time Series* (New York: Academic Press, 1977).

CHRISTINE HEKMAN, 'Purchasing Power Parity and Structural Change', unpublished Ph. D. dissertation, Graduate School of Business, University of Chicago, February 1977.

SAUL H. HYMANS, 'On the Use of Leading Indicators to Predict Cyclical Turning Points', *Brookings Papers on Economic Activity, No. 2* (Washington: Brookings Institution, 1973) pp. 339–75.

PETER ISARD, 'The Price Effects of Exchange-Rate Changes', in P. B. CLARK, D. E. LOGUE, and R. J. SWEENEY (eds), *The Effects of Exchange Rate Adjustments* (London: Department of the Treasury, 1977) pp. 369–86.

HARRY G. JOHNSON, *Further Essays in Monetary Economics* (London: Allen & Unwin, 1972).

PIETER KORTEWEG and ALLEN H. MELTZER, 'Inflation and Price Changes: Some Estimates and Tests of Alternative Theories', draft, March 1977.

ROBERT E., LUCAS, JR., 'Some International Evidence on Output-Inflation Trade-offs', *The American Economic Review*, Manasha, Wisconsin, Vol. 63, June 1973, pp. 326–34

H. LEE MOON, *Purchasing Power Parity* (New York: Marcel Dekker, 1976).

STEPHEN P. MAGEE, 'Currency Contracts, Pass-through and Devaluation', *Brookings Papers on Economic Activity, No. 1* (Washington: Brookings Institution, 1973) pp. 303–25.

—— 'U.S. Import Prices in the Currency-Contract Period', *Brookings Papers on Economic Activity, No. 1* (Washington: Brookings Institution, 1974) pp. 117–68.

—— 'Contracting and Spurious Deviations from Purchasing Power Parity', JACOB A. FRENKEL and HARRY G. JOHNSON (eds), *Studies in the Economics of Exchange Rates* (Reading, Mass.: Addison-Wesley, 1978), ch. 4 pp. 67–74.

—— and STEPHEN D. THOMPSON, *Exchange Rates and US Employment*, a Study for the Joint Economic Committee, US Congress, unpublished.

LAWRENCE H. OFFICER, 'The Purchasing-Power-Parity Theory of Exchange Rates: A Review Article', *International Monetary Fund Staff Papers*, Washington, Vol. 23, 1976a, pp. 1–60.

—— 'The Productivity Bias in Purchasing Power Parity: An Econometric Investigation', *International Monetary Fund Staff Papers*, Vol. 23, 1976b, pp. 545–79.

RICHARD J. ROGALSKI and JOSEPH D. VINSO, 'Price Level Variations as Predictors of Flexible Exchange Rates', *Journal of International Business Studies*, Vol. 8, Spring-Summer 1977, pp. 71–81.

E. SLUTZSKY, 'The Summation of Random Causes as the Source of Cyclic Processes', *Econometrica*, Bristol, Vol. 5, 1937, pp. 105–47.

GEORGE J. STIGLER, 'The Economics of Information', *Journal of Political Economy*, Vol. 69, June 1961, pp. 213–25.

7

Currency of Invoicing and Forward Covering: Risk-reducing Techniques in British Foreign Trade

STEPHEN CARSE and GEOFFREY E. WOOD

This paper[1] follows the pioneering work of Sven Grassman in the description and analysis of payment and financing procedures in international trade.[2] In his study of Swedish foreign trade, Grassman analysed currency of invoicing practices, use of the forward market and the variability of credit terms, relating his findings to a wide range of issues in international finance, such as the relationship of reserve movements to the trade figures and the explanation of the Swedish balancing item.

Our focus here, although very much narrower, was prompted by certain very striking results obtained by Grassman. In particular these were, firstly, that most goods traded internationally were invoiced in their exporter's currency (in 1968, 66.1 per cent of Sweden's exports and 58.8 per cent of her imports were invoiced in the exporter's currency) and, secondly, that only a small part of Sweden's trade was covered forward (6.0 per cent of her imports and 6.8 per cent of her exports). These results undermine the two popular beliefs that some international currency (sterling or the United States dollar) acts as a vehicle for the conduct of international trade and that most international traders rely on the forward market for protection against exchange-rate fluctuations.

Grassman did not develop any systematic explanations of his results. For this reason and also perhaps because of the feeling that Swedish trade, because of its particular commodity composition, may somehow be 'special' and not representative of what is done in the rest of the world, the implications of these results for official exchange-rate policy have never been considered. It is to this question that this paper is addressed.

Our approach is as follows. First, we describe the exchange-control restrictions which limit the extent to which British firms engaged in foreign trade can protect themselves from exchange-rate changes. We then develop certain hypotheses about how firms thus circumscribed will behave. The hypotheses which are developed are designed particularly to reveal the implications of our data for exchange market stability. These hypotheses are then tested against our data. By that means, we build up certain 'stylised facts' about behaviour in this area. The implications of these stylised facts first for the short-run behaviour of the exchange market, and then for government policy towards international capital flows, are then discussed.

EXCHANGE-CONTROL RESTRICTIONS

Exchange-control regulations in the United Kingdom compel British firms to seek security in sterling; that is to be concerned with the sterling value of their profits. These exchange-control regulations require that all foreign currency earnings be converted into sterling and thus prevent British firms from maintaining a diversified portfolio of foreign currencies.[3] In addition to this restriction, firms are also constrained in how they can protect the sterling value of their receipts from currency fluctuations.

British importers who have to pay their supplier in foreign currency can buy that currency only when they are actually about to make the payment due. Similarly, British exporters, whenever they receive foreign currency, are required to convert it immediately into sterling. The room for accelerating or retarding currency conversion is very slight, for if a bank is open to receive (say) a foreign-currency-denominated payment which has been made to one of its customers, then it will be able to convert that currency to sterling as the regulations require, since banks in the United Kingdom are allowed to maintain (within limits set by the Bank of England in negotiation with the individual banks) small net foreign-currency positions. Thus the longest that an exporter could legally hold foreign currency he had received would be three days over a bank holiday weekend, provided of course that he received the payment after banking hours. An importer has even less room for manoeuvre, as he can obtain the foreign currency he needs to make a payment only within banking hours. By the nature of illegal transactions they cannot be quantified; but the exchange-control regulations are strictly enforced, and slippage is thought to be small. Firms, then, cannot protect themselves by buying or selling spot foreign exchange in advance of their need for – or receipt of – it.

Firms are, however, allowed to protect themselves in the forward market. Exporters can sell expected receipts forward, up to six months in advance of when they will actually receive a foreign currency payment. The treatment of importers is in this respect *not* symmetrical with that of exporters. They can take forward cover as long in advance of an expected payment as they wish, and up to six months beyond the actual expected date of importing the goods. In other words, if a firm contracts to import some goods in a year's time and payment will be due six months after that, then it can take forward cover, to the extent of that payment, for eighteen months ahead (at any rate in principle – in practice they may have difficulty obtaining cover of such maturity).

A point worth making explicitly is that the above-summarised exchange-control regulations apply equally to multinational and to purely national British companies. Enforcement must of course be harder in the former case, but it is attempted. Again, transactions which escape the regulations cannot be quantified. It is (perhaps not surprisingly) the view of the exchange-control authorities that such transactions are both few and small.

SOURCES OF RISK

Having discussed how risk-avoiding behaviour is constrained, it is next necessary to consider the kinds of risk to which firms engaged in foreign trade are exposed. Two kinds of risk can be distinguished: *exchange risk* and *price risk*.[4] The former is the risk a firm bears when it has an open position in a foreign currency. The latter arises when a firm is holding an inventory of goods. The meaning of the former is quite plain; it is the risk of a change in the value of a foreign currency relative to the firm's home currency. The precise nature of price risk does, however, require elaboration.

In that the price of a firm's inventory can always change, even if the firm only trades domestically, price risk is always present – and present for every firm. It is, however, present in quite different ways for two different kinds of good. Some goods are traded on international markets, have their price determined by world supply and demand, and differ in price between countries only by transport costs and, if they exist, tariffs.

Markets in such goods can be centralised – for example, wheat – but need not be – for example, petroleum. Firms which deal in such goods cannot 'ride out' temporary demand or supply fluctuations by keeping price unchanged and varying their inventory, for if, for example, they were to maintain price during a temporary fall in demand, they would sell nothing. In that sense, they are much more exposed to price risk than a firm which deals in a heterogeneous commodity and which can meet temporary fluctuations in demand or supply by varying inventory at a constant price. They are, however, also guaranteed that exchange-rate changes will be fully reflected in the price of what they sell: since the *world* price is fixed, a 10 per cent sterling devaluation (for example) will raise the sterling price of their product by 11.1 per cent, except to the surely second-order extent that such an exchange-rate change affects world supply and demand. On the other hand, a trader in imported heterogeneous goods may find that he could not adjust – at any rate, fully – his sterling selling prices after such a devaluation.[5]

In summary, 'exchange risk' and 'price risk' are present for traders in both types of goods. The greater price risk for traders in one type of good is, however, not necessarily an unmixed disadvantage, in that it does provide almost automatic adjustment of the home currency selling price to exchange-rate changes. The potential usefulness of such adjustment can be very simply shown by an example.[6] This example will also help to point us towards our testable hypothesis.

EXPLOITATION OF RISKS

Consider a British importer who habitually holds an inventory of his import – say German motor-cars. Suppose he can habitually owe his supplier an amount of Deutschemarks equal to the total value of his inventory. Then, if a depreciation of sterling against the Deutschemark occurs, so long as he can raise the sterling price of his cars by the same amount he has neither gained nor lost. In other words, in certain circumstances an *unfavourable* effect from exchange risk can open up the possibility of a *favourable* effect from price risk.

There is also, of course, another possibility. So far we have assumed that the importer had been invoiced in Deutschemarks. Suppose that he was not, but was invoiced, in sterling, his home currency. Then he was *never bearing* exchange risk, and was exposed to price risk only. In the case of our hypothetical importer he could gain by raising the sterling selling price of his inventory; but had the exchange-rate change been in the other direction and competitive pressures forced him to drop his price, he would have lost. The moral of the second part of the example, then, is that being invoiced in one's home currency, although it *can* be a risk-reducing procedure, is not invariably one.

Another risk-reducing procedure is covering the transaction forward. If our importer (invoiced in Deutschemarks again) had bought his Deutschemarks forward, when he raised the sterling price of his inventory he would have made an additional gain rather than just avoided a loss. That does not, however, unambiguously mean that he should always cover forward. The first reason for this is that since there are generally wider buy – sell spreads on the forward market than on the spot market, he would be incurring larger transaction costs. A second reason is that one currency can stand for quite long periods at either a forward premium or a forward discount as against another. If the importer were continually buying forward a currency which stood at a forward premium against his own, his profits would be continually reduced as a result, unless he could adjust either his selling or buying price in compensation – and of course, if he could thus adjust, he would surely do so even if he did not cover forward!

Summarising then, the distinction between exchange risk and price risk shows that in certain circumstances these two sources of risk can be offsetting. It also shows that invoicing (or being invoiced) in one's home currency is not necessarily risk-reducing, and reminds us too that use of the forward market, although at times contributing positively to profits, can also prove a steady drain from profits. (It may appear tempting to make some more systematic statement – that, for example, forward covering reduces the variance of profits at the cost of also reducing their level. Unfortunately no such statement is possible. Once forward cover has been taken on a particular transaction, that transaction is free of exchange risk. But if a trader is regularly engaged in foreign trade he *must* face exchange-rate fluctuations: whether or not he takes forward cover determines only whether he is affected by spot market or forward market fluctuations. In other words, the reason that no simple systematic statement can be made is that the forward market provides protection only to an individual transaction, and not to a series of transactions. It may of course be rational to cover forward continually – a firm can have good reasons, such as high penalties attached to bankruptcy, for being particularly averse to an unexpected foreign exchange loss.)

HYPOTHESES TO BE TESTED

The hypotheses to be tested can most simply be developed by

considering the choices facing a British firm engaged in foreign trade.

Recollect that such a firm has to convert all its earnings to sterling. It can only (again because of exchange controls in the United Kingdom) take up a position in foreign currency in association with its foreign trade; there is no question of the firm diversifying into a portfolio of foreign currencies. These restrictions are imposed on British firms by institutional factors. We do, in addition, impose one simplifying assumption. This is that the decision to trade is taken before the firm decides how to handle the risk associated with that trade. We do not explore, or allow for, any interaction between the two decisions, but rather consider only how the risks associated with a predetermined value of trade are handled. We do of course assume that the firm is risk-averse.

We also assume that the firm cannot vary the date on which it makes (or receives) payment – that is, that it can neither lead nor lag. The purpose of this assumption is two-fold. First, since leading and lagging are ways of anticipating exchange-rate changes, they provide some protection against their consequences. Ruling out leading and lagging simplifies the hypotheses we are about to test. Second, and more important, we wish to explore in the final section of this paper the consequences for exchange market stability of restrictions on capital movements, and 'leads and lags' are a form of capital movement.

A firm in the situation we have described then faces two decisions. One concerns whether to invoice in the domestic, or a foreign currency (the latter including, of course, the international vehicle currency, should there be one). The second is whether or not to cover any resultant foreign-currency commitment; in effect, whether to enter the forward market, since exchange-control regulations prohibit the taking of an offsetting spot transaction.

The second of these decisions can concern either sellers or buyers — that is either exporters or importers — but it is not taken in negotiation with the trading partner. The first decision can, however, be a subject for negotiation. In making the first decision the risk-averse exporter will prefer to invoice in home currency despite the presence of forward markets which could theoretically make him indifferent to the choice of currencies. For forward market imperfections can exclude the possibility of using this form of risk cover. In particular, wider buy—sell spreads in the forward market than in the spot market may make transaction cost prohibitively high, whilst it is difficult to obtain cover in certain currencies and of long maturities. Moreover, these imperfections tend to become accentuated during times of exchange market uncertainty, precisely when the exporter will need to give extra consideration to the invoicing decision.

In negotiations, then, whether or not price risk can offset exchange risk will plainly be a consideration. This factor will also be relevant in the decision on whether or not to cover any exchange risk. Accordingly, it is now useful to introduce the concepts of 'tradeables I' and 'tradeables II'.

Tradeables I and Tradeables II

It has long been an accepted practice in international economics to impose on the world the stylised fact that goods can be divided into two categories – tradeables (which can be traded internationally) and non-tradeables (which can not). The most popular example of the latter category is haircuts. In a study by R. I. McKinnon, a further dividing of tradeables into groups I and II was carried out.[7]

Tradeables I are, in McKinnon's words, 'those in which producing firms can control (set) the market prices for their own particular products. Such firms face a downward-sloping short-run demand curve, and there is some product heterogeneity. In such markets, prices do not fluctuate to keep the market more or less continually cleared – supply is, with regard to short-run fluctuations in the equilibrium quantity, kept equal to demand by changes in inventories.'

Tradeables II are commodities where price does fluctuate to keep the market clear, and where firms cannot vary their price and choose the amount they sell. McKinnon cites motor cars as an example of tradeables I, and wheat as an example of tradeables II.[8] In the terminology above, the exposure to price risk is (other things being equal) always greater for dealers in tradeables II than for dealers in tradeables I.

The distinction between tradeables I and tradeables II leads to our first hypothesis. Exporters of tradeables I are not accustomed to quickly varying price so as to clear their market or offset transitory variations in costs. They are, therefore, not readily able to exploit price risk to offset exchange risk. They can perhaps use the forward market, but, as argued above, they would prefer to invoice in home currency as a means of obtaining home-currency certainty. Importers of tradeables I are also unaccustomed to quickly varying their selling price, but as the goods are frequently sold on retail markets rather than at a contract price as negotiated between the exporter and importer, the importer has somewhat more price flexibility than the exporter. This leads us to expect that exports of tradeables I will be invoiced in their exporter's currency. Our expectation of this is reinforced by two other factors. First, importers are sometimes less concentrated than their suppliers. Second, as was shown in the above example, for the importer to be invoiced in his home currency is not invariably risk-reducing for him. This, it will be recollected, is because, if the importer is invoiced in his home currency which then between invoicing and settlement appreciates against that of his supplier, he may incur a loss if he is forced as a result of competitive pressures, which arise from the price-stickiness of his competitors, to drop his home-currency selling price immediately upon the appreciation. It may be conjectured that when tradeables I are shipped to a non-producer of them – cars to a less developed country, for example – they become, through lack of local competition, as price-flexible as tradeables II. Thus, should the importer's currency depreciate, the price of the imported goods in the importer's currency would rise more or less proportionately. The exchange risk and price risk would cancel out and one could thus hypothesise that such trade would have a lesser tendency to be invoiced in the exporter's currency. But the exporter would in this case almost certainly possess more market power than the importer, and be unwilling to invoice in a currency the market for which was much thinner than that for his own.

What of tradeables II? This is rather more straightforward. In this case, the value of any inventory cannot be maintained even temporarily by price rigidity. Price risk will offset exchange risk almost automatically, by the smooth and (in this case) inevitable workings of the market. Hence, one might conjecture that neither exporter nor importer would much care what currency the trade was invoiced in. Such a hypothesis would be very hard to test, since it is hard to conceive of any distribution of currencies of invoicing which would be inconsistent with it. Accordingly, it is worthwhile pushing the analysis a little further. Many tradeables II are actually traded in worldwide markets which are fairly centralised, for example, coffee, tea, and cocoa (the London commodity exchanges), shipping (the Baltic Exchange), wheat (at Chicago) and cotton (also at Chicago). Prices on these exchanges are quoted in the exchange's home currency – that is in sterling or the United States dollar. Not all tradeables II are traded on such centralised exchanges, but they need not be for a common currency to be used in invoicing them. Petroleum products, nowdays always invoiced in United States dollars, are an example of this. We therefore test, as hypothesis II, that tradeables II in British trade are invoiced in either sterling or United States dollars, irrespective of the exporting country (and irrespective of whether they are a British export or import).

Before going to report the results of testing these hypotheses, two difficulties must be faced. The first is classifying goods as tradeables I or tradeables II. To do this, we make use of the Standard International Trade Classification (SITC). Tradeables I are regarded as being defined by SITC sections 5 to 8, but excluding divisions 67 and 68, and tradeables II by SITC sections 0 to 4, together with divisions 67 and 68. The definitions of these categories comprise the appendix to this chapter.

This classification is of course somewhat intuitive, and the need to classify simply means that we are testing a joint hypothesis – the hypothesis that we aim to test plus the correctness of our classification of a good to the category of tradeables I or tradeables II. This does not however concern us too much, mainly because while there are undoubtedly 'marginal' goods, the bulk of each category does comprise goods that are, if there is any sense at all in the classification scheme, quite unambiguously either tradeables I or tradeables II. Unless our classification is *systematically* wrong, the hypothesis we aim to test will be tested.

The second preliminary difficulty arises from the existence of multinational firms. When a multinational firm is trading between one arm and another, it does not matter which 'arm' bears the exchange risk. Sometimes, for that reason, we expect that multinationals, when trading within the firm, to behave differently from purely national firms, and sometimes we do not. We do not, however, pursue the distinction here, as we are interested in invoicing (and covering) practices in the aggregate.

Testing the Hypotheses

The data used to test the hypotheses contained in this paper were obtained from mail questionnaires and relate to a sample of 1252 export invoices and 800 import invoices dated February 1975. The total value of the export sample was £16.4m. The total value of the import sample £12.1m. Because we were not in a position to use the full import sample we have aggregated in our survey, less certainty should be attached to the import analyses. In particular, it seems that the sub-sample of import invoices includes a lower proportion of tradeables II commodities than expected. Some caution should thus be attached to the import figures until the results of the full sample analysis are known.

It is now convenient to restate and test hypotheses I and II.

Hypothesis I: tradeables I are invoiced in their exporter's currency.

This hypothesis is supported, as we found that 75.7 per cent (by value) of exports and 55 per cent (by value) of imports of tradeables I in the United Kingdom were invoiced in their exporter's currency. Both these percentages are significantly different (at the 5 per cent level) from 50 per cent. (Why being different from 50 per cent is crucial will emerge below.)

Hypothesis II: tradeables II are invoiced in sterling or the United States dollar.

This hypothesis was also supported; we found that 86.4 per cent (by value) of exports of tradeables II, and 87.6 per cent of imports of tradeables II were invoiced in sterling or the United States dollar. Of tradeables II trade so denominated, 37.3 per cent was in dollars, suggesting a declining vehicle currency role or sterling. The aggregate figures were significantly different (at the 5 per cent level) from 50 per cent.

Aggregating and reclassifying, we can also say that 75.9 per cent of British exports are invoiced in sterling, while 72.1 per cent of British imports are invoiced in foreign currency.

Taking Forward Cover

It was shown above that tradeables I are generally invoiced in the currency of the exporter, while tradeables II, in which dealers are both able and accustomed to use price risk to offset exchange risk, are generally invoiced in either sterling or the dollar so as to exploit the advantages of using a vehicle currency.

Dealers in tradeables II, although not as a general rule invoicing in their own currency, will none the less not see themselves as exposed to exchange risk – because price risk will provide protection from that. That does not hold for tradeables I. These are invoiced mainly in the currency of their exporter and this, by the nature of tradeables I, leaves British importers of the goods exposed to exchange risk. Accordingly, as hypothesis III, we test whether British importers of tradeables I cover forward to a greater extent (that is whether more of them do it, and to a greater percentage by value of trade) than importers of tradeables II.

It should be noted that, even for tradeables I, there is some measure of price risk. If an importer of tradeables I finds he has to pay in an appreciated currency, and he carries inventory, then he may be able to raise his selling price and use price risk to offset exchange risk. But this ability to set two risks against each other will be restricted, primarily by two factors. If the importer is selling his products in competition with domestic producers rather than other importers, the effect of the exchange-rate change on his competitors' costs will, in the short run, be rather muted. This will limit his ability to raise prices. Second, even if he could raise prices by the full amount of the appreciation the exchange loss would only be exactly offset if inventories exactly equalled his foreign currency debt. This second point can go either way – it can lead to either windfall losses or windfall gains; but a risk-averse importer, fearing a £1 loss more than he values £1 of gain, would still take some forward cover. On balance therefore these two points imply that, even for tradeables I, *all* exchange risk can be eliminated by partial forward cover.

Hypothesis III: more imports of tradeables I are covered forward than imports of tradeables II.

Testing hypothesis III, we find that it too is supported. Indeed, the support is quite striking. We found that 28.1 per cent by value (14.2 per cent by number) of British imports of tradeables I were covered forward, while only 25 per cent by value (12.9 per cent by number) of imports of tradeables II were covered forward. (The percentages for tradeables I and tradeables II were significantly different at the 5 per cent level.)

TABLE 7.1

A: Currencies in Foreign Trade Invoicing in the United Kingdom

	Exports Tradeables			*Imports Tradeables*		
	I	*II*	*All*	*I*	*II*	*All*
Seller's currency	75.7	77.3	75.9	55.0	46.3	53.5
Buyer's currency	17.1	18.3	17.3	27.8	31.5	27.9
US$ as a third currency	6.4	4.2	6.0	13.9	21.7	15.5
Other third currencies	0.8	0.2	0.8	3.3	0.5	3.1
Total	100.0	100.0	100.0	100.0	100.0	100.0

B: Proportion of Foreign Trade Covered Forward

	Tradeables I	*Tradeables II*	*All tradeables*
Exports covered forward	3.5 (0.9)	4.7 (6.6)	3.7 (1.9)
Imports covered forward	28.1 (14.2)	25.0 (12.9)	26.9 (13.5)

NOTES
1. The proportion of traders who covered forward is in parentheses.
2. The figures for all traded goods in exports and imports imply that 15.3 per cent of British foreign trade is transacted at forward exchange rates (assuming there is a visible trade equality of imports and exports).

Summarising so far, we have found that 75.9 per cent of British exports are invoiced in sterling (the exporter's home currency) and that 72.1 per cent of British imports are invoiced in foreign currency. We also found that about only 15 per cent of British trade was covered forward. A summary of results is given in Tables 7.1A and B. These results are consistent with those of Sven Grassman.[9] We have also shown that this pattern of invoicing and covering is explicable; that it arises from risk-aversion (in combination with exchange controls in the United Kingdom). It therefore appears justifiable to draw out certain implications of those observations.

STABILITY OF THE FOREIGN EXCHANGE MARKET WITH CAPITAL IMMOBILITY

Consider the time profile of a foreign-trade transaction as displayed schematically below. The process starts with an order being placed and the contract signed (t_0), and only at some subsequent time (t_1) are the goods exported. Delivery takes place at a later date still (t_2). Payment takes place on a date (t_3).

THE TIME PROFILE OF A TYPICAL FOREIGN TRADE TRANSACTION

t_0	t_1	t_2	t_3
Order placed	Registration by Customs of exporting country	Delivery (and registration by Customs of importing country)	Payment

In principle it would be possible for a contract to be written in such a way that the contract is denominated in one currency but is settled in another. Such a splitting of the unit-of-account and means-of-payment functions of money has in the past been known in the oil industry, where some of the Gulf States formerly demanded payment in sterling for accounts that were denominated in dollars. We have, however, not come across any examples of this practice and we therefore assume that, except where the contract is denominated in the importer's own currency, he needs to enter the foreign exchange market on or before t_3 in order to discharge his obligation. We found that, typically, firms do not attempt to cover their positions in advance of payment, either through the forward market or by buying the needed currency spot prior to t_3; the latter practice is indeed specifically precluded by British exchange-control regulations. Where a contract is denominated in the importer's or a third currency, the exporter needs to enter the foreign exchange market on or after t_3 in order to convert his proceeds into domestic currency. Given that British exchange-control regulations again require almost immediate conversion into sterling, one can legitimately assume that, except for the 15 per cent of trade that is covered forward, all the payments made at t_3 involve demand or supply in the British foreign exchange market at that time.

If the credit period is constant and there are no other private capital movements, the participants in the foreign exchange market at a time t_3 are the traders who have to fulfil contracts signed at some earlier time t_0. (We abstract for the time being from the forward market.) Importers from both countries come to the market with a demand, or exporters with a supply, that is predetermined in terms of the currency in which the contract was denominated. It is easy to see that which currency is used to denominate contracts is of fundamental importance in determining the stability of a freely-floating exchange rate (that is, when there is no central bank intervention whatsoever) in such a market. If contracts are denominated in the currency of the exporter, a depreciation of the domestic currency will reduce the foreign-currency value of the predetermined volume of exports being paid for at a predetermined domestic-currency price, while leaving the foreign-currency value of import payments unchanged.[10]

Since export payments provide the supply of foreign exchange while import payments provide the demand, the supply of foreign exchange will fall relative to the demand, that is, the excess demand for foreign exchange will increase. This will intensify the depreciation. If, on the other hand, contracts are denominated in the currency of the importer, a depreciation of the domestic currency will leave the foreign-currency value of exports unchanged, while reducing the foreign-currency value of imports, thus reducing the excess demand for foreign exchange and relieving the pressure for depreciation.[11]

This simple but important result may be stated formally as a theorem and proved.

It should be emphasised that the following result holds only in the short run, defined as the period before which either trade volumes or home-currency prices respond to an exchange-rate change.

Theorem: with zero capital mobility, a freely-floating exchange rate would be globally unstable if all trade contracts were denominated in the exporter's currency, and globally stable if all trade contracts were denominated in the importer's currency.

Note: for the sake of brevity in the presentation of the theorem, the phrase 'invoiced in the exporter's currency' means that in the case of the United Kingdom, for example, exports are invoiced in sterling and imports are invoiced in the exporter's currency or any other currency except sterling.

Proof

Let x = value of exports due for settlement in currency of denomination;
X = value of exports due for settlement in foreign currency;
m = value of imports due for settlement in currency of denomination;
M = value of imports due for settlement in foreign currency;
r = exchange rate (units of foreign exchange/unit of domestic currency).

Postulate that the exchange rate appreciates when there is excess supply of foreign exchange, that is:

$$\dot{r} = \alpha(X - M)$$

Case A: all contracts are denominated in the exporter's currency.

Then $X = xr, \qquad M = m$

so $\dot{r} = \alpha(xr - m)$

and $$\frac{\partial \dot{r}}{\partial r} = \alpha x > 0$$

that is, the exchange rate is unstable.

Case B: all contracts are denominated in the importer's currency.

Then $X = x, \qquad M = mr$

so $\dot{r} = a(x - mr)$

and $$\frac{\partial \dot{r}}{\partial r} = -\alpha m < 0,$$

that is, the exchange rate is stable.

The evidence indicates quite decisively that in Britain, as in the other industrial countries, exports are denominated overwhelmingly in domestic currency, while imports are denominated predominantly in foreign currency. One can therefore conclude that, in the absence of capital mobility, the foreign exchange market would be dynamically unstable. This instability is global: it is not a case of an unstable equilibrium being surrounded by two stable equilibria.[12]

The same set of facts that imply the dynamic instability of a freely-floating exchange rate also imply that a J-curve effect follows the devaluation of an adjustably-pegged rate. The usual explanation of the J-curve is that, when an industrial country devalues, the foreign-currency price of its exports falls by more than that of its imports. In themselves, these price adjustments tend to lead to an increased trade deficit, although of course their purpose is to prompt volume adjustments that are normally expected to outweigh the price effects in due course. Since, however, the price adjustments are made quickly, while the volume responses normally take some time to come into play, the initial effect of devaluation is to increase the trade deficit.

From time to time economists have expressed doubts as to whether this J-curve really exists. The practice of denominating export contracts in domestic currency and import contracts in foreign currency, however, implies that such an effect must exist, at least over the time interval $(t_3 - t_0)$. If a devaluation occurs at time t_0, it is not until t_3 that there will be any opportunity for a non-perverse response of the trade balance, defined on a payments basis, to occur. The earliest possible occasion for a non-perverse response of the trade balance on a transaction basis – that is, as it is measured in the United Kingdom by the trade statistics – is somewhat sooner, at t_1; while the earliest possible occasion for a positive response on the import side is t_2. The more relevant concept of the J-curve, however, is the length of time during which actual payments show an increased deficit and, with no capital movements, this is at least until t_3. Whether, and for how long, a J-curve persists beyond t_3 depends on the considerations that have traditionally been taken to underlie the J-curve: namely the speed with which prices are adjusted following an exchange-rate change, the extent to which those price adjustments imply a terms of trade deterioration, and the speed with which trade volumes respond to the changes in relative prices and competitiveness. The study undertaken in this paper is unable to throw any light on these factors; all it can do is to show that a short-term J-curve effect certainly exists in the United Kingdom.

The principal policy implication of the existence of a J-curve is that, following a devaluation, the authorities should be prepared to allow and to finance an increased trade deficit for some period of time. Only if such financing were impossible, because devaluation had been delayed until reserves were already depleted to the minimum tolerable level and it was impossible to induce a capital inflow, would it be rational to deflate income to the level compatible with 'external balance' during the period when the J-curve effect persists.[13] Since, however, the average period ($t_3 - t_0$) is almost certainly less (some twelve weeks) than the period needed for demand management policy to have an impact on the level of output and imports, this policy implication has little to do with the short-term J-curve that results from invoicing practices: it depends upon the longer-term, and less certain, J-curve that results from the delay in adjusting trade contracts to the changes in competitiveness. The important policy implication arising from invoicing practices is that, discussed above, which arises with a floating exchange rate.

ROLE OF THE FORWARD MARKET

In the preceding analysis we have abstracted from the possibility that transactions are covered in the forward market. This abstraction is in fact entirely natural as long as one is also abstracting from capital mobility, for in that event the instability of the spot exchange market is unaffected by the existence of a forward market. Some fraction of the contracts due for settlement on a date t are settled at a rate that has been determined at some previous time. Importers who have covered forward receive their foreign exchange from foreign importers who have also covered forward at a rate that in general differs from the spot rate. But, on the assumption of zero capital mobility, the values of trade transactions whose forward contracts mature on a date t must be balanced. Hence introduction of the forward market cannot alter the conclusion that the foreign exchange market is unstable when capital is immobile and trade contracts are denominated in the exporter's currency.

Its introduction does, however, have interesting implications when we allow capital mobility, for the widely held belief that dynamic stability of a freely-floating exchange rate requires some group to take an open position in foreign exchange, that is to speculate, is modified, at least in principle, in the case where a forward market exists. Suppose that there were a certain group of traders who not only cover their transactions forward, but who also decide whether or not to sign a contract according to the forward rate currently prevailing. Suppose, also, that the spot rate were declining and that there was no group prepared to stem this decline by taking an open position. If the decline in the spot rate were not accompanied by a decline in the forward rate, interest arbitrageurs would buy the currency spot and sell it forward. Their attempt to do this would depress the forward rate, which would, by the hypothesis assumed above, cause an increase in export contracts, and/or a diminution of import contracts, signed and covered forward. If trade responses were sufficiently sensitive to variations in the forward rate, the net demand for the currency in the forward market by forward-rate-sensitive traders would increase as the forward rate fell, thus matching the supply being provided by the interest arbitrageurs, who would in turn maintain the spot rate. It is therefore possible to envisage circumstances in which, despite denomination of export contracts in the currency of the exporter, the foreign-exchange market was stable even without speculation. The assumptions, however, needed to construct this case – notably the assumption that there exists a substantial body of traders who vary the number of contracts signed in the light of the forward rate, then promptly covering forward, whose collective demand for foreign exchange is elastic on a day-to-day basis – appear to us sufficiently remote from reality to justify regarding this case as a theoretical curiosity, particularly as so small a part of British trade is covered forward at all.

POLICY IMPLICATIONS

We have shown that the invoicing practices common in British foreign trade produce short-run instability of the foreign exchange market. We also showed that, while the introduction of the forward market could, once capital mobility is allowed, eliminate that instability without anyone taking an open position in a currency, the conditions necessary for this are, because of the small amount of British trade covered forward, certainly not present.

The principal policy implication which we draw from these results is that the government should make a joint, consistent decision on its policies toward exchange-rate management on the one hand and capital mobility on the other. If it intends to allow the exchange rate to float in more than name, then it should eliminate obstacles to short-term capital mobility, including exchange-control regulations governing the timing of trade payments. (Quite different considerations apply to the decision as to whether flows of long-term capital should be restricted – such as whether there may be a discrepancy between social and private returns because taxes and wage increases generated by investment accrue to foreigners when capital is exported.)[14]

Our own preference on this issue is to opt for a genuinely floating exchange rate, coupled with the elimination of obstacles to capital mobility. This is not to say that we advocate completely free floating with no management at all, but rather that such management as is undertaken should be done primarily through improving the information base of the private sector, for example by establishing and publishing a 'reference rate' designed to guide the private sector as to government estimates of the equilibrium rate, with that rate reinforced through intervention only to a very limited extent.[15] Such behaviour would encourage the taking of open positions, which our analysis leads us to conclude is of the greatest importance for short-run exchange market stability. This preference arises from a conviction that exchange-rate changes are a desirable part of the adjustment process, but are virtually impossible to effect through the adjustable peg in a world of high capital mobility (as the world would remain with any feasible tightening of exchange control) without major crises. Further, the invoicing practices which produce short-run exchange-rate instability are, as we have shown, rooted in micro-economic efficiency considerations; any policy which changed these practices with the aim of producing short-run stability we would therefore regard as undesirable.

SUMMARY AND CONCLUSIONS

Following Sven Grassman, we have investigated invoicing and forward covering practices in foreign trade. We found for the United Kingdom, as Grassman found for Sweden, a predominance of invoicing in the exporter's currency and very limited use of the forward market. This behaviour we showed was not chance, but explicable in terms of risk-aversion. On the basis of these results we then showed, first, that without capital mobility the exchange market was in the short run globally unstable; and, second, that, even with capital mobility, use of the forward market was so limited as to require the taking of open positions before the exchange market would be stable in the short run. We therefore concluded, on the basis of our analysis, that our preferred exchange-rate regime was one of managed floating (the management being largely confined, we stress, to improving the private sector's information base in ways such as that outlined in the above paragraph). Such a regime, in our view, would produce short-run exchange market stability without interfering with efficient micro-economic decision-making by firms.

APPENDIX: DIVISION AND SECTION TITLES OF THE STANDARD INTERNATIONAL TRADE CLASSIFICATION (REVISED)

Division	00	Live animals (excluding zoo animals, dogs and cats)
	01	Meat and meat preparations
	02	Dairy products and eggs
	03	Fish (not of British taking) and fish preparations
	04	Cereals and cereal preparations
	05	Fruit and vegetables
	06	Sugar, sugar preparations and honey
	07	Coffee, tea, cocoa, spices and manufactures thereof
	08	Feeding stuff for animals (not including unmilled cereals)
	09	Miscellaneous food preparations
Section	0	Food and live animals
Division	11	Beverages
	12	Tobacco and tobacco manufactures
Section	1	Beverages and tobacco
Division	21	Hides, skins and furskins, undressed
	22	Oil, seeds, oil nuts and oil kernels
	23	Crude rubber (including synthetic and reclaimed)
	24	Wood, lumber and cork
	25	Pulp and waste paper
	26	Textile fibres not manufactured and their waste, old clothing and other textile articles: rags
	27	Crude fertilisers and crude minerals (excluding coal, petroleum and precious stones)
	28	Metalliferous ores and metal scrap
	29	Crude animal and vegetable materials, not elsewhere specified
Section	2	Crude materials, inedible, except fuels
Division	32	Coal, coke and briquettes
	33	Petroleum and petroleum products
	34	Gas, natural and manufactured
	35	Electric energy

Section	3 Mineral fuels, lubricants and related materials
Division	41 Animal oils and fats
	42 Fixed vegetable oils and fats
	43 Animal and vegetable oils and fats, processed, and waxes of animal or vegetable origin
Section	4 Animal and vegetable oils and fats
Division	51 Chemical, elements and compounds
	52 Mineral tar and crude chemicals from coal, petroleum and natural gas
	53 Dyeing, tanning and colouring materials
	54 Medicinal and pharmaceutical products
	55 Essential oils and perfume materials; toilet, polishing and cleansing preparations
	56 Fertilisers, manufactured
	57 Explosives and pyrotechnic products
	58 Plastic materials, regenerated cellulose and artificial resins
	59 Chemical materials and products, not elsewhere specified
Section	5 Chemicals
Division	61 Leather, leather manufactures, not elsewhere specified, and dressed furskins
	62 Rubber manufactures, not elsewhere specified
	63 Wood and cork manufactures (excluding furniture)
	64 Paper, paperboard and manufactures thereof
	65 Textile yarn, fabrics, made-up articles and related products
	66 Non-metallic mineral manufactures, not elsewhere specified
	67 Iron and steel
	68 Non-ferrous metals
	69 Manufactures of metal, not elsewhere specified
Section	6 Manufactured goods classified chiefly by material
Division	71 Machinery, other than electric
	72 Electrical machinery, apparatus and appliances
	73 Transport equipment
Section	7 Machinery and transport equipment

Division	81	Sanitary, plumbing, heating and lighting fixtures and fittings
	82	Furniture
	83	Travel goods, handbags and similar articles
	84	Clothing, knitted or crocheted articles including elastic or rubberised fabric and articles of fur
	85	Footwear, gaiters and the like
	86	Professional, scientific and controlling instruments; photographic and optical goods; watches and clocks
	87	Miscellaneous manufactured articles, not elsewhere specified
Section	8	Miscellaneous manufactured articles
Section	9	Commodities and transactions not classified according to kind

NOTES

1. This paper reports some of the results of a study of financing procedures in British foreign trade, undertaken in collaboration with the late Fred Hirsch and with John Williamson. We are indebted to the Ford Foundation for its financial support of the research programme, and to John Spraos for his most useful comments on the paper.
2. Grassman (1973a and b).
3. Firms engaged regularly and substantially in foreign trade are sometimes allowed to maintain foreign currency accounts of strictly limited size, with their bank in the United Kingdom. The limits on the size of these 'hold' accounts are low and are strictly enforced, so that their existence does not substantially modify this statement. Hold accounts are allowed so as to reduce transaction costs on firms who both import and export using foreign currency. Foreign-currency receipts can only be held where a payment in that same currency is soon to be made.
4. This nomenclature is due to Aliber (1976).
5. This conjecture is supported by some work by Williamson and Wood (1976) who showed that the prices of motor-cars were very imperfectly arbitraged internationally, and also by Isard (1977).
6. It is convenient to note here why we do not need to make use of the distinction between two types of risk that is fairly widely used in the literature on foreign-exchange exposure – that between transaction exposure and translation exposure. Transaction exposure is the exposure to risk between the time a transaction is initiated and the time it is paid for; it is what we have called exchange risk. Translation exposure arises from having assets (and/or liabilities) in more than one currency; the balance-sheet value of these, when translated to one accounting currency for the enterprise, can of course be affected by an exchange-rate change, and the firm's net worth, as measured by its balance sheet, can change in the absence of any transactions.

Since we are concerned only with flows of goods and their associated payments, we refer only to transaction exposure.

7. In this section of the paper we make use of some recent work by R. I. McKinnon (forthcoming). We are greatly indebted to Professor McKinnon for allowing us access to this work.
8. This kind of classification is not novel, although its application in this area is. The distinction is very similar to that in macro-economics between 'flexprice goods' (in Hicks' term) or goods traded in 'auction markets' (a term used by, among others, R. J. Gordon) and, on the other hand, 'fixprice goods' which are traded on 'customer markets'.
9. Sven Grassman (1973).
10. Magee (1973) discusses the implications for all four combinations of currency invoicing practices in importing and exporting.
11. It can now of course be seen why what matters is that more than 50 per cent of exports be denominated in sterling while more than 50 per cent of imports be denominated in foreign currency; for if that is so, the above arguments all hold.
12. As in the traditional analysis of the 'static stability' of the foreign exchange market. See Kemp (1964).
13. Incidentally, during this period, devaluation cannot play the traditional role assigned to an expenditure-switching policy of avoiding the need to depress output below the 'internal balance' level – the income level consistent with 'external balance' (assuming zero capital mobility) actually declines as long as the J-curve effect persists.
14. A discussion of the factors relevant to the decision as to whether to restrict long-term capital exports can be found in Williamson (1973).
15. For discussion of the 'reference rate' proposal see Ethier and Bloomfield (1975) and Williamson (1975).

REFERENCES

R. Z. ALIBER, 'The Firm Under Pegged and Floating Exchange Rates', *Scandinavian Journal of Economics*, Stockholm, Vol. 78, No. 2, 1976.

W. ETHIER and A. I. BLOOMFIELD, 'Managing the Managed Float', *Princeton Essays in International Finance*, Princeton, No. 112, 1975.

SVEN GRASSMAN, *Exchange Reserves and the Financial Structure of Foreign Trade* (Farnborough, Hampshire: Saxon House, 1973a).

—— 'A Fundamental Symmetry in International Payments Patterns', *Journal of International Economics*, Amsterdam, Vol. 3, May 1973b).

P. ISARD, 'How Far Can We Push the Law of One Price?', *American Economic Review*, Vol. 67, December 1977.

M. C. KEMP, *The Pure Theory of International Trade* (Englewood Cliffs: Prentice-Hall, 1964) Ch. 18.

R. I. MCKINNON, *Money in International Exchange: the Convertible Currency System* (London: Oxford University Press, 1979).

STEPHEN P. MAGEE, 'Currency Contracts, Pass-through, and Devaluation', *Brookings Papers on Economic Activity*, Washington, No. 1, 1973.

J. WILLIAMSON, 'Payments Adjustment and Economic Welfare' *IMF Staff Papers*, Washington, Vol. 20, November 1973.

J. WILLIAMSON, 'The Future Exchange Rate Regime', *Banca Nazionale del Lavoro Quarterly Review*, Rome, Vol. 28, June 1975.

J. WILLIAMSON and GEOFFREY E. WOOD, 'The British Inflation: Indigenous or Imported', *American Economic Review*, Vol. 66, September 1976.

International Money and Reserves in the World Economy

K. ALEC CHRYSTAL

The aim of this paper is to draw attention to some issues which have been somewhat neglected in international monetary economics. The argument to be developed is based upon a view of the world as a monetary system, particular attention being given to the role of money as a transactions medium in an international context.It is not intended to convey the impression that the transactions motive is the only, or even the dominant, reason for international money holdings. But it will be shown that, if there is any value in this approach at all, it does raise serious questions about the role of the IMF Special Drawing Rights (SDRs).

In what follows, Section I will briefly draw attention to some of the existing ideas in this field, Section II will discuss the connection between offical reserves and private international money balances. Finally Section III will analyse the role of centrally created reserves such as the SDR. At the outset, however, it should be stressed that many of the steps in the ensuing argument depend upon acceptance of monetary-theoretic propositions which may themselves be subject to dispute. Nonetheless, it is sufficient for present purposes to achieve recognition that the scenario to be developed is a possible one. Only time and a great deal more research will establish its true validity.

I EXISTING LITERATURE

There are two distinct schools of thought concerning the role of money in the international payments system. The first, which has come to be called the 'vehicle currency hypothesis', is associated with the names of A. K. Swoboda and R. I. McKinnon. Further support for this view has come from C. P. Kindleberger, K. Brunner and A. Meltzer, and Richard. N. Cooper[1]. The second, the 'symmetry hypothesis', arises from the evidence provided by Sven Grassman on the invoicing pattern of Swedish foreign trade.[2]

According to the vehicle-currency hypothesis there is a demand in the international economy for a circulating medium of exchange, just as there is in a domestic economy. There will be information and resource gains to traders because of alleged transactions economies of scale in money holdings. Thus, the balances required to conduct all trade in one currency would be less than the sum of those required if the same aggregate value of trade were conducted in several different currencies. Swoboda derives this result from the inventory model of W. Baumol[3] and, whilst doubts have been raised as to the precise empirical value of this model by C. Sprenkel,[4] there would seem to be absolutely no reason to expect the contrary to be true.[5] That is to say, a widely acceptable statement should be one that says that, *ceteris paribus*, money balances held to conduct trade in one currency will not exceed those held to conduct the same value of trade in a number of different currencies.[6] If such a proposition is acceptable then the addition of informational gains makes the use of an international medium unambiguously beneficial. The currencies which will actually be used are clearly those of the dominant trading nations and, in this respect, the dollar is to be regarded as the paradigm vehicle currency.

Whilst there is some aggregate evidence available[7] relating aggregate external money balances to trade, the symmetry view has flourished on the basis of a different kind of evidence. Grassman has shown that Swedish foreign trade is dominantly invoiced in the currency of the exporter, to a much lesser extent in the currency of the importer and hardly at all in third-party currencies. There was little apparent change in this pattern between 1968 and 1973 (save for a decline in the use of sterling and rise in the use of the Deutschemark,[8]) despite the fact that the latter observation post-dates the onset of floating exchange rates. None the less it would have to be admitted by the Grassman school that *some* of Sweden's foreign trade is invoiced in third-party currency and that some commodity types are dominantly invoiced in dollars – these, of course, being largely homogeneous primary commodities.

It is apparent that the relationship between invoicing patterns and demand for stocks of currencies is in fact complex. It could be argued that invoicing patterns tell us little about the fundamental nature of the world monetary system but rather a lot about the market position and associated pricing policies of various industries. Industrial exporters with a somewhat differentiated product, or who are merely supplying overseas sales subsidiaries, will have no good reason to set their prices in other than their own currency. This will be especially true when exchange rates are fixed but will continue to be so unless floating rates inflict sufficient losses of sales to make the cost of pricing in an alternative currency worthwhile. Even here, however, the existence of forward markets for most currencies would suggest that only long-term contracts will, necessarily, be serious candidates for change.

Is the symmetry hypothesis necessarily inconsistent with the existence of vehicle currencies? Clearly it is if we take the vehicle-currency hypothesis in its original form – that is, if it is asserted that a larger proportion of trade in goods and services is settled in terms of vehicle currency. But consider the question in a different form. Does perfect symmetry of invoicing patterns preclude the existence of 'transaction balances' of vehicle currencies? The answer is no. In order to arrive at this conclusion, however, the hypothesis has to be formulated in a slightly different way. Consider the dollar to be the potential vehicle currency. The United States is the largest country in world trade and their money market is the largest in the world. The dollar may not be the 'money' in all goods markets but it can still be the money in all foreign exchange markets. Cross-markets do not exist for all currencies in the world but every currency has a market with the dollar (if it has a market at all) Currency traders, at least, will wish to hold working balances of dollars. But what of goods traders?

Consider a goods trader who has stochastic payments and receipts in a number of different currencies. He can adopt any combination of three possible strategies. First, he can convert all foreign currency balances into domestic currency virtually instantaneously. Second, he can run an inventory of every currency in terms of which he trades, switching from one to another only when he has to make payment in a currency of which he has a zero balance. Or, third, he can convert balances of most external currencies into dollars unless he has a known payment to be made in another currency in the foreseeable future. If it is conceded that transactions costs in dollars are significantly lower than for any other currency, that the probability of the next payment being in dollars is higher than for any other currency and that there may be inventory economies of scale, then strategy three would appear likely to dominate. When to this is added the greater probability that if trade *finance* is involved it will be dollar-denominated, the strategy of matching asset and liability denominations would seem to make the case for holding dollar balances rather than any other currency virtually impregnable.

This analysis clearly hangs critically on the difference in transactions costs between the dollar and other currencies as well as between spot and forward markets. Many readers who have been accustomed to ignoring transactions costs may find it hard to believe that these could be significant, let alone significantly different. The evidence, such as it is, however, is strongly supportive of this view. Swoboda reports that:

> In London, which is probably the most important foreign exchange centre, the brokerage fee on U.S. dollar transactions is only $\frac{1}{5}$ of the fee on Canadian dollar transactions, and roughly $\frac{1}{8}$ to $\frac{1}{10}$ of the fee on other major currencies. In Rome, the brokerage fee for dollars is approximately $\frac{1}{2}$ of the fee on other major currencies whereas in Belgium the figure is about $\frac{1}{4}$ (except for the Canadian dollar). In Germany the brokerage fee on U.S. dollar and pound sterling transactions is $2\frac{1}{2}$ to 3 times lower than that on other currencies. Finally, the French practice of charging .01 centimes per dollar or per continental monetary unit is equivalent to charging .02 per cent on dollar transactions and three to five times more on continental currency transactions.[9]

Proof of this point, would, of course, require more recent information on transactions costs in both spot and forward markets. But at the very least it is worth considering as a possibility.

The conclusion of this section is then that, irrespective of the evidence relating to invoicing patterns, there is some reason to believe that the world economy has a demand for balances of vehicle currencies or what may more conventionally be called international media of exchange. Such balances clearly exist and there is every reason to expect that growing world trade will be associated with a growing demand for them. This is what international liquidity discussions should largely be about and it is noticeable that, so far, there has been no need to say anything about the official sector of the system. It is therefore now necessary to turn to a discussion of the relationship between the private-sector holdings of international money and official-sector holdings of international reserves.

II OFFICIAL RESERVES AND PRIVATE MONEY

It is customary to consider private money holdings separately from official reserve holdings. There is, however, in many cases a considerable degree of interdependence between the official sector and the private sector. The nature of this interdependence has now to be highlighted. It is convenient to proceed by considering various types of monetary system.

Consider, first, the pure gold standard system, where it is assumed that gold is the money internally and externally. This is an extreme case, but it is an interesting one because here the domestic money supply and international reserves are one and the same thing. Clearly official reserves would simply be official sector holdings of gold. But there would be no reason in such a system to distinguish between private and official holdings. Overall payments deficits or surpluses would simply lead to a corresponding fall or rise in the domestic gold balances. Private traders hold their international money balances for themselves but these are also the domestic money.

The second case is slightly more complex and may be called the modified gold standard. Here international payments continue to be made in gold, but domestic circulation is predominantly in deposit notes. Notes exchange for gold at a fixed rate but the fixing is achieved by the banking system as a whole and there continues to be no clear distinction between the official and private sector, at least in so far as the monetary system is concerned. There is now, however, a clear difference between reserves and money supply, although reserves have two functions. First they are the 'backing' for the domestic paper issue (but only those held by the banks), and second they are the country's holdings of externally acceptable money (which may be held privately or by deposit-taking institutions). It is this second function that is of specific interest, so the first function will be deliberately neglected.

Consider then a country's gold holdings, held for purposes of international trade. Every trader trading abroad will require at his disposal a stock of gold from which he can meet his net external debts. This gold could be held by traders themselves, in which case the international reserve could be thought of as the sum of traders' balances. Here the gold inventories required could presumably be analysed in the standard way. The possible existence of transactions economies of scale, however, means that such dispersal of gold holdings would not be a long-run equilibrium. If traders' balances could be pooled in some way, then the jointly held reserve could be smaller than the sum of individual balances. This obviously permits the possibility of a profitable banking operation. Any bank would be able to bribe traders to deposit gold in exchange for bank paper and, as a result, the bank would have scope for further profitable lending.

Another way of looking at the same phenomenon is to ask what the required trading reserve would be if traders were able to hold a joint reserve on which all could draw. The presumption is that the joint reserve required would be smaller than the sum of the individual reserves for any given level of trade, and its validity would depend on the signs of the individual covariances of net cash flows. If such economies of pooling do indeed exist, it would be no surprise to find the number of deposit-taking institutions involved to be small. In some well-documented cases the reserve-holding institution *evolves* to be unique.[10]

This last step in the argument is an important one which is worth stressing. It is being suggested that there are sound economic reasons why the trading reserve of an economy could come to be centrally held since, as a result, the size of reserve required could be minimised. In this respect the centralised reserve can be thought of as being held on behalf of the trading sector and its optimal size will depend on exactly the same factors as would individual reserves. Centralisation of reserves is of course a matter of degree, depending upon the number of institutions involved. But central banks should be seen as part of this spectrum – not qualitatively separable.

For any given level of external trade, the more gold that traders hold for themselves the less will be held in any centralised reserve and vice versa. Thus we have arrived at the conclusion that, if there has evolved a centralised holding of the trading reserve, there is a relationship between individual and central holdings. The greater is the former, the smaller will be the latter and the greater is the latter, the smaller will be the former, *ceteris paribus.*

Clearly there are many loose ends in the above model, especially with regard to the position of banking reserves in general. But the value of the exposition is that the trade-reserve argument carries over particularly easily to the modern floating exchange-rate case. In the latter situation the analysis is even simpler because the trading reserve and the banking reserve are quite distinct. Consider each country to have its own internal fiat money. Exchange rates are market-determined but traders require working balances of dollars upon which they may draw, the dollar being the only international money. Consider the domestic central bank to be a deposit-taking institution (the existence of a banking 'buffer' between the central bank and traders adds an extra step but no unavoidable difficulty).Traders have the effective choice of holding their dollar deposits in foreign banks or placing them with the central bank. If the central bank issues traders with a dollar-denominated liability then the above analysis goes through *mutatis mutandis*. The bigger the proportion of dollar deposits held through the central bank, the smaller they will be overall. And the same interdependence exists between central bank dollar assets and traders' external dollar assets.

The analysis, however, is rather more complex to the extent that the central bank issues a domestic currency liability to traders in exchange for a dollar deposit. This is an interesting case because it is very close to a situation in which the central bank is not a deposit-taking institution but instead runs an active foreign exchange buffer. That is to say, if the central bank buys foreign exchange when its traders are selling and sells when they are buying, the effect is the same as issuing a domestic denominated deposit in exchange for foreign currency. This is an important step because it implies that a central bank can be thought of as holding reserves on behalf of its trading sectors whether or not it is in fact a deposit-taking institution. If the central bank has no active reserve, then traders will wish to hold larger inventories of foreign exchange than they otherwise would. This is obviously because exchange-rate uncertainty is reduced by central bank smoothing operations. An interesting corollary of this argument could be that, at least in so far as overall reserve holdings are concerned, rigidly fixed exchange rates accompanied by foreign-exchange controls could be optimal. The latter would amount to enforced pooling of excess foreign balances and the former could minimise required working balances.

It is important, at this point, to be aware of an assumption which is being implicitly made. This is that foreign currency holding involves a real opportunity cost. It might be objected that this is not appropriate in the modern world, since reserves are held in interest-bearing deposits. This does not, in fact, change the picture. Virtually all large-scale deposits are in interest-yielding form for whatever term they are made. What matters is that, because they are highly liquid, the interest is less than could be obtained if liquidity were not required. In other words, so long as short-term interest rates are less than those on long-term investments then reserve holdings have an opportunity cost. If centralising reserve holdings reduces transactions demand, resources will be released which can be invested more profitably. The existence of such an opportunity cost will continue to be presumed.

A number of points have now emerged which can be summarised.

First, for *any* degree of exchange-rate variability a country's foreign exchange holdings may be reduced to the extent that they are centrally held. This implies that official reserve holdings are not solely associated with fixed exchange rates. They can be thought of as substitutes for private inventories which will be demanded whatever the exchange-rate regime. The relation between central bank and trading sector does not require the bank to take deposits, although, of course, many central banks are deposit-taking institutions. Secondly, it would seem reasonable to suggest that the assets held by central banks in their active reserve should be just those that traders would wish to draw on to meet net external payments. There need not,of course, be a direct correspondence, but it is likely that the characteristics required of an intervention currency and of a vehicle currency will be identical, especially with regard to the 'depth, breadth and resilience' of the market for that particular currency. As a very minimum a central bank would need to hold an active reserve of *marketable* currency. This latter point is rather obvious but it does have implications for the SDR which will arise below. Finally, it is now clear that the *primary* need for international money balances arises in the international trading sector – it always has done so and it always will. It is the existence of separate currency areas which generates an international monetary problem. The role of the official sector and of supranational reserve assets can only be assessed in the light of the needs of the private sector, and attention is now turned to an evaluation of the SDR.

III CENTRALLY-CREATED RESERVES AND THE SDR

In the fixed exchange-rate world of the two decades which followed the Bretton Woods agreement, it was the position of official reserves that was given overwhelming attention. The critical problem, as perceived by Robert Triffin, was agreed to be how to provide for a sufficient growth of official reserves (usually synonymous with international liquidity) without becoming overdependent upon the dollar as a reserve currency. The danger of this would be that the ratio of United States gold reserves to dollar liabilities could become so small that confidence in the dollar would become fragile. The SDR was invented as a way of providing for an increase in official reserves without raising dependence upon the dollar. Indeed it is still widely believed that the SDR will provide for the future growth of reserves and, as a result, will reduce dependence on all reserve currencies.

In this section it will be first argued that since the SDR is not marketable, it cannot be used either as a vehicle currency or an intervention currency and, as a result, will never replace assets that can. Secondly, it will be noted that the SDR is best thought of as a credit instrument rather than as 'money'. And, finally, it will be suggested that there is a logical possibility of SDR creation leading to an increase of official foreign exchange holdings, rather than a decrease as has previously been presumed.

The fact that the SDR is, at best, money between central banks and cannot be used in foreign exchange markets has been noted elsewhere, notably by Richard N. Cooper.[11] It is worth stressing, in the light of the above analysis, however, that the basic international monetary problem is to provide a monetary instrument which is available to all actors in the system and especially to private traders. This is required to facilitate transactions between people who live in different currency areas. It could, of course, be argued that the SDR would ease this problem to the extent that its existence increased the stability of exchange markets. But, the SDR *itself* cannot do this, since it cannot be used in exchange markets. Rather, it is only useful to the extent that it increases availability of other currencies. Traded currencies, such as the dollar, will continue to be held by private traders and, of course, the active proportion of official reserves will also continue to consist of foreign exchange.

It would appear, therefore, that if the SDR were to be a desirable reserve asset it must be because of its pecuniary yield characteristics, since it yields no utility through its marketability. The set-up of SDRs, by which net users pay interest to net holders, though, makes the characteristics of the SDR as a reserve asset rather strange. H. G. Grubel has recently applied the optimal quantity of money analysis to the SDR.[12] He argues that the optimal welfare allocation will be achieved where the interest rate on SDRs is just equal to the market rate (for the same risk characteristics). Since the initial allocation yields no interest to the holder, whatever the interest rate set, this argument is entirely inappropriate. Indeed, if the interest rate on the SDR were considered equivalent to a market interest rate, then the welfare gains from *any* initial allocation would be exactly zero, since any foreign exchange acquired in return for SDR would incur the rate of interest which would have been paid for such a loan anyway. Increasing overdraft facilities at market interest rates when a market is already in equilibrium has no effect whatsover. Only if the increased supply of credit lowers interest rates will there be an increase in demand. For the optimal quantity of money argument to go through, either interest should be paid to all holders (through perhaps increased allocation) or the valuation of the SDR should be set in such a way that it appreciates against a typical bundle of currencies. If governments regard the present SDR allocation as net wealth they are deluded; it is merely a credit facility.

What then is the effect of an SDR allocation? The presumption which underlay the introduction of the SDR was that there would be an increase in total reserves which was less than the value of the SDR allocation itself. That is to say that central banks would react in such a way as to reduce the foreign exchange component of reserves in absolute value. It is not clear how this would come about, but a necessary condition on the demand side is that holders regard the marginal utility of SDRs as exceeding that of substitutes. But if, as is not entirely inconceivable, the marginal utility of the SDR is widely regarded as below that of say dollar assets, then it becomes quite possible for an SDR allocation to lead to an increase in foreign-exchange reserves. Whether or not this actually happens is, of course, an empirical matter, but that it is at least a logical possibility should be recognised.

Consider there to be two different kinds of central bank in the world. First, there are the 'banker' central banks whose currencies are acceptable as official-sector reserves. And, secondly, there are the ordinary central banks whose liabilities only serve as money in their own country. So far as the ordinary central banks are concerned, each has a reserve which is the outcome of its overall monetary and exchange-rate policy and the composition of the reserve is presumably determined by regard to the characteristics of marketability, yield and risk. Now let each be given an allocation of SDRs. Is the resulting portfolio an optimal one? The answer is clearly no if the marginal utility of any foreign exchange asset exceeds that of SDRs. Such a situation is not unlikely since the interest on the SDR is a fraction below that on a basket of currencies, in addition to which marketability will presumably yield utility. In other words the typical ordinary central bank could be looking to increase the foreign-exchange component of its portfolio by drawing upon its SDR facility, either because the interest cost of using SDRs is exceeded by the interest yield on say, dollar assets, or because the latter provide utility as an intervention currency, whereas SDRs do not.

The position of banker central banks is different in one important respect. This is that, even if they also regard the marginal utility of SDRs as less than that of other reserves, they may still find SDRs preferable to their own liabilities. In other words, a banker central bank may not wish to accept SDRs (in addition to its allocation) in exchange for other elements of its reserve portfolio but it might be prepared to accept them in exchange for its own liabilities. The sense in this is clear when it is realised that it would, in effect, be printing its own reserves. Even if they do not want SDRs they may be 'designated' as recipients by the IMF. A numerical example could serve to illustrate the possible reaction process.

TABLE 8.1

Numerical Example as Illustration of the Possible Reaction Process

	Banker central banks				*Non-banker central bank*	
	A		*B*		*C*	
	SDR	FE	SDR	FE	SDR	FE
Round 1	100	0	100	0	100	0
Round 2	100	0	200	0	0	100
Round 3	200	0	100	100	0	100
Round 4	100	100	100	100	100	0

NOTES

1. FE = Foreign-exchange reserves; SDR = Special drawing rights.
2. Numbers are additional to original position.

Consider the situation depicted in Table 8.1. There are two banker central banks, A and B, and one non-banker, C. In the first round all are given an allocation of 100 SDRs. Central bank C decides it would like to use its SDRs to obtain foreign exchange (FE) so it goes to B and B takes C's SDRs, issuing its own liabilities in exchange. B now has 200 SDRs and C has 100 of FE. Banker B now has more SDRs than its own allocation so it may decide to go to A and offer SDRs in exchange for A's liabilities. After round three, then, A would have 200 SDRs, and B would have 100 SDRs and 100 FE. If C were now to restore its allocation by repurchasing from A 100 SDRs with the FE, which is B's liability, all central banks would have restored their SDR allocation (as encouraged by the rules) but foreign exchange reserves would have risen, in this case by 200. Clearly, in practice, adjustment is restricted by the IMF rules but these have recently been relaxed – with the intention of making the SDR more attractive! Only round three looks unlikely since it is not clear why A should accept SDR from B. If, however, it knows that round four is in prospect, then the two combined leave A with more FE than before. This is clearly desirable. Such a process may of course take a long time to complete a circuit, and obviously exaggerates the likely effect. None the less, even after the first round, foreign-exchange reserves have risen and may never fall again. All that is required for foreign-exchange reserves to rise is that some central bank should issue its own currency in exchange for SDRs.

This portfolio adjustment process is only one of many possible scenarios but it does seem that there is a chance that an SDR allocation could be followed by an increase in the foreign exchange element of reserves. Indeed, the process described is little more than a legitimate form of what used to be known as 'incest'. The difference between the initial and ultimate situation is that banker A and banker B have created reserves for themselves by exchanging liabilities. This was always possible under the Bretton Woods system but was regarded as being against the rules of the game. Now the existence of SDRs may obscure, even from central bankers, what is going on. All that is required for this 'multiplier' process to continue is for there to exist at least one banker central bank prepared to accept SDRs for its own liabilities and one other central bank looking to obtain foreign exchange for SDRs. A foreign-exchange-reserves contraction would require banker countries to buy back their liabilities as a result of an increase in their SDR holdings. This seems no more likely than the opposite.

The story does not end with the portfolio adjustment phase because central banks will adjust their monetary policies as a result of the higher levels of reserves. None is likely to react to an apparent increase in reserves by a contractionary monetary policy, so the world money supply will increase. Any resulting inflation will reduce the real value of reserves. This need not affect the composition of reserves unless, as has been suggested, typical central banks wish to increase the proportion of foreign exchange in their reserve portfolio. This they can do by running a less expansionary monetary policy than the banker countries and acquiring foreign exchange through the market. A process such as this is, of course, sufficient on its own to generate an SDR multiplier, even in the absence of the portfolio adjustment process described above. If the foreign-exchange component of reserves were to decline, as a result of central bank spending, then, in the absence of asset settlement, these reserves would flow into the private sector. A direct money supply increase would result. So this outcome is not one that should be generally encouraged.

It is clear that the period since the introduction of the SDR has indeed been associated with a rapid rise in the foreign-exchange component of reserves. It would, however, be unwise to attempt to attribute such events to the existence of the SDR, since the conventional story of the United States deficit must be heeded. None the less, it would be equally unwise to ignore the possibility that the SDR issue was a contributory factor in the collapse of the system. It is typical to regard the SDR as a good idea which came along too late. Further serious thought should be given to the role of the SDR in the light of the above analysis. The truth might just be that the SDR is a bad idea that should never have come at all.

The mistake in analysis which encouraged the belief that the SDR could reduce dependence upon foreign-exchange reserves is the same mistake that encourages the community of nations to believe that by strong words they can make the SDR evolve into the 'major reserve asset' of the international monetary system. As presently constituted the SDR is not a reserve asset at all, it is a credit facility. Unless there is some major rethinking, the future of the SDR will be small and its contribution to solving the basic international monetary problem will be minor.

IV CONCLUSION

The basic function for which international monetary institutions are required is to facilitate transactions between a diversity of currency areas. It seems clear that the world economy has evolved balances of marketable currencies which can fruitfully be viewed as international media of exchange. Indeed they fulfil all the classical functions of money. Any supranational asset which is to increase the efficiency of the world monetary system must be provided with demonstrably superior characteristics to existing accepted currencies. The SDR as presently constituted has little or nothing to offer. Indeed it is not even clear that future SDR issues will not lead to increased holdings of foreign exchange.

Private traders will require international money balances, whether or not central banks intervene to smooth exchange rates. If there were no such interventions it is possible that private demand would rise so as to more than offset the fall in demand for official sector reserves. In other words, the *total* demand for international money balances could well be greater under a regime of floating exchange rates than one of fixed exchange rates. On this basis it is clear that central banks might fruitfully be advised to pursue a policy of at least smoothing exchange-rate fluctuations, since they may thereby achieve a resource saving for their trading sector.

It is clear, however, that the above analysis highlights only monetary aspects of the world economy. The simple solution to this basic problem would be to have just one world money. Some would argue that such a solution would cause as many problems as it solved, but of course they would not be strictly monetary problems. Rather they would be regional problems. Perhaps the best politically feasible solution, in the long run, will be to have just one supranational international money and a genuine symmetry of national currencies. But the SDR, as presently constituted, can never perform this job. The experiment has been one small step for man in the wrong direction!

NOTES

1. See Swoboda (1968), McKinnon (1969), Brunner and Meltzer (1971), Kindleberger (1972) and Cooper (1972).
2. Grassman (1973) and (1976).
3. Baumol (1952).
4. Sprenkel (1969).
5. Indeed, Sprenkel's evidence that the size of money balances is larger than one would expect confirms the potential importance of money balances in the world economy.
6. A similar pattern is reported for other major countries in Page (1977).
7. Chrystal (1975, 1976, 1977).
8. This is quite consistent with the evidence in Chrystal (1977) which shows substitutability between sterling and Deutschemarks.
9. Swoboda (1969), p. 136.
10. The role of the Bank of England is a clear example, see Bagehot (1873): '. . . But the danger to the depositing banks is not the sole or principal consequence of this mode of keeping the London reserve. The main effect is to cause the reserve to be much smaller in proportion to liabilities than it would otherwise be.'
11. Cooper (1972).
12. Grubel (1977).

REFERENCES

W. BAGEHOT, *Lombard Street* (London: H. S. King, 1873).

W. BAUMOL, 'The Transactions Demand for Cash, an Inventory Theoretic Approach', *Quarterly Journal of Economics*, Cambridge, Mass., Vol. 66, No. 4, November 1952, pp. 545–56.

K. BRUNNER and A. MELTZER, 'The Uses of Money: Money in the Theory of an Exchange Economy', *American Economic Review*, Manasha, Wisconsin, Vol. 61, No. 5, December 1971, pp. 784–805.

K. ALEC CHRYSTAL, 'Demand for International Media of Exchange', University of Essex, Ph. D. thesis, 1975.

—— 'Some Evidence in Defence of the Vehicle Currency Hypothesis', University of Essex Discussion Paper, No. 93, November 1976.

—— 'Demand for International Media of Exchange', *American Economic Review*, December 1977, pp. 840–50.

RICHARD N. COOPER, 'Eurodollars, Reserve Dollars and Asymmetries in the International Monetary System', *Journal of International Economics*, Amsterdam, Vol. 2, No. 4, September 1972, pp. 325–44.

SVEN GRASSMAN, *Exchange Reserves and the Financial Structure of Foreign Trade* (Farnborough, Hants: Saxon House, 1973).

—— 'Currency Distributions and Forward Cover in Foreign Trade: Sweden Revisited, 1973', *Journal of International Economics*, Vol. 6, No. 2, May 1976 pp. 215–21.

HERBERT G. GRUBEL, *The International Monetary System*, 3rd edition (London: Penguin, 1977).

CHARLES P. KINDLEBERGER, 'The Benefits of International Money', *Journal of International Economics*, Vol. 2, No. 4, September 1972, pp. 425–47.

RONALD I. MCKINNON, *Private and Official International Money: the Case for the Dollar*, Princeton Essays in International Finance No. 74 (Princeton: Princeton University Press, 1969).

S. A. B. PAGE, 'Currency of Invoicing in Merchandise Trade', *National Institute Economic Review*, London, August 1977.

CASE SPRENKEL, 'The Uselessness of Transactions Demand Models', *Journal of Finance*, New York, December 1969, pp. 835–47.

A. K. SWOBODA, *Eurodollars: a Suggested Interpretation*, Princeton Essays in International Finance No. 64 (Princeton: Princeton University Press, 1968).

—— 'Vehicle Currencies and the Foreign Exchange Market', in R. Z. Aliber (ed.), *International Market for Foreign Exchange* (New York: Praeger, 1969) p. 36.

9

Reciprocity in Trade Negotiations under Flexible Exchange Rates

RICHARD BLACKHURST[1]

The two related topics suggested by the title may be introduced by posing in a simplified form the two questions I will attempt to answer.

> (*a*) Textbook discussions of the gains from freer trade typically say little or nothing about the trade policies of other countries – so why, we may ask, are countries traditionally so concerned with the need to 'achieve reciprocity' in trade negotiations? Or, more succinctly, if freer trade is beneficial, why not adopt it unilaterally?

And

> (*b*) Is the answer to the first question dependent on what is assumed about the exchange rate?

To answer these questions it is necessary to depart from the essentially long-run analysis of comparative statics – with its assumptions of perfect wage/price flexibility and perfect factor mobility – and to focus primarily on the short run. That is, the answer to the first question involves several considerations which arise only during the transition between two equilibrium positions, while the second question has little relevance outside the short run since, in the long run, exchange rates and price levels are always adjustable.

Most references to reciprocity in the context of trade negotiations have in mind reciprocal reductions in barriers that have a *direct* effect on trade flows, such as tariffs, quotas and government procurement procedures. The focus in this instance is on reciprocity that can, at least in principle, be quantified – usually in terms of the stimulus to the level of trade in the products in question. To distinguish this use of the term from the two alternatives noted below, it may be labelled 'economic reciprocity'. All references in this paper, unless otherwise noted, are to economic reciprocity.

Reciprocity may also be used to refer to an exchange of concessions during negotiations on issues that affect trade flows only indirectly, such as a new safeguard clause, the issue of whether to have an injury requirement for countervailing duties, and so forth. This may be labelled 'issue reciprocity'. A third use is what Robert Hudec refers to as 'legal reciprocity', defined as 'the subjection of all members to the same or similar rules'.[2]

The three types of reciprocity overlap and blend into one another. And while it is possible to have trade-offs between the categories – such as a concession on the safeguard clause being exchanged for reductions in certain tariffs – the usual practice is not to mix economic reciprocity with the other two types (the reason for this will become clear later in the paper).

The use of the term 'negotiations' should also be clarified. Negotiations carried out within the framework of the General Agreement on Tariffs and Trade may be divided into the major negotiating rounds (of which the current Tokyo Round is the seventh) and negotiations that occur separate from the major rounds, such as those involving safeguard actions and the creation or enlargement of customs unions. Although reciprocity is an issue in both categories of negotiations, this paper is concerned only with the major rounds of trade negotiations.

The paper is divided into three sections. Section I is concerned with a theoretical analysis of the role of reciprocity, first under fixed exchange rates and then under flexible exchange rates. The former is necessary, even though the paper is concerned ultimately with the role of reciprocity under flexible rates, because current policies and attitudes toward reciprocity – as well as the literature on the subject – are completely dominated by experience inherited from a fixed exchange-rate past.[3] Section II examines the role of reciprocity in practice, as it evolved during the thirty years since the founding of GATT. In Section III the motivations behind the traditional insistence on reciprocity are analysed in the light of the economic analysis of the role of reciprocity under flexible exchange rates.

I ROLE OF RECIPROCITY IN A SIMPLE MODEL

In this section the economic rationale for reciprocity is analysed from the viewpoint of a single country, using a model whose principal simplifying assumptions are as follows:

(*a*) using labour and capital, the country produces three final consumption goods: an export good X, some of which is consumed domestically, an import-substitute good M, and a non-traded 'home' good H; the domestic version of the import good M_d and the foreign version M_f are perfect substitutes for one another; the three commodities are partial substitutes for one another both in consumption and in production;

(*b*) in the short run, capital in the form of plant and equipment is characterised by immobility (it is specific to the industry) and wage flexibility (it is a residual claimant on revenue), labour is characterised by partial mobility and partial wage flexibility, and prices exhibit some downward rigidity;[4]

(*c*) the country is a sufficiently small participant in world markets that variations in the quantities it buys and sells have no impact on world market prices;

(*d*) a non-discriminatory 20 per cent tariff on M is the only restriction on international trade;

(*e*) the decline in government revenue, and the increase in national income which results from the more efficient use of labour and capital (each the result of the tariff reduction), are both small enough that their respective impacts can be ignored; and

(*f*) in the absence of tariff reductions, the country under review and the 'rest of the world' are at full employment and have constant price levels, balanced balance of payments and stable *per capita* and aggregate national incomes.

In addition to these assumptions, there are also certain assumptions regarding the monetary variables. The choice in this instance was dictated by a desire to minimise the discussion of the monetary repercussions of balance-of-payments disequilibria, an aspect on which there exists a fairly extensive literature.[5] In particular, I assume that:

(*g*) the central bank's short-run policy is to maintain a nominal money supply such that desired and actual real cash balances are equal to one another; and (*h*) the government's policy in the short run is to use, whenever necessary, transfer payments to maintain aggregate expenditure at its full-employment level.

Evidence on the behaviour of governments in dealing with actual balance-of-payments problems suggests that the latter two assumptions are not unrealistic.

RECIPROCITY UNDER FIXED EXCHANGE RATES

It is useful to begin the analysis of a decision to insist on reciprocity – defined in this section as an insistence that other countries simultaneously reduce their tariffs by the amount required to produce a balanced expansion of trade at the given exchange rate – by looking first at what would happen in a world of fixed exchange rates if our country unilaterally eliminated its tariff. Unilateral elimination of the tariff may be taken as a proxy for any situation in which, as a result of a reduction in trade restrictions – multilateral or unilateral – a country's imports initially increase by more than its exports.

Beginning with the import sector, we note first that because M_d and M_f are perfect substitutes, the price of the domestically produced version of M must decline to the world market level, since at any price above the world market level sales of M_d would be zero. With the units of M defined so as to make the world price equal to $US1.00, and an initial exchange rate of one US dollar equals one domestic dollar ($D1.00), the domestic price declines from $D1.20 to $D1.00.

As a result of the decline in the domestic price of M, consumers switch some of their expenditure from X and H to M. The price decline also puts pressure on wage rates of capital and labour in the M_d industry. Assume that output of M_d declines as a result of some workers leaving or being laid off; other workers accept a lower wage, and there is a reduction in capital's wage as the utilisation of plant and equipment declines.[6] The increase in imports is equal to the sum of the increased consumption and the decline in domestic production.

Next, assume that the adjustment in the H sector – to the leftward shift of the demand curve caused by the decline in the price of M – takes essentially the same form, involving a combination of lower wages and a decline in employment, and a decline in the price of H (the latter effect will, in turn, produce a leftward shift of the demand curve for M).

In the X sector there is a leftward shift of the domestic demand curve – due to the decline in the prices of M and H – and export sales increase (the shift of the demand curve has no effect on the price of X because its price is set in the world market). In addition *some* of the labour released from the M_d and H industries will seek work in the X industry; the ones who are willing to accept a lower wage than before (needed to induce X to raise its labour – capital ratio) will be hired and the domestic supply curve for X will shift to the right. The net increase in exports is equal to the sum of the decline in domestic consumption and the increase in domestic production.

Each of the three goods markets is in temporary equilibrium, with domestic supply and demand equal in the H market, and foreign trade taking up the excess demand and supply in the M and X markets, respectively. The factor markets, in contrast, are in disequilibrium. The wage of capital has fallen in the M_d and H sectors (not necessarily by the same amount) and increased in the X sector (the increase in X's labour–capital ratio raises capital's wage). Similarly, labour wage rates have declined in all three sectors and wage differentials have widened, but not by enough to avoid some unemployment.

In addition to the disequilibrium in factor markets, the balance of payments will also be in disequilibrium. Keeping in mind the assumption that the government uses transfer payments to maintain aggregate expenditure at its full employment level, it may be shown that there will be a balance-of-payments deficit equal to the sum of the net decline in expenditure on the home good and the decline in the domestic production of the import substitute good, less the increase (if any) in the production of X.[7] The larger (smaller) the absolute value of the cross-elasticity of demand between H and M (X and H), the larger the supply elasticity of M_d, and the smaller the degree of wage flexibility and factor mobility, the larger will be the initial deficit.[8]

In summary, the unilateral elimination of the tariff has landed the country in a situation in which (i) factor markets are in disequilibrium, with some factors unemployed, and with each factor's wage rate varying between industries, and (ii) the balance of payments is in deficit and international reserves are declining.

The next question concerns what can be done to improve the situation. One possible alternative open to the government is to terminate the transfer payments, cease reintroducing into the money supply the domestic currency proceeds from the net sale of foreign exchange and simply wait for the situation to correct itself – presumably through a decline in income and demand in the short run, and later through a relative decline in domestic wages and prices. But the combination of the downward stickiness of wages and prices in the short run, the political commitment of most governments in the post-war period to the maintenance of full employment, and insufficient foreign exchange reserves, is almost certain to rule out this alternative.

Aside from the uninteresting option of reintroducing the tariff or some other interference with trade, the country has two additional alternatives. One is to devalue the domestic currency. In this instance the key consideration is the knowledge that in the post-war period most countries resisted – at least initially – suggestions that a balance-of-payments disequilibrium be corrected via a change in exchange rates. Another alternative is to seek a solution through the use of monetary and fiscal policies. The difficulty is that, if the country attempts to correct the balance-of-payments deficit by introducing restrictive monetary and fiscal policies to force the domestic price level to fall relative to that of other countries, the unemployment problem will worsen. Alternatively, if expansive monetary and fiscal policies are used to reduce unemployment, the payments deficit will worsen as the demand for imports rises and as some exports are diverted from foreigners to domestic consumers.[9]

These considerations go a long way toward explaining why unilateral tariff reductions were not a common feature of the post-war period. On the other hand, there were six major tariff-cutting rounds while the Bretton Woods system was operating, and most observers agree that substantial progress has been made in reducing tariffs. The explanation is, of course, that the tariff reductions were not unilateral. Countries have been willing to reduce tariffs, but nearly always on the condition that trading partners agree to 'reciprocate' by simultaneously reducing some of their tariffs.

This raises the question of the way in which the situation just described would have differed if the rest of the world had eliminated its tariffs on X – and on M, since some of the other countries will also be importing our country's import good – at the same time as our country eliminated its tariff on M.

When the rest of the world eliminates its tariffs on X, the price of X in the rest of the world will decline, and consumption of X will increase, causing its price in the world market to rise, at least in the short run.[10] For our country, this appears as an upward shift of the world demand curve for its exports. Reciprocity, therefore, mitigates the unemployment problem because the X industry will be *actively* expanding output to meet the new demand, whereas before, when the tariff reduction was unilateral, the X industry expanded only passively. That is, in the previous situation there was only the opportunity to sell additional output at the going world price; now, the jump in the world price of X makes the industry anxious to expand output *and* willing to offer higher wages, if necessary, to attract capital and labour.

Just as the increase in world demand for X caused the world market price of X to be bid up, the removal of tariffs on M will lead to an increase in the world market price of our import good. Because the decline in the domestic market price of M is smaller than it would have been in the absence of reciprocity, the initial impact of the tariff elimination on the M_d industry is less severe.[11]

As for the industry producing the non-tradeable home good, the nominal price of its product may rise or fall depending on the details of the situation; however, we know that in the new equilibrium the price of H, as well as the price of M, will have declined relative to the price of X.[12]

Reciprocity will also reduce the potential deficit in the balance of payments, perhaps turning it into a temporary surplus. The short-run differences, relative to the previous (unilateral reduction) situation, are as follows. Production of X will increase by a larger amount because the industry will be actively expanding and willing to bid up money wages when necessary. The initial switch in expenditure from X to M will be approximately the same (because the relative price change between X and M is approximately the same), but the switch from X to H will be larger because the decline in the price of H relative to the price of X does not in this instance come about solely through a fall in the price of H (which I assume exhibits some downward stickiness); therefore the initial decline in the domestic consumption of X is larger. This, together with the larger increase in the production of X, both work to ensure a larger increase in export earnings.

The higher world price for M will also act to reduce the initial deficit by simultaneously moderating the increase in the consumption of M (since in this instance the price of M initially declines relative to the price of H by less than the amount of the tariff, and therefore the initial expenditure switch from H to M is smaller), and reducing the decline in the production of M_d relative to what would have occurred initially at a post-tariff-elimination price of \$D1.00.[13]

While it is true that the difficulty of estimating in advance the impact of a given tariff reduction makes it unlikely that the increases in imports and exports will exactly match, and granting that a lack of sufficient geographic and occupational mobility will continue to present adjustment problems, it is clear that under fixed exchange rates the short-run unemployment and payments problems will be less severe if the tariff reduction is reciprocal rather than unilateral.[14] This is an important conclusion because it offers—within a context which recognises the constraints facing policy-makers—a rigorous economic defence of the central importance traditionally attached to reciprocity.[15]

UNILATERAL LIBERALISATION UNDER A FLEXIBLE EXCHANGE RATE

In a world without financial flows between countries, unilateral trade liberalisation would affect a freely-floating exchange rate through developments in the trade account—that is, with the appearance of the first tendency toward an import surplus, the exchange rate would begin to depreciate and it would continue to depreciate until the adjustment to the change in relative prices was complete.

Once we allow for the fact that people hold stocks of financial assets denominated both in their domestic currency and in foreign currencies, it is no longer true that the exchange rate changes in response to pressures at the trade level. Anticipation of trade-account developments provides the rationale for the depreciation, and the size of the depreciation is dictated by the magnitude of those developments. But the mechanism that actually brings about the depreciation is the behaviour of holders of financial assets, not the behaviour of importers and exporters.

Consider a simple example in which (i) the unilateral tariff elimination comes as a surprise, and (ii) the public accepts as correct the government's estimate that the liberalisation will require an 8 per cent depreciation (the depreciation must be less than the size of the eliminated tariff because the new balance is achieved partly through an expansion of exports and, thus, the new equilibrium level of imports must exceed the pre-liberalisation level). The anticipated depreciation will create a disequilibrium in the markets for stocks of financial assets denominated in domestic and foreign currencies. Because the existing stocks of such assets are very large relative to trade flows in the short run, and because of the speed with which capital can flow between assets denominated in different currencies, capital market developments will dominate and both the spot and forward exchange rates will depreciate immediately by the full 8 per cent.

Space limitations preclude a detailed discussion of the implications of asset–market determination of exchange rates for international commercial policy.[16] As far as this paper is concerned, the most important implication concerns the possibility that the timing of the exchange-rate change will differ from the timing of the unilateral trade liberalisation. Two common characteristics of decisions to liberalise trade are prior public debate and a staging of the reductions over a period of time. In either instance developments in asset markets could cause the exchange rate to depreciate in advance of the liberalisation. If this happened, there would be a transitory distortion of relative prices between the liberalising country and the rest of the world. Short of introducing new restrictions on capital flows, the only way the advance depreciation of the spot rate could be avoided is through an appropriate change in the interest-rate differential between assets denominated in the depreciating currency and assets denominated in other currencies.

Returning to the analysis of developments at the trade and production level, assume that the tariff is removed unilaterally and that the possible problems associated with the exact timing of the depreciation are sufficiently minor that they can be ignored.

In the market of the export commodity the depreciation causes an upward shift in the foreign demand curve for *X expressed in domestic currency* (the world market price in US dollars remaining unchanged) – a development similar in many ways to what happened in the export goods market under fixed rates and reciprocity. In particular, employment problems associated with the adjustment to unilateral tariff elimination will be less difficult under flexible exchange rates because the export industry will be 'actively' expanding its level of employment and output in response to the higher price (as when there is reciprocity under a fixed exchange rate), in contrast to the 'passive' expansion (at an unchanged price) under a fixed exchange rate and no reciprocity.

With the world market price of the import good unchanged at $US1.00, the combination of the tariff removal and the depreciation will cause the import supply curve *expressed in domestic currency* to shift down by less than the amount of the tariff elimination – the same result as with the fixed rate plus reciprocity. In the same way, the situation of the *H* industry is similar to its situation when there is reciprocity. While its nominal price may decline or increase, depending on the details, the new pattern of *relative* prices will involve a decline in the price of *H* relative to the price of *X*, and an increase in the price of *H* relative to the price of *M* – in short, the post-elimination pattern of equilibrium relative prices will be approximately the same as with reciprocity. (It will not be exactly the same because the price-distorting foreign tariffs remain unchanged in the unilateral situation.) Again depending on the details of the situation, output of *H* may either increase or decrease.

There is, lastly, the question of the balance of payments. The answer this time is easy. With a truly flexible exchange rate, the rate will vary so as to keep the balance of payments in balance.

In summary, a comparison of the results with those of the fixed rate plus reciprocity case suggests the general conclusion that, from a purely economic point of view, whatever employment and balance-of-payments advantages reciprocal reduction has *vis-à-vis* unilateral reduction in a fixed-rate world are fully shared by unilateral reduction in a flexible-rate world. The point is not that exchange-rate depreciation eliminates transitional adjustment problems, but rather that it offers as much help as does reciprocity – or perhaps even more help considering that the stimulus under the depreciation alternative is much more decentralised both geographically and occupationally.

ALLOWING FOR MANY TRADEABLE GOODS

In some instances, relaxing one or more of the first six assumptions of the model does not alter the conclusions in an important way. For example, if consumers consider M_d and M_f as imperfect substitutes for one another, the model is simply expanded to include four commodities rather than three; or if the country has some monopsonistic power in the world market for M, and/or some monopolistic power in the world market for X, the analysis must allow for possible terms-of-trade effects. On the other hand, if quantitative restrictions (QRs) are introduced into the model, the equivalence between reciprocity and depreciation disappears because depreciation is of no help to an export industry facing a QR.

Moving from a world of three commodities into a world of many commodities also affects the conclusions of the simple model. First, it becomes possible to take into account the implications of allowing for trade in inputs. An extensive literature on the theory of effective protection is available and there is no need to discuss it in detail.[17] Among its principal implications for commercial policy are (i) the impact of a general tariff reduction on the output of a particular import-substitute industry can be positive or negative, depending on the relation between the tariff cut on the commodity itself and the tariff cuts on its inputs; and (ii) export industries which suffer from negative effective rates of protection (caused by tariffs on inputs) can get a direct boost from tariff reduction independent of reciprocity or exchange-rate depreciation.[18]

The second change is that in a multiple-product world it is very likely that changes in commercial policy and changes in exchange rates will have different effects within the import and the export sectors. Consider, for instance, the following two examples.

(*a*) A country unilaterally removes tariffs on some, but not all, imports and allows the exchange rate to depreciate to maintain trade balance. The domestic prices of the import goods not covered by the liberalisation will rise as a result of the depreciation, causing domestic consumption of these goods to decline and their domestic output to expand (thus developments in the exempted subset of the import sector parallel developments in the export industry).

(*b*) A country, some of whose exports already enter foreign markets free of duties and other restrictions, decides to reduce its tariffs. If it insists on reciprocity, only those export industries which currently face foreign tariffs are potential recipients of direct benefits from the negotiations, whereas if the tariff elimination is unilateral, all export industries will benefit directly from the subsequent depreciation.

Allowing for several tradeable goods affects the earlier findings in different ways. The conclusion regarding the rationale for insisting on reciprocity in a fixed-exchange-rate world is untouched. But the conclusion that the impact of tariff reduction on the long-run pattern of production, consumption and trade is largely independent of what is assumed about exchange-rate flexibility and reciprocity is no longer valid. We know that some exports already enjoy duty-free treatment, and that trade liberalisation seldom covers all imports, which means that the pattern of post-reduction prices among tradeable goods will differ according to whether reciprocity or an exchange-rate change is used to maintain trade balance.

Another consideration is that, historically, governments have pursued reciprocity, partly out of a desire to minimise the transitional employment and balance-of-payments problems, and partly out of a desire to focus the benefits of trade liberalisation on particular export industries in order to obtain political support for trade liberalisation. Reciprocity, therefore, may be subdivided into 'aggregate reciprocity' and 'special interest reciprocity'. As far as aggregate reciprocity is concerned, there is a strong parallel between the benefits of exchange-rate depreciation and the benefits of reciprocal tariff reductions by trading partners. From the standpoint of special interest reciprocity, however, exchange-rate depreciation *may be* less attractive than reciprocal tariff cuts because the benefits cannot be directed to particular export industries. This formulation, in turn, draws attention to the empirical question of the relative importance which governments attach to the opportunity to favour *particular* export industries. This question is taken up in Section III.

II RECIPROCITY IN PRACTICE

In this section the analysis shifts from the simple model to what is loosely described as the 'real world'. Three facets of the role of reciprocity in post-war trade negotiations are examined – the degree of importance attached to reciprocity, the definition of reciprocity and the factors that motivate governments to seek reciprocity.

IMPORTANCE ATTACHED TO RECIPROCITY

Although the view of trade negotiations as an opportunity for exchanging concessions is very old, its modern history may be dated from the passage of the United States Reciprocal Trade Agreements Act of 1934. This approach to trade negotiations clearly enjoyed the support of other countries, for it had a major impact on the drafting of the rules and procedures that were to govern the post-war multilateral trading system. Discussing the origins of the legal obligations in the charter of the stillborn International Trade Organisation, Robert Hudec states:

> The dominant purpose of a trade agreement was the exchange of tariff reductions. The concept of a balanced exchange was central. The appearance of a sound bargain was usually regarded as essential to the political support of such agreements, and trade policy officials themselves were not opposed to the idea, for they saw that their own tariff reductions would contribute most to general trade liberalization if they were used to pry similar concessions from others. The word for the idea of balanced exchange was 'reciprocity'.[19]

Reciprocity is hardly mentioned – and never defined – in the text of the General Agreement on Tariffs and Trade. The only explicit references of any consequence are the general reference in Article XXVIII *bis*., and the statement in Article XXXVI (added in 1965) to the effect that the developed countries do not expect reciprocity from the developing countries.[20]

Despite the paucity of explicit references to reciprocity in the General Agreement, there can be little doubt as to the pervasive influence of the concept on the negotiations. Consider the following items, drawn from a vast amount of available evidence.

(i) Discussing the Dillon Round of negotiations (1960–62), Gerard and Victoria Curzon note,

> [The point at which] a supplier ceased to be important, and therefore no longer liable to be asked to 'pay' for a concession negotiated by someone else, was not defined. . . . In practice, the line was drawn at 10 per cent, which meant that a country supplying 10 per cent or less to a particular market was not asked for 'payment'.
>
> . . . [An] implication of this rule was that if one important trading nation refused to participate, the item was dropped and the scope of the negotiations was seriously reduced. In the interests of preserving reciprocity, no participant would agree to reduce its tariffs on any product on which a non-participant supplied more than 10 per cent of its imports.[21]

(ii) In each of John Evans' two books based on his extensive experience with post-war trade negotiations up to and including the Kennedy Round, there is a separate chapter devoted exclusively to reciprocity.[22]

(iii) The Declaration issued at the end of the Ministerial Meeting in Tokyo in September 1973, setting the stage for the current negotiations, states: 'The negotiations shall be conducted on the basis of the principles of mutual advantage, mutual commitment and overall reciprocity. . . .'[23]

(iv) Finally, as an indication that the forty-year period between the United States Reciprocal Trade Agreements Act and the Trade Act of 1974 did not dull the attraction of reciprocity for the United States Congress, the latter Act establishes:

> . . . a procedure that requires the President, after the completion of multilateral trade negotiations, to determine whether all major industrial countries have granted concessions substantially equivalent to those granted by the United States. If a determination is made that a country has not made substantially equivalent concessions, the President shall recommend to Congress legislation providing for denial of concessions to those countries with respect to duties or other import restrictions.[24]

This array of evidence leads to the inescapable conclusion that the desire for reciprocity has played a pre-eminent role in post-war trade negotiations.

DEFINING RECIPROCITY

Someone unfamiliar with trade negotiations could be forgiven for presuming that a concept as central as reciprocity would have a specific, operative, generally accepted definition. In fact, there is no official definition of what constitutes reciprocity. As a result, it is necessary to rely on personal reports of participants and on inferences drawn by experienced observers from the behaviour of the negotiators. Ernest Preeg, a member of the United States' negotiating team during the Kennedy Round, writes: '. . . in view of the various factors that compose reciprocity, it was clear that no single measure, but a series of different or complementary measures would be required.' He then goes on to list what he believed to be the four principal measures – average depth of cut, trade volume offered for concession, loss of duties collectible and projected trade impact. Regarding the fourth measure he continues:

> The impact of tariff and other concessions on future trade might be considered the main criterion of reciprocity. It is not possible, however, to calculate the effect precisely. . . . These projections, when carried out during the Kennedy Round, were primarily for internal use, although statements about qualitative differences in the value of offers rested on some kind of assumption as to the expected trade-creating effects of the concession.[25]

In his book on the GATT John Jackson mentions the fallacies of the third measure, and indicates support for the fourth measure,[26] while John Evans stresses the fourth exclusively: 'Usually, though there were exceptions, the aim of the negotiator was even more precise: to see that the expected increase in his country's exports should at least equal any likely increment in its imports.'[27]

The analysis in Section I offered a strong *a priori* rationale for an emphasis on measuring (defining) reciprocity in terms of the anticipated impact of tariff reductions on trade flows. The authorities cited above seem to agree that, despite the computational problems, this is the principal measure which has been used in post-war trade negotiations up to and including the Kennedy Round.

MOTIVATIONS FOR SEEKING RECIPROCITY

Gerard and Victoria Curzon identify four reasons behind the desire for reciprocity, to which I have added a fifth:[28]

(1) ease transitional employment problems;
(2) avoid balance-of-payments problems;
(3) minimise terms-of-trade effects;
(4) political motivation; and
(5) speed up the overall pace of trade liberalisation.

They credit the first two – already discussed extensively in Section I – with being the source of 'the broad outline to a country's negotiating position'. The terms-of-trade consideration enters the picture when the participants believe they have monopsonistic or monopolistic power in the world market for certain products, reciprocity being seen as a way of reducing the likelihood that reductions in trade barriers will affect the terms of trade adversely.

Their fourth reason is a generalised version of the 'special interest reciprocity' mentioned at the end of Section I. They first argue that 'reciprocity helps to create a constituency for tariff agreements in the export sector, which would not exist if a government proposed to reduce tariffs unilaterally', then state that this is probably the most important motivation behind the pursuit of reciprocity because the difficulties of estimating the economic effects of a tariff bargain, plus the fact that they are often spread out over a period which exceeds the current government's term in office, act to focus attention 'upon balancing out of the immediate political pressures and counter-pressures on the home front'.[29] In developing this argument, they note that Richard N. Cooper has expressed a similar opinion: 'The principle of reciprocity is designed to hold out the promise of export gains to certain sectors of the economy, and thereby to establish a counterweight to those who will be hurt by increased imports. . . . Reciprocity attempts to build pluralistic support for tariff reductions.'[30]

A somewhat broader, long-term view of trade negotiations is implicit in the fifth reason for seeking reciprocity. According to this view, a country which actively desires to liberalise its trade should not reduce its restrictions unilaterally, but rather should make the reductions conditional on similar reductions by the more recalcitrant countries, since in the end the sum total of trade liberalisation will be greater than it would have been had the country acted unilaterally.

The first three reasons involve reciprocity in a 'protective role', defending the country against real or imagined problems associated with unilateral reductions in trade barriers. Numbers (4) and (5), in contrast, play a 'positive role', offering apparent advantages in terms of mobilising the support of domestic groups – and of foreign governments – for trade liberalisation. All five reasons are part of the heritage from the fixed-exchange-rate past. If the move to more flexible exchange rates is to have an impact on the role of reciprocity in trade negotiations, it must be through its effect on one or more of the five.

III IMPLICATIONS FOR RECIPROCITY OF THE ABANDONMENT OF THE BRETTON WOODS SYSTEM OF FIXED EXCHANGE RATES

Section I covered in detail the implications of the switch to flexible exchange rates for the first two reasons for seeking reciprocity, concluding that reciprocity and exchange-rate changes are virtually perfect substitutes as solutions to the transitional employment and balance-of-payments problems associated with reductions in trade barriers.

One potentially important aspect of the balance-of-payments motivation, however, was not mentioned. The Curzons argue that: 'Even in a flexible exchange-rate world [a reciprocity-induced balanced expansion of trade] is of some importance, since currency depreciation is not without its real cost.'[31] Harry G. Johnson supported their view, adding that the 'internal politico-economic rationale for reciprocity might become much stronger with floating rates than with fixed rates . . .'[32]

This aspect of the balance-of-payments rationale for reciprocity is much less convincing than it appears at first glance. The issue is not whether the public is indifferent to exchange-rate changes, but rather the extent to which such a change can be 'sold' to the public as a possible inconvenience worth bearing in pursuit of greater benefits. This could be included in the government's campaign to sell trade liberalisation to the electorate and it seems plausible that the public could be persuaded that any inconveniences associated with a possible equilibrating exchange-rate change would be more than compensated for by the gains from freer trade. Moreover, when exchange-rate depreciation is part of the package, the appeal for public support can be broadened to include those export industries that currently face low or zero duties and that would not benefit from reciprocal reductions in tariffs.[33]

Public reaction to the dramatic change in the pattern of exchange rates that occurred in 1971–73 supports the view that exchange-rate changes that occur for understandable and seemingly plausible reasons do not generate excessive amounts of criticism.[34] Discussions in the popular press also suggest that the public's perception of the trade implications of exchange-rate changes is increasing, with such headlines as 'The Lower Dollar May Be a Plus', 'How a Rising Yen Could Help the U.S.' and 'Strong Pound Hurts Exports' becoming commonplace.[35]

A country that relied on exchange-rate depreciation to balance its external position following trade liberalisation, *and* that had a system in which the general level of wages was indexed to the consumer price index, could have a problem – although this is by no means certain because trade liberalisation will put downward pressure on domestic currency prices of goods whose barriers are reduced, while the exchange-rate depreciation is working in the opposite direction on the prices of all tradeable goods. More specifically, the answer depends on, among other things, the proportion of tradeable goods in the consumption basket, on the relative importance (within that proportion) of products whose restrictions were reduced, and on the price response of non-traded goods to the price developments among tradeable goods.

Third on the list of reasons for seeking reciprocity is the desire to minimise the possible terms-of-trade effects of trade liberalisation. There are at least three considerations that argue against the importance of this third motivation.[36] First of all, a large majority of the examples used to illustrate the existence of power in world markets – petroleum, coffee, phosphate, computers and so forth – involve situations in which the alleged market power is in the hands of sellers rather than buyers. In such situations, *export* restrictions – seldom discussed in trade negotiations – are the preferred terms-of-trade device.[37]

Second, much of the empirical evidence offered in support of the existence of monopsonistic power in world markets is open to question, in part because of statistical and methodological problems and in part because the analysis often is short-run (one to two years after a devaluation or tariff reduction), whereas the interesting question is whether a country can, by its own actions, produce a *lasting* change in the price of something it buys (or sells) in the world market.[38]

Finally, there is the practical consideration that the literature on post-war commercial policy-making suggests that policy-makers and negotiators have attached little or no importance to the issues of the terms-of-trade effects of trade liberalisation. In short, governments worry about lots of things when they are considering trade liberalisation, but terms-of-trade effects do not seem to be very high on the list.

For the fourth reason on the list – the political motivation – the implications of the switch to flexible exchange rates are more subtle. The Curzons and Cooper support the view that governments attach considerable importance to what I have labelled 'special interest reciprocity'; and a casual reading of their remarks might suggest that there is no reason why this desire to favour certain export industries – as a way of generating political support for trade liberalisation — would disappear simply because the major countries have switched to flexible exchange rates. In fact many people do take it for granted that nothing has changed in this regard. They know that all of the effort on the import side involves specific industries, they see evidence of a parallel approach on the export side, and there seems to be no reason why flexible exchange rates should alter this situation.

It is not that simple, however. To begin with, there is a paucity of evidence of industry-specific producer efforts on the export side that are comparable in scope and intensity to the efforts on the import side whenever a new round of trade negotiations is proposed.[39] A more important consideration, with respect to the above quotations from the Curzons and Cooper, is that both refer to reciprocity under fixed exchange rates. If the exchange rate is believed to be fixed, the government obviously cannot seek support among exporters for trade liberalisation by pointing out the stimulus to exports that comes with exchange-rate depreciation. Nor would it be very helpful to lecture the export sector on the symmetry between import taxes and export taxes, because most export industries also sell in the domestic market and therefore would be adversely affected by the deflationary pressure that would necessarily accompany unilateral trade liberalisation under a fixed exchange rate.[40] In these circumstances, the *only* incentive it can offer to the export sector in exchange for political support is the promise of reciprocal tariff reductions by trading partners. Furthermore, it would not make sense to appeal to all exporters because some would be already enjoying zero or low-duty treatment in foreign markets. Under these circumstances, a government seeking support in the export sector has little alternative but to point out to certain industries that foreign tariffs on their goods are high and that the government will work hard during the negotiations to get those tariffs reduced.

There is a crucial distinction between this process and its counterpart on the import side. Governments clearly desire to discriminate among import-substitute industries, and they do this by exempting certain products from part or all of the general reductions in duties. The decision as to which import-substitute industries will be so favoured is based almost entirely on the amount of political pressure which the threatened workers and owners in a particular industry can bring to bear on the government. The import side, therefore, involves the government reacting to strong industry-specific pressures that originate *outside* the government. The situation on the export side, in contrast, traditionally involves efforts by general interest groups that favour trade liberalisation and (usually) the government. To the extent that industry-specific proposals are involved, they generally originate *within* the government as part of its efforts to secure, in a fixed-exchange-rate world, political support for trade liberalisation.

This view of the differences in the nature and origin of the pressures on the import and export sides is supported by two studies of United States commercial policies. In the summary chapter of their section on pressure groups, Bauer, de Sola Pool and Dexter observe: 'The anti-protectionist forces draw more support from persons identified with the general interest and in turn direct more of their efforts to public education. . . . Protectionists almost always used such pinpointed mobilization of directly involved special interests.'[41]

Robert Baldwin's recent study of the political economy of United States trade policy arrives at a similar conclusion. Throughout the study the references to protectionist pressures are industry-specific, while the sources of pro-liberalisation pressure are general. The government frequently makes concessions to import-competing industries to obtain their support (or abstention) on trade legislation, but there are no examples of concessions or promises being given to secure the support of particular export industries. Summarising the results of a statistical analysis of voting on the United States Trade Act of 1974, Baldwin observes: 'The problem with a statistical analysis of these [export-oriented] industries is that relatively few testify strongly in favor of liberalization.'[42]

The distinction regarding the nature and origin of the pressure is crucial. If there were a strong parallel between the industry-specific political response on the import side and the political response on the export side, governments would never consider the benefits of exchange-rate depreciation as a substitute for the benefits of conventional reciprocity because depreciation cannot deliver industry-specific benefits.[43] Given, however, that governments generally do not attach intrinsic importance to the opportunity to discriminate between export industries, it is not unreasonable to assume that they would be willing to accept exchange-rate depreciation as a viable substitute for reciprocity.

Fifth on the list of advantages of reciprocity is the argument that an insistence on reciprocity speeds up the pace of overall trade liberalisation because the pro-liberalisation countries are able to use their willingness to reduce trade barriers to persuade other countries to join in the move to freer trade. While this view clearly has some merit, it does not require much reflection to figure out that it is very much a double-edged argument. Suppose, for example, that one major trading country were strongly opposed to trade liberalisation, especially as regards its own trade (because protectionists were in a dominant political position), but also as regards world trade (because it did not want the rest of the world to get the income gains that come with liberalisation) – not at all an implausible combination of attitudes. In such a circumstance, the protectionist country would be beside itself with joy if the rest of the world were to announce that the negotiations were conditional on the participation (that is, reciprocity) of all major countries.

The obvious point of this example is that the argument could go either way, which is unfortunate because there is no way to determine conclusively which tendency in fact dominates – do the pro-liberalisation countries pull along the unenthusiastic countries, with the result that the overall pace of liberalisation is speeded up, or do the recalcitrant countries act as such a drag that the overall pace is slower than it would be if the pro-liberalisation countries acted unilaterally?[44]

When thinking about this question, it is important to be explicit regarding what is being assumed about exchange rates. Under a system in which all exchange rates were explicitly or implicitly viewed as unalterably fixed, reciprocity could be said to speed up trade liberalisation, but only in the banal sense that without reciprocity there would be virtually no liberalisation at all. The question of which tendency dominates is interesting only if unilateral reduction by one country, or multilateral reduction among a subset of countries, is a feasible alternative – which is to say that it is an interesting question only if the relevant exchange rates are flexible or 'changeable' and if there is an acceptance of the equivalence of reciprocity and exchange-rate depreciation as far as help with the transitional problems is concerned.

Although it is impossible to arrive at a definitive conclusion as to which tendency dominates – the pro-liberalisation or anti-liberalisation – it is possible to draw some inferences from an analysis of the ways in which the pursuit of reciprocity has affected the 'negotiating atmosphere'. To begin with, it can be argued that an insistence on strict reciprocity increases the influence of those countries that wish to minimise the extent of trade liberalisation. They can prevent a negotiating round from being initiated simply by informing the others in advance that they will not participate, or they can agree to a round of negotiations and then force everyone else to settle for only limited liberalisation. The essence of the problem is that countries that desire both substantial liberalisation and full reciprocity have no direct leverage over the go-slow countries. To find leverage they must engage in what is referred to inelegantly in the international relations literature as 'issue-linkage' – that is, they must look for issues outside the scope of the negotiations, *and* be willing to make sacrifices/concessions on the other issue(s) as the price of getting the go-slow countries to engage in meaningful trade liberalisation.[45] It is not implausible that an arrangement such as this, in which the degree of progress is heavily dependent on a coincidence of wants among the major countries, contributes to a slowing-down rather than to a speeding-up of the pace of trade liberalisation.

Another aspect relevant to the question of whether the pursuit of reciprocity speeds up or slows down the rate of trade liberalisation is the tendency for the concern with reciprocity to create a 'bargaining chip' mentality *vis-à-vis* trade negotiations. John Evans' comments on this point, based on his extensive experience with post-war trade negotiations, are as follows:

> . . . the existence of tariff bargaining is in itself a sufficient reason for the insistence on reciprocity; . . . Thus, the cost a government incurs when it reduces or binds a tariff may be measured less by any possible disadvantages from increased imports than by the value it believes a negotiating partner would place on that action. Once this simple, and observable, fact is recognized, it becomes less difficult to understand how a number of governments intent on the reduction of tariffs for their mutual benefit can be diverted from that purpose into a contest in which each seems as much concerned with denying benefits to its partners as with obtaining benefits for itself.[46]

A third consideration is that it is likely to become increasingly difficult to estimate the impact of reductions in barriers on trade flows. This is partly a result of the gradual shift in emphasis in negotiations from tariffs to non-tariff barriers[47] and partly a result of the growing interdependence of countries (a development that makes the repercussions of changes in trade barriers both quantitatively more important and – because the interactions among commodities are more important and more numerous – increasingly difficult to predict).[48] The concern is that this decrease in the already low degree of confidence surrounding estimates of the trade effects of changes in tariffs and other restrictions could, if combined with the traditional insistence on reciprocity, lead to the adoption of a more cautious and miserly approach to trade liberalisation.

This concludes the discussion of the five principal reasons advanced to explain why governments have traditionally preferred reciprocal reductions in trade barriers to the alternative of unilateral reductions. Only the employment, balance-of-payments and political-motivation arguments for reciprocity emerge clearly and unambiguously valid. Of the remaining two, the terms-of-trade argument offers only a minor (if any) incentive, while the 'speed up the pace of liberalisation' argument is at best ambiguous in a flexible-exchange-rate world. Furthermore, the three valid arguments for reciprocity have something important in common – all of the benefits which reciprocity brings in terms of helping with transitional employment problems, helping with transitional balance-of-payments problems and helping governments marshal domestic support for trade liberalisation, may be obtained through a depreciation of the exchange rate.

The implications of this conclusion for trade negotiations are encouraging. In addition to increasing the degree of flexibility in the negotiations and improving the scope for innovative ideas, freeing countries from the strait-jacket of reciprocity brings three specific advantages. The first concerns the choice of a tariff-cutting formula. Authors such as John Evans describe the automatic tariff-cutting formula approach as one which offers countries the opportunity to free themselves from the traditional concern with reciprocity – each country simply agrees to reduce its tariffs by a certain percentage, which is cranked out of the common formula; there is no need to haggle over strict reciprocity.[49] One of the reasons why the linear approach of the Kennedy Round was combined with the traditional technique of basing reciprocity on quantitative estimates of the effects of the tariff cuts on individual imports and exports of each country (inherited from the days of commodity-by-commodity bargaining) was the fear of many countries that an automatic approach would produce unbalanced expansions of imports and exports and thereby create balance-of-payments and employment problems – a concern which, as we have seen, was valid under the system of fixed exchange rates which was in effect throughout the 1960s. With the advent of flexible exchange rates, there is no longer any reason to worry about this aspect of the simple formula approach.

Other beneficiaries of the switch to flexible exchange rates are the trading blocs which participate in trade negotiations as a single unit because they have a common set of trade restrictions – that is, the customs unions and common markets. Under fixed exchange rates, the negotiators for a trading bloc face the difficult task of trying to come up with an agreement in which reductions in a common tariff schedule will lead to a balanced expansion of imports and exports in several countries, each with its separate trade pattern. Such a situation can easily create an incentive for an approach to the negotiations which is more cautious and less ambitious than the individual approaches that would have been adopted had the members been participating separately. The availability of the option of using exchange-rate changes to achieve a balanced expansion of trade within the area, as well as with the rest of the world, therefore represents a particularly liberating change for those customs unions and common markets whose member countries allow their currencies to float *vis-à-vis* one another.

The third advantage involves a fundamental principle of the GATT which has been bruised a good deal during the post-war period.[50] Among the various threats to the 'most-favoured-nation' principle which are lurking in the wings is one which is illustrated by the following quotation from the prestigious Committee for Economic Development:

> If it should turn out that some major trading unit of the free world should be unwilling or unable to undertake trade liberalization that is substantially equal to what is generally desired, the rest of the free world nations should consider how they could nevertheless enhance their continued economic progress through the benefits of expanded trade, not excluding from consideration a departure from the unconditional most-favoured-nation principle, valuable as that principle is.[51]

There is a similar message in the United States Trade Act of 1974.[52]

That the pursuit of reciprocity could bring both the generally pro-trade-liberalisation Committee for Economic Development and the legislature of a country which traditionally has been a vocal defender of non-discrimination in trade to the point of raising the possibility of an entirely new kind of departure from the most-favoured-nation principle is surely one of the most damaging indictments of the whole concept of reciprocity. By removing any rationale for *insisting* on reciprocity, the switch to flexible exchange rates will lend a bit of needed help to one of the most important principles to come out of the destructive disorder that characterised international commercial relations in the 1930s.

One other item should be mentioned. It is well known that under the current monetary system the determination of exchange rates is not left entirely in the hands of private buyers and sellers. All central banks, as a matter of course, feel free to intervene in exchange markets, ostensibly for the purpose of smoothing out 'erratic' movements. This facet of the current international monetary system obviously has implications for trade negotiations. For example, if a country which was anxious to liberalise its trade were to knowingly reduce its restrictions by more than its trading partners reduced theirs, on the assumption that its exchange rate would depreciate and bring about a balanced expansion of trade, and then found that its trading partners were intervening in the exchange market to prevent their currencies from appreciating (because they liked the emerging export surplus), there would be considerable tension and ill-will. The simplest and most direct way of precluding this type of problem is for countries to strictly abide by the new Article IV of the International Monetary Fund, which includes the obligation to 'avoid manipulating exchange rates or the international monetary system in order to prevent effective balance-of-payments adjustment or to gain an unfair competitive advantage over other members'.[53]

SUMMARY OF THE IMPLICATIONS FOR TRADE NEGOTIATIONS

It is important to emphasise that I do *not* conclude that, in a flexible-exchange-rate world, unilateral tariff reduction is a first best policy for a single country or for the world. Under the right conditions, multilateral negotiations and reductions clearly offer the most productive approach to trade liberalisation. If all of the major countries are interested in trade liberalisation at the same time and to the same degree, then negotiations for mutual reductions in barriers are likely to lead to a greater degree of liberalisation than would occur if the participants engaged in independent, simultaneous, unilateral reductions. This would also avoid the repeated realignment of exchange rates that is likely to occur if the liberalisation is unsynchronised. The only implication which the analysis in this paper would have for such a situation would be that the participants are now free to let floating exchange rates take over the job of ensuring a balanced expansion of post-reduction trade.

When these ideal conditions do not hold, the conclusion regarding the high degree of substitutability between reciprocity and exchange-rate depreciation takes on added importance. Suppose the situation is the opposite of the first one, namely that there is a single country that wishes to reduce or eliminate one or more of its trade restrictions and that no other country has any interest in trade liberalisation. In the past this country would have faced a serious dilemma, knowing that a unilateral reduction would involve either the creation of serious transitional employment and balance-of-payments problems or a violation of the international admonition against exchange-rate changes. With the adoption of flexible exchange rates, all this has changed. And the conclusion is that the country should liberalise unilaterally and let the exchange rate depreciate to ensure a balanced expansion of trade.

Most of the time, of course, the actual situation lies between these two extremes. This makes it difficult to be specific about the implications of the analysis. If only a few major countries are interested in a new round of negotiations at a particular point, but there is a very good chance that within a year or so the other countries will decide to join in (and none of the original supporters are likely to drop out), then it probably would be a good idea to wait. Alternatively, if there was little prospect of persuading the other countries to join in, then the interested subset should go ahead with their own 'semi-multilateral' reciprocal most-favoured-nation reductions, letting the subsequent exchange-rate changes bring about the necessary balancing of the trade expansion both between the participants themselves and between them and the non-participating countries.

Postponing trade liberalisation means postponing the date at which the country begins to receive the flow of benefits (that is, the increase in national income) that comes with the more efficient use of its factors of production. It follows that a comparison of the advantages of reducing trade barriers at two alternative dates must be based on a comparison of the discounted present value of two streams of benefits. This draws attention to the possibility that most-favoured-nation trade liberalisation *now* by one or a few countries could raise its/their welfare (and thus world welfare) by more than it would be raised if it/they waited for full multilateral liberalisation at some point in the future.

Long-held, deeply felt beliefs are not easily relinquished – even when it is apparent that they have lost much of their original validity – and it is safe to assume that we are not going to see any revolutionary changes in attitudes toward reciprocity; at least not in the near future. To an extent, it is appropriate that there should be some resistance to a major change in thinking about reciprocity. Full, multilateral, reciprocal reductions remain the best approach to trade liberalisation (provided that the cost in terms of delays and less ambitious reductions is not excessive) and it is desirable that efforts be made to follow that path. The widespread incidence of quantitative restrictions, against which exchange-rate changes are ineffective, is another reason why there is certain to be continuing interest in reciprocity.

A third source of resistance is the prevalence of the belief that an insistence on reciprocity can be defended on grounds of 'fairness' and 'equality of access'.[54] The emotional appeal of this view, particularly among businessmen and politicians, is so strong that there is probably little to be gained by stressing the point that it is based on the demonstratably mistaken belief that most (all?) of the benefits of reductions in a country's trade barriers typically accrue to foreigners. A better approach would be to supplement explanations of the gains to the liberalising country with the following question directed to the export sector: to what extent should a country deny itself the benefits of trade liberalisation simply because its trading partners either do not want, or are too short-sighted to see, the benefits that come with freer trade?

As far as an answer to that question is concerned, it is not unreasonable to assume that as export industries become more aware of the way in which they are doubly penalised by their own country's import barriers – which both increase the cost of their inputs *and* reduce aggregate exports through a relative appreciation of the exchange rate – the 'fairness' argument for reciprocity may yield some ground to the desire for expanded production and profits.

In summary, the pursuit of reciprocity can easily become costly in terms of delays and lost opportunities. Under fixed exchange rates there was an understandable reluctance to respond to these costs by giving way on reciprocity because the alternatives of devaluation or domestic deflation were themselves considered very costly. By virtually eliminating the cost of opting for an exchange-rate change instead of reciprocity, the switch to flexible exchange rates has provided countries with a practical alternative that can be drawn on whenever the costs of pursuing the reciprocity alternative threaten to become excessive.

NOTES

1. Any opinions, conclusions or recommendations expressed in this paper are my own and are not intended to reflect the views of the Secretariat of the General Agreement on Tariffs and Trade. I would like to thank John Black, Hans Genberg, Frieder Roessler, Jan Tumlir and the participants in the IESG Conference for comments on previous drafts. Because some differences of opinion may remain, primarily regarding the relative importance

attached to certain aspects of the argument in the latter part of the paper, the usual remark to the effect that I assume responsibility for any errors is of more than routine importance.

2. Hudec (1978); see also Hudec (1975).
3. On a purely numerical basis, most countries still peg their currencies to another currency, or to a basket of other currencies; however, on a trade-weighted basis, it is a predominantly flexible-rate world, with nearly three-quarters of world trade in mid-1975 accounted for by countries whose currencies were floating independently or jointly. See International Monetary Fund (1975).

   This is a convenient place to mention that as far as this paper is concerned, it makes no difference whether an exchange rate is freely flexible, subject to managed floating (in accordance with the new IMF rules), or simply readily adjustable; the crucial point is the willingness to have exchange rates that adjust to domestic developments, as opposed to the Bretton Woods system which emphasised adjusting domestic developments to a given exchange rate. For this reason, the analysis is applicable also to countries that still peg their currency, as long as there is sufficient willingness to adjust the rate when necessary.
4. The assumption that labour's wage, and prices, have *some* downward flexibility is plausible in a world subject to inflation since real wages and prices can decline without the necessity of a reduction in nominal values, provided, of course, that sufficient 'money illusion' exists. Throughout the paper I assume that sufficient money illusion does exist.
5. See Frenkel and Johnson (1976) and the references cited therein.
6. Measured in terms of the actual payments to capital, there is an unambiguous decline. As far as the rate of return on capital is concerned, it can be said to decline only so long as the firms refuse to write down the value of their existing capital stock in response to this *permanent* change.
7. First, we know that the increase in value of imports ($\dot{C}_{mf}$) is equal to

   (1) $\dot{C}_{mf} = \dot{C}_{xm} + \dot{C}_{hm} - \dot{M}_d$

   where $\dot{C}_{xm}$ = expenditure switched from X to M

   $\dot{C}_{hm}$ = expenditure switched from H to M

   $\dot{M}_d$ = change in production of M_d, valued at world market price.

   Next, the increase in sales of X abroad ($\dot{X}_f$) is equal to

   (2) $\dot{X}_f = \dot{C}_{xm} + \dot{C}_{xh} + \dot{X}$

   where $\dot{C}_{xh}$ = expenditure switched from X to H

   $\dot{X}$ = increase in production of X.

   The change in the balance of payments $\dot{B}$ is

   (3) $\dot{B} = \dot{X}_f - \dot{C}_{mf}$

   Substituting the first two expressions into the third, we obtain

   (4) $\dot{B} = \dot{C}_h + \dot{M}_d + \dot{X}$

where $\dot{C}_h = (\dot{C}_{xh} - \dot{C}_{hm})$, that is, the net change in expenditure on H. The first two terms on the right side are each negative and, therefore, additive.

8. The existence of a deficit means that the central bank is, on net, exchanging foreign exchange for domestic currency, and therefore the domestic money supply (as well as international reserves) will decline continuously if nothing is done. It is assumed, however, that the central bank has a (short-run) policy of adjusting the nominal money supply so as to insure an equality between actual and desired real cash balances (because the tariff elimination caused the domestic price level to decline, some reduction in the nominal money supply is necessary).
9. If we allow for international capital movements, there is in principle a way out of this dilemma. A restrictive monetary policy would cause interest rates to rise, attract an inflow of foreign capital (or reduce the outflow of domestic capital), and thereby correct the balance-of-payments disequilibrium. In the meantime, an expansive fiscal policy would be utilised to reduce the level of unemployment. See Mundell (1962). This is essentially a short-run policy in which foreign exchange is obtained indirectly by borrowing it from private foreign holders—rather than directly from the IMF or through the use of the SWAP agreements—and used to finance the trade deficit. Assuming this change in capital flows cannot be maintained indefinitely, there is still the need to transfer factors out of the M_d (and perhaps the H) industry and into the X industry (the problem is as much one of the distribution of employment among industries as it is of the aggregate level).
10. What happens to the price in the long run depends on whether the industry—on a world-wide basis—is characterised by constant, increasing, or decreasing costs. This also holds for the import good.
11. A less formal way of describing this situation is to say that if several other importing countries are reducing their trade barriers at the same time, competition from low-cost exporters will be 'spread around a bit'.
12. In order for the price of H to rise at all the H industry must receive more orders from former buyers of X than it loses to the M sector, and/or lose more labour and capital to the X industry than it gains from the M sector; but this can happen only so long as its own price remains below the new price of X. For a more detailed analysis of developments in the home goods sector see McDougall (1966), especially p. 221; see also McDougall (1970), especially p. 159; Komiya (1967); and Corden (1971), especially pp. 103–4.
13. The differential consumption effects under the reciprocity alternative also benefit the H industry in the short run – that is, the initial expenditure switch from X to H is larger, and the initial expenditure switch from H to M is smaller, than under the unilateral reduction alternative.
14. A further minor complication is that the timing of the impact of the reductions in trade barriers on trade flows may vary among commodities. Thus an agreement that leads to a balanced expansion of trade at the end of five years will not necessarily yield a balanced expansion during the intervening years.
15. This suggests a rationale for the fact (noted in the introduction to the paper) that economic reciprocity is seldom traded off against legal or issue reciprocity. For instance, an agreement to exchange a tariff cut for a

concession on a new safeguard clause could not be expected to produce a balanced expansion of trade for the parties involved.

16. For a discussion of the asset–market approach to exchange rates see, for example, Branson and Halttunen (and the references cited therein) in this volume. As with most of the literature to date on this topic, they confine their analysis to monetary disturbances.
17. See Corden (1971); Grubel and Johnson (1971).
18. A third implication, implicit in the first two, is that a unilateral tariff reduction could result in a tendency toward an export surplus, and thus require an *appreciation* of the exchange rate. If all tariffs were eliminated, this could occur only if the tariff structure consisted, on net, of negative effective rates of protection. Alternatively, it could occur if the tariff reductions were selective and focussed primarily on the reduction or elimination of negative effective rates. See Johnson (1966) and Corden (1971) Ch. 5. The relevance of this point to commercial policy is limited by the fact that empirical investigations have not turned up any examples of a tariff structure of the requisite type, nor examples of tariff reductions with a demonstrable bias toward the elimination of negative effective rates.
19. Hudec (1975) p. 19.
20. GATT (1969). For a discussion of the latter point, see Patterson (1966) pp. 342–3.
21. Curzon and Curzon (1976) Vol. 1, p. 173. In their article, the Curzons characterise reciprocity as one of the four pillars of GATT's approach to trade liberalisation (the other three are non-discrimination, expansion of trade via reduction of trade barriers and international trade order).
22. Evans (1967) and (1971).
23. GATT Press Release (GATT/1134), 14 September 1973.
24. Barth and Nemmers (1976) p. 143. The reason why the United States is the only country mentioned in this section is the easier availability of official statements on trade policy, which results from the particular institutional arrangements regarding trade policy formulation in that country – namely that the United States Congress has plenary authority over tariffs and other trade restrictions, but has periodically delegated *some* of that authority to the President on a temporary basis. There is no evidence to suggest that the attitude of any of the other major countries towards the principle of reciprocity differs in an important way from that of the United States.
25. Preeg (1970) pp. 132–3.
26. Jackson (1969) p. 241.
27. Evans (1971) p. 21.
28. Curzon and Curzon (1976) pp. 158–9; I have revised the order slightly. The first three are discussed also by Jacques L'Huillier (1977).
29. Curzon and Curzon (1976) p. 159.
30. Cooper (1971).
31. Curzon and Curzon (1976) p. 158.
32. Johnson (1976) p. 24.
33. In a paper written in 1972 (prior to the widespread adoption of floating exchange rates), Jan Tumlir first notes the employment and balance-of-payments arguments for reciprocity, and then observes that increased exchange-rate flexibility would 'not only reduce the technical difficulty of

trade negotiation by lessening the importance of reciprocity, but also alter the balance of domestic interests impinging on the negotiator by giving the export sector a reason to press for even unilateral reductions in the national tariff'. Tumlir (1973) p. 288.

More recently Yeager and Tuerck have noted that fixed exchange rates tend to 'hide' the fact that import restrictions harm a country's export industries by causing an appreciation of the exchange rate relative to its level in the absence of such restrictions [Yeager and Tuerck (1976) p. 107]. As the public becomes progressively more accustomed to floating exchange rates, those firms in the export sector that are not already aware of this point should get the message.

34. Discussing the passage of the United States Trade Act of 1974, Robert Baldwin notes that 'the passage of a liberal trade bill would probably not have been possible without the depreciation of the dollar in 1971 and 1973 and the eventual adoption of a floating exchange system for the major trading nations.' Baldwin (1977) p. 27.
35. *Business Week*, New York, 15 August 1977 and 24 October 1977, and *International Herald Tribune*, Paris, 2 November 1977.
36. This view is not inconsistent with the analysis in Section I in which reciprocal tariff reductions were assumed to produce increases in the world market prices of both the import and export goods. Behind that analysis was the assumption that if a country unilaterally cut its tariff, world prices would be unaffected, while if a majority of countries simultaneously cut tariffs, the subsequent increase in demand for traded goods would (at least temporarily) cause the world market prices of each country's imports and exports to rise by approximately the same amount. In either case, the small country's terms of trade remain essentially unchanged.
37. It would be possible for a country to take advantage of monopolistic power in the world market for one of its export goods by using trade restrictions to produce a relative appreciation of the exchange rate. This, however, would be second-best (compared to a direct restriction on the particular export good) because the export decline induced by the appreciation would affect all export goods, including those for which there would be no terms-of-trade gain to offset the welfare loss from the decline in the volume of trade.
38. Because consumers and producers do not adjust instantaneously to the appearance of price differentials between different sources of the same product, it is often possible for a country to affect its terms of trade in the short run, the length of the short run being a function of such factors as the availability and distribution of market information, the degree of standardisation of the product, industry practices regarding the duration of purchase contracts, and so forth. Although transitory terms-of-trade gains or losses have an impact on national welfare (equivalent to the discounted present value of a temporary flow), such efforts generally are very small relative to national income and, in any case, are not what most people have in mind when they talk about terms-of-trade effects – or, perhaps more accurately, these temporary effects are often treated as though they were permanent.
39. There can be little doubt that the desire to favour particular groups of producers in the economy has influenced governments in deciding whether

particular tariffs should be reduced. But, again, there is no reason to believe that these considerations have determined their attitude toward the reduction of the general level of tariffs or toward reciprocity of tariff negotiations. Evans (1971) pp. 28–9; see also Baldwin (1977) p. 36. There are trade disputes which do involve specific export products, but generally they occur outside the trade negotiating rounds and are the result of an *increase* in foreign protection. The well-known 'chicken war' between the United States and the European Community is an example of such a situation. Moreover, there always will be a limited number of situations in which a government will not be indifferent regarding which of its export industries get a boost. Probably the two leading current examples of this are countries that are anxious to do some 'next-higher-stage processing' of unprocessed or semi-processed raw materials, and the importance that certain countries attach to obtaining reductions in their trading partners' import restrictions on agricultural products. These concerns, however, involve a relatively small number of the larger countries, and the degree of concern (that is, the degree of willingness to 'pay a price' to achieve these goals) is uncertain.

40. The symmetry refers to the fact that any measure that permanently reduces the level of imports also permanently reduces the level of exports, and vice versa. See A. P. Lerner (1936).
41. Bauer, de Sola Pool and Dexter (1972) p. 397.
42. Baldwin (1977) p. 36.
43. This needs to be qualified slightly. If those export industries which currently face zero (or very low) duties in their principal foreign markets were to organise an effective political lobby, the pressure would be in the direction of unilateral tariff cuts (to include duties on their tradeable inputs) combined with exchange-rate depreciation.
44. John Evans stresses this dual nature in the chapter on reciprocity entitled 'The Two Faces of Reciprocity' in Evans (1967).
45. Describing the pre-1971 post-World War II period, the Curzons state: 'Attempts to use totally unconnected political or economic levers with which to extract trade concessions are rare and are deeply resented when they do in fact occur.' Curzon and Curzon (1976) p. 163. See also Frieder Roessler (1978).
46. Evans (1971) pp. 32–3.
47. The dispute during the Kennedy Round over the 'valuation' of an agreement to bind a duty was a minor preview of what may be in store. See Preeg (1970) p. 133.
48. For a discussion of the post-war growth in trade interdependence see Blackhurst, Marian and Tumlir (1977).
49. 'A linear reduction of all tariffs by equal percentages . . . would have represented a clean break with reciprocity.' Evans (1967) p. 32.
50. See Patterson (1966); Gerard Curzon (1965), especially Ch. III; Jackson (1969), especially p. 24; Hudec (1975), especially pp. 204–8; and Evans (1967), especially pp. 319–21.
51. Committee for Economic Development (1964) p. 41.
52. United States 93rd Congress, *Trade Act of 1974*, 3 January 1975, Sec. 126. This section of the Trade Act appears to be open to two interpretations: (i) the United States would refuse to extend reductions in restrictions to the

offending country, or (ii) the United States would withdraw, on an MFN basis, all reductions in restrictions on products of export interest to the offending country. The first alternative would violate the MFN principle, while the second would have undesirable consequences for 'third countries' whose export interests overlap with those of the offending country; the latter situation could give rise to retaliatory withdrawals, or even lead to an unravelling of the entire agreement.

53. International Monetary Fund (1976) p. 107.
54. There is a very strong element of this in the 1974 United States Trade Act; see Wolff (1976). Again, there is no reason to believe that this view is any less prevalent in other countries.

REFERENCES

ROBERT E. BALDWIN, 'The Political Economy of Postwar Trade Policy', *Bulletin*, New York University, 1977, No. 4.

M. BARTH and B. NEMMERS, 'A Road Map to the Trade Act', *Law and Policy in International Business*, Washington, 1976.

R. A. BAUER, I. DE SOLA POOL and L. A. DEXTER, *American Business and Public Policy: the Politics of Foreign Trade*, second edition (New York: Aldine-Atherton Press, 1972).

RICHARD BLACKHURST, NICOLAS MARIAN and JAN TUMLIR, *Trade Liberalization, Protectionism and Interdependence*, GATT Studies in International Trade No. 5 (Geneva: GATT Secretariat, 1977).

COMMITTEE FOR ECONOMIC DEVELOPMENT, *Trade Negotiations for a Better Free World Economy* (New York: CED, 1964).

RICHARD N. COOPER, 'Tariff Issues and the Third World', *The World Today*, London, September 1971.

W. M. CORDEN, *The Theory of Protection* (Oxford: Clarendon Press, 1971).

GERARD and VICTORIA CURZON, 'The Management of Trade Relations in the GATT', in Andrew Schonfield (ed.), *International Economic Relations of the Western World 1959–1971* (Oxford: Oxford University Press, 1976).

GERARD CURZON, *Multilateral Commercial Diplomacy* (London: Michael Joseph, 1965).

JOHN EVANS, *U.S. Trade Policy: New Legislation for the Next Round* (New York: Harper & Row, 1967).

—— *The Kennedy Round in American Trade Policy* (Cambridge, Mass: Harvard University Press, 1971).

J. A. FRENKEL and HARRY G. JOHNSON (eds), *The Monetary Approach to the Balance of Payments* (London: Allen & Unwin, 1976).

General Agreement on Tariffs and Trade, *Basic Instruments and Selected Documents* (Geneva: GATT Secretariat, 1969) Vol. IV.

HERBERT G. GRUBEL and HARRY G. JOHNSON (eds), *Effective Tariff Protection* (Geneva: GATT Secretariat and the Graduate Institute of International Studies, 1971).

ROBERT E. HUDEC, *The GATT Legal System and World Trade Diplomacy* (New York: Praeger, 1975).

—— *Settlement of International Trade Disputes*, Thames Essay No. 16 (London: Trade Policy Research Centre, 1978).

INTERNATIONAL MONETARY FUND, *Annual Report* (Washington: IMF, 1975).

—— *Proposed Second Amendment to the Article of Agreement to the International Monetary Fund* (Washington: IMF, 1976) p. 107.

HARRY G. JOHNSON, 'A Model of Protection and the Exchange Rate', *Review of Economic Studies*, Edinburgh, April 1966.

—— *Trade Negotiations and the New International Monetary System* (Geneva and London: Graduate Institute of International Studies, and the Trade Policy Research Centre, 1976).

JOHN H. JACKSON, *World Trade and the Law of the GATT* (New York: Bobbs-Merrill, 1969).

R. KOMIYA, 'Non-traded Goods and the Pure Theory of International Trade', *International Economic Review*, Japan, June 1967.

A. P. LERNER, 'The Symmetry Between Import and Export Taxes', *Economica*, London, August 1936, reprinted in Richard E. Caves and Harry G. Johnson (eds), *Readings in International Economics* (Homewood, Illinois: Richard D. Irwin, 1968).

JACQUES L'HUILLIER, 'La notion de réciprocité dans les négociations tarifaires', in *Les relations internationales dans un monde en mutation* (Geneva: Sijthoff-Leiden, for the Institut Universitaire de Hautes Etudes Internationales, 1977).

I. A. MCDOUGALL, 'Tariffs and Relative Prices', *The Economic Record*, Melbourne, June 1966.

——'Non-traded Commodities and the Pure Theory of International Trade', in McDougall and R. H. Snape (eds), *Studies in International Economics*, Monash Conference Papers (Amsterdam: North Holland, 1970).

ROBERT A. MUNDELL, 'The Appropriate Use of Monetary and Fiscal Policy under Fixed Exchange Rates', *International Monetary Fund Staff Papers*, Washington, March 1962, reprinted in his *International Economics* (New York: Macmillan, 1968).

GARDNER PATTERSON, *Discrimination in International Trade: the Policy Issues* (Princeton: Princeton University Press, 1966).

ERNEST PREEG, *Traders and Diplomats* (Washington: Brookings Institution, 1970).

FRIEDER ROESSLER, 'The Rationale for Reciprocity in Trade Negotiations Under Floating Exchange Rates', *Kyklos*, Basel, Vol. 31, Fasc. 2, 1978.

JAN TUMLIR, 'Trade Negotiations in the Field of Manufactures' in Paul Streeten (ed.), *Trade Strategies for Development* (London: Macmillan, 1973).

L. B. YAEGER and D. G. TUERCK, *Foreign Trade and U.S. Policy: the Case for Free International Trade* (New York: Praeger, 1976).

ALAN WOLFF, 'The U.S. Mandate for Trade Negotiations', *Virginia Journal of International Law*, Spring 1976.

Index